Investment in Indian Agriculture

About the Authors

S. Bisaliah, PhD in Agriculture Economics from University of Minnesota, has been engaged in teaching, research, development work and academic administration for the last four decades. He had served as Chairman, Karnataka State Agricultural Price Commission, contributing for policy and programme formulation for agriculture development. The international working experiences of Prof Bisaliah include: Monitoring and Evaluation Expert, World Bank Forestry Project (Nigeria), thrice consultant to FAO (Rome), twice consultant to Economic and Social Commission for Asia and Pacific, and once Consultant to World Bank-FAO. He has 170 research articles and policy reports on agriculture/rural development and capital formation in agriculture.

S. Mahendra Dev is Director, Indira Gandhi Institute of Development Research (IGIDR), Mumbai, India. Earlier he was Chairman of the Commission for Agricultural Costs and Prices, Govt. of India, Delhi and Director, Centre for Economic and Social Studies, Hyderabad (1999 to 2008). He received his PhD from the Delhi School of Economics and his Post-doctoral research at Yale. He has more than 100 research publications in national and international journals and has written extensively on agricultural development, poverty and public policy, food security, employment guarantee schemes, social security, farm and non-farm employment. He has been a consultant and adviser to many international organisations, such as UNDP, World Bank, International Food Policy Research Institute, ILO, FAO and ESCAP. He has been a member of several government committees including the Prime Minister's Task Force on Employment and Rangarajan Commission on Financial Inclusion and is presently member of the expert group on poverty.

Saifullah Syed, presently working in the Policy Assistance and Support Service of the Food and Agriculture Organization (FAO) of the United Nations, holding the position of Senior Policy Officer, joined FAO in 1983. Prior to that he was working for the Organization for Economic Cooperation and Development (OECD). He completed his MSc in Economics from Birkbeck College, University of London and PhD in Economics from University of Paris-Dauphine, France. His field of specialisation includes: modelling for policy analysis; providing policy assistance and advice for sustainable agriculture and rural development and international trade. Dr. Syed has published several research papers and is co-author of the book: *Agriculture in the Cook Islands: New Directions* (1993). His current research interest is in policies for promoting investment in agriculture. He is leading a Japanese Trust Fund Project on policies for promoting investment in agriculture, which led to initiation of work for this book.

Investment in Indian Agriculture

Macro and Micro Evidences

S. Bisaliah
S. Mahendra Dev
Syed Saifullah

ACADEMIC FOUNDATION
NEW DELHI

www.academicfoundation.com

First published in 2013
by

ACADEMIC FOUNDATION
4772-73 / 23 Bharat Ram Road, (23 Ansari Road),
Darya Ganj, New Delhi - 110 002 (India).
Phones : 23245001 / 02 / 03 / 04.
Fax : +91-11-23245005.
E-mail : books@academicfoundation.com
www.academicfoundation.com

In association with

Indira Gandhi Institute of Development Research (IGIDR), Mumbai.

Cataloging in Publication Data--DK
Courtesy: D.K. Agencies (P) Ltd. <docinfo@dkagencies.com>

Bisaliah, S.
Investment in Indian agriculture : macro and micro
evidences / S. Bisaliah, S. Mahendra Dev, Syed Saifullah.
p. cm.
Includes bibliographical references (p.).
ISBN 9788171889549
ISBN 8171889549

1. Agriculture--India--Finance. 2. Saving and investment–
India. 3. Agriculture and state--India. 4. Poverty–
Government policy--India. 5. Agriculture--Economic aspects–
India. I. Mahendra Dev, S., joint author. II. Saifullah, Syed,
joint author. III. Title.

DDC 338.130954 23

Typeset by Italics India, New Delhi.
Printed and bound in India.

Contents

List of Tables and Figures

Tables

Figures

Preface

The book, *Investment In Indian Agriculture: Macro and Micro Evidences*, is a product of joint efforts of the authors with the financial support from Food and Agriculture Organization (FAO), Rome, under the Japanese Trust Fund Project. The Policy Division of FAO has been addressing various issues of capital formation in and for agriculture sector of developing countries. The present work represents one such effort with macro and micro (farm) level data of India with the hope that the experiences of and evidences from India in the area of investment in agriculture and its impact on output/productivity and poverty alleviation would provide some useful messages for other developing countries in formulating and implementing policy and programme designs.

The theme of the book is structured and sequenced in such a way so as to address four issues. First, what are cross-country experiences on the relationship between capital formation and growth, and between growth and poverty especially in agriculture sector? Second, how has been the macro level experiences of India in growth of investment in agriculture, complementarity between public and private sector investment, and relationship between capital formation, agriculture growth and poverty? Third, what do farm (micro) level evidences suggest about the growth of capital stock, composition, capital intensity and productivity, and the importance of agriculture capital stock in influencing farm level gross value of output and productivity of labour engaged in agriculture? Related to this is the issue of determinants of capital formation attempted in the study. The differential performance of different sample states and farm groups with respect to these aspects of agriculture capital stock has also been analysed. Fourth, what are the possible pathways and policy directions derived from macro and micro evidences for influencing investment in agriculture? Following the present study, the authors have lined up another study, 'Investment Portfolio of Farm Households: Micro Level Evidences From India'. This proposed study on investment portfolio management by farmers would be a complementary volume to the present study.

This book would not have been completed but for the financial support provided by FAO, support of Mr Jeena of Commission for Agriculture Costs and Prices (CACP), Ms Dhritisri Sarkar in data processing, Ms Kalavathi in providing secretarial assistance, and Dr N.S. Viswanath for editorial support. The authors remain grateful to all of them.

—S. Bisaliah,
S. Mahendra Dev,
Syed Saifullah.

1 Introduction

The story of economic growth and development in India during the last two decades or so has produced useful experiences and evidences on the 'impact' of economic reforms in the perspective of economic globalisation. These experiences and evidences would provide insights into how to navigate further reform process in the country as well as lessons for many other countries engaged in reforms for growth and development. First, the general performance record of India during the last two decades has led the economy from low growth to high growth trajectory so as to be labelled as one of the fastest growing economies. Mainly, service sector–led growth pattern has become quite visible during this period of economic reforms. Second, the performance record of India during the same period with respect to inclusive growth (equity dimension of growth) has been far from satisfactory. Realising that the growth/development dualism has deepened and broadened, the core objective of Twelfth Five Year Plan (2012-2017) is set as 'faster, more inclusive and sustainable growth.'

The major challenge is to identify the sectors, regions and socio-economic groups where the pattern of 'inclusive' growth could lead to broad-based virtuous growth/development, and which itself could be a source of growth and sustainability. Agriculture is identified as one of the major areas of focus for making growth more inclusive (Dev, 2008). A kind of agriculture growth cycle has been registered in India—peak growth rate of about 3.5 per cent in 1980s, decelerated growth rate of around 2.6 per cent from the mid-1990s to the mid-2000s, marginal recovery in the middle of 2000s, and again slip to decelerated growth. This kind of agriculture growth cycle has established the vulnerability of Indian agriculture to external and weather shocks. Deceleration in agriculture growth since mid-1990s has given rise to many concerns such as the inability of the sector to meet rising demand for agri-food products, the need for agri-food production sector to move on to high growth trajectory to sustain high GDP growth rate, the growing rural–urban development divide, the persisting food inflation, and 'inability' of the country to meet the Millennium Development Goal (MDG) of halving poverty by 2015. Further, the spatial and social analysis of poverty and hunger (Bisaliah, 2009b) has led to the inference that poverty in India is predominantly rural. Indian agriculture is no longer predominant in terms of its share (around 16%) in national GDP, but it is a predominant sector in terms of dependent population (two-thirds of country's population depending on this sector for livelihood). Further it generates employment for over 50 per cent of country's workforce and contributes for about 16 per cent of the country's exports. Added to these, agriculture forms the single largest occupation in the private sector in the country, and it forms a critical edifice of the strategy for overall development of the economy (HLC, 2009).

Notwithstanding the decline in the share of agriculture to national GDP, the predominant role of agriculture in India has been very well recognised. Hence, the deceleration in growth of agriculture has become one of the major concerns. The context, complexity and concerns of Indian agriculture development, and the major drivers and directions of growth have been analysed (Bisaliah, 2009c). The major concerns and challenges recognised are: technology fatigue, productivity fatigue, degradation and depletion of nature resource base, stagnation in area under irrigation, lagging regions (such as rainfed areas) and farm groups (such as marginal and small farms), inadequate rural infrastructure (such as roads, electricity, markets), lack of diversification of rural economy, falling investment in agriculture especially public investment, and so on. In addition to all these, there is a need for producing more output per unit of bundle of resources. This warranty a paradigm shift from increase in productivity from a single resource (partial productivity) to productivity of entire set of resources used in production i.e., total factor productivity (TFP). In a major study on TFP in Indian agriculture, Chand *et al.* (2011) have estimated that share of TFP to output growth (in crop and livestock sector) was 17.8 per cent during 1985-86 to 2006-07, and 14.7 per cent during 1990-91 to 2006-07. This implies small and declining share of TFP to output growth in these sectors and output growth has been mainly input–led growth. Annual TFP growth estimated to be around 0.42 per cent in crop and animal sectors between

1990-91 to 2006-07 is too low for generating and sustaining TFP–led agriculture growth in India. India has to maintain a steady growth in TFP to ensure food security and achieve the projected growth of food and non-food commodities. But TFP growth depends on public policies such as investment in research, extension, education, infrastructure (irrigation, roads, electricity supply and so on) and natural resource management (Chand *et al.*, 2011).

It is obvious from the preceding section that TFP–led growth in crop and livestock is possible, if adequate investment is made on determinants of TFP, among many lines of investment in agriculture. Several studies have argued that investment is the single most important factor in the growth process (Lewis, 1955; Rostow, 1960). In view of the importance of investment in economic growth, there has been considerable interest in factors governing investment during different periods and stages of development (HLC, 2009: Chapter XIII). While public investment is governed largely as a matter of political economy compulsions and by availability of funds, variety of factors determine private investment, the determinants of which change over time, space and sector of investment. Four broad results on investment in agriculture, investment and agriculture growth, and agriculture growth and poverty need to be made explicit to place this study on investment in agriculture in the proper perspective, and these will be examined in detail in subsequent chapters. First, cross-country studies (details in Bisaliah, 2010a) have drawn the inference that agricultural capital stock and productivity of labour engaged in agriculture are positively related, and productivity of labour and prevalence of poverty and hunger are inversely related. Second, the study on India (Bisaliah, 2004; 2010a) has led to the inference that capital formation in/for agriculture, and output/productivity growth are positively related, and output/productivity growth in agriculture and the rate of poverty reduction are also positively related, implying that agriculture is a pro-poor sector. Third, India represents a typology of growth wherein accelerated growth in national GDP, decelerated growth in AGDP and slow rate of poverty reduction co-exist. Fourth, there has been a loss of momentum in investment in agriculture in India since mid-1990s, much more so in public investment. Hence, trends in farm sector investment (HLC, 2009: Chapter XIII) reveal that agriculture is losing its share in investment particularly more rapidly during the decade of 1990s and onwards led mainly by the loss of momentum of public sector investment. In fact, the share of public sector in the total investment in agriculture has declined, more pronounced in 1990s (28%) and in 2005-06 (23%), as compared to what it was in 1980s (45%). In brief, declining investment in agriculture over time has been considered as one of the binding constraints on the performance of agriculture sector and on the realisation of other development policy goals like reducing poverty controlling prices of food articles and generating productive jobs in rural sector. However, it is understandable that investment is only one element that establishes connections and communications between capital formation and agriculture growth and agriculture growth and poverty reduction, and it can be both the trigger for and outcome of specific national policies and strategies on natural resource management, land tenure, education, research and development, rural infrastructure, adaptation to climate change, and so on (FAO, 2011). In fact the policy brief by FAO (2011) has recognised some broad aspects relating to agriculture investment—saving and investment behaviour of farmers, fixed capital investment and property right, factors governing investment at farm level, policy options for foreign direct investment, policy options for forging the link between domestic savings and agriculture investment, between public investment and private investment, and for sustaining these links.

Given the decline in the momentum of investment in agriculture in India, decelerated growth in farm sector, and decline in the rate of poverty reduction, and recognition of importance of agriculture for inclusive growth—all these have led to many issues on investment in agriculture both at research and policy levels. Before examining the major issues on investment in agriculture, a brief reference to structure of investment in agriculture is in order (HLC, 2009: Chapter XIII). There are two components of investment in agriculture—gross fixed capital formation (GFCF), consisting primarily investment in physical assets; GFCF and change in stock of inventories would constitute what is called gross capital formation (GCF). However, investment in agriculture is predominantly in the form of physical assets, and inventory of stocks are relatively of less important. Capital formation through investment in agriculture leads to augmentation of capital stock which in turn contributes for increasing the productivity of land and labour, increase in production and value addition. Public sector investment in rural infrastructure could have the positive inducement effect on private sector investment: public investment enhances growth in productivity, production, agri-business development and development of non-farm economy in rural area. Private sector investment assumes the form of investment by corporate sector (big private companies and unorganised entities like sugar cooperatives and milk cooperatives) and by farm households. The investment by farm households consists of investment on farm equipments, machinery, irrigation, land improvement and so on. The share of farm household investment in total private investment in agriculture is estimated to be about 90 per cent (HLC, 2009: Chapter XIII), establishing the dominance of household investment in private investment.

Keeping the backdrop on capital structure in agriculture, major issues to be addressed in the area of investment in agriculture are detailed as below (For details see Bisaliah, 2009a and FAO, 2011):

- Which are the observed typologies and investment growth cycles across countries?
- Whether growth rates and composition of investment in agriculture vary across countries and over a period of time? Has structure of capital formation changed with economic globalisation across countries since 1980s? Added to this is the issue whether structure of foreign capital inflow for investment in agriculture of needy countries has altered since 1980s?
- How important are foreign loans and grants to supplement domestic savings so as to ensure a targetted level of investment in agriculture?
- What are the determinants of public and private investment in agriculture?
- Whether private investment in agriculture can be a substitute for public investment? How is the complementarity between public and private investment through inducement effect on private investment?
- What policies and development environment would promote public and corporate sector partnership in stimulating investment on rural infrastructure and non-farm rural economy?

- How is the relative importance of subsidies and public investment for agriculture in promoting and sustaining TFP-led agriculture growth at farm level?
- What pathways and policy options for private sector investment to have positive impact on growth in agriculture productivity/ production at farm level so as to realise general development policy goals?

FAO with support from Japanese Trust Fund Project is engaged in addressing these issues by documenting and analysing the experiences and evidences of different countries through its cross-country studies. Even though these issues are structured for exploration through cross-country studies, these are appropriate for study of various issues of capital formation in Indian agriculture through investment by different stakeholders, and inferences derived and lessons learnt from this study on India would be quite valuable for other countries engaged in mobilising and stimulating investment in agriculture, to address the problems of poverty, food security and rural transformation through agriculture development.

The specific objectives set out for the present study are:

- To document and analyse the cross-country experiences on the relationships between capital and general economic growth, and between general economic growth and poverty, as well as the relationships between capital formation in agriculture, growth and prevalence of poverty and hunger.
- To analyse macro evidences on trends in investment and composition, growth cycle of capital stock in/for agriculture, investment behaviour of private and public sector, complementarity between public and sector investment, and on relationship between capital formation in agriculture, agriculture growth and poverty.
- Analyse micro (farm level) evidences on growth of capital stock and its composition, capital intensity and productivity, importance of farm level capital stock *vis-à-vis* other determinants of gross value of output and productivity of labour engaged in agriculture, and to identify the determinants of capital formation by farm households.
- To identify the pathways and policy options for influencing investment in agriculture by both public and private sector.

The first objective of the study is addressed in Chapter 2, second objective in Chapter 3, third objective in Chapter 4 and Chapter 5, and the last objective in Chapter 6.

2 Capital, Growth and Poverty

Relationships and Evidences

A search for sources of growth in growth models and evidences from empirical growth accounting studies would form the analytical frame to identify the role of capital as a deep driver of growth. Further, the nexus between growth and poverty, and between agriculture growth and poverty needs to be derived from empirical studies so as to provide basis for designing development policies and programmes. Hence, the present chapter focusses on identifying the broad concept of capital, the role of capital in growth models, results and inferences from cross-country regression studies as a part of growth accounting research, relationship between capital stock and agriculture growth and poverty. In view of this, the present chapter is designed to address six basic questions on capital, growth and poverty. First, how has the concept of capital been broadened and deepened to identify 'capital' as one of the key drivers of growth? Second, what role is assigned to capital in broad streams of growth models? Third, what are the inferences from growth accounting studies so as to place the concept and role of capital in proper perspective? Fourth, how is the relationship between general growth and poverty and agriculture growth and poverty? Fifth, what are global/regional perspectives on the relationship among agriculture capital stock (ACS), productivity of labour engaged in agriculture and prevalence of hunger and poverty? Sixth, what developing countries can learn from addressing these questions with respect to capital, growth and poverty?

The Concept of Capital: Broadening and Deepening

The concept and measurement of capital has been an important area of both theoretical and empirical debate among economists (Robbinson, 1953-54; 1956; Harcourt, 1972; Harcourt and Laing, 1973). One of the important lines of arguments of Ranson (1987) has been the advancement of the institutional theory of capital, wherein evolution of the concept of capital has been traced. Ranson (1987) places emphasis on institutionalist definition of capital that at the core of institutional theory of production is technology (technology generation, transfer and utilisation as subsystems), specifying a complex of materials, skills and equipment. Thus technology serves the function of capital. Further, technology is disseminated and improved largely through education and research institutions, while it is applied through economic institutions. More efficient institutions permit increasing the rate of output with the prevailing technology. Hence the theory locates creative potency not in capital accumulation as such, but in workmanlike operations of education and research institutions as well as economic institutions. The message for developing countries is quite clear: capital formation is a necessary condition for supporting growth, but the sufficient conditions assume the form of institutions to raise production possibilities by diffusing skills necessary to apply, borrow or improve technology. Further developing countries have to realise that capital stock is to be maintained, if output is to remain constant, must be expanded if growth is to occur, and that must be improved if development is to occur.

Capital in the Matrix of Deep Drivers of Growth

One of the ways to examine the role of capital in growth is to place it in the matrix of deep drivers of growth. The systematic search for the deep drivers of economic growth goes back at least to Solow (1956; 1957), and numerous factors have been suggested and studied as engines of growth since the 1980s, thanks to the research works of Romer (1986; 1987; 1989) Lucas (1998 and 2002) and others. In the context of the present section, a brief survey of some engines of growth (Hughes *et al.*, 2008) and the relevance of different types of capital in the matrix of deep drivers of growth is in order. Human capital (Schultz, 1961; Becker, 1964; Lucas, 1998), as well as learning by doing (Arrow, 1962), knowledge capital generated through investment in R&D (Romer, 1990), social capital as an umbrella term for variety of concepts such as trust, social networks, honesty and civic engagements and so on (Hall and Jones, 1999; Kumar and Medsusaka, 2006), institutional capital (governance) and structures, physical capital (equipment), infrastructure capital (David, 1993; World

Bank, 1994), and natural resource capital (physical and biological environment) could be considered as deep drivers of economic growth. The UN Millennium Project (UNECLAC, 2005) recognises physical capital, social capital, human capital, infrastructure, knowledge capital, natural capital and public institutional capital as deep drivers of growth, among others. However, Lucas (2002) recognises that human capital is a very broad concept and therefore difficult to measure. The study by Temple (1999) rightly classifies the causes of growth into proximate causes (physical capital, human capital, and R&D) and wider influences on growth (population growth, openness in international trade, financial system, inequality, government spending on infrastructure, natural resources, intellectual property rights (IPR) and tax systems).

In brief, economic growth is engineered mainly by three immediate drivers *viz.*, labour, capital (in the broad sense) and multifactor productivity or total factor productivity (MFP/TFP, details later). TFP is residual that captures everything that is not measurable like physical and human input. Further the drivers of TFP are human capital, social capital and governance, infrastructure capital, natural capital and knowledge capital and so on.

Capital in Growth/Development Theory

Three major streams of advancement in growth/development theory and the role of capital in the growth/development process could be identified (Stern, 1989; Solow, 1994; Temple, 1999). The major focus of these advancement is to answer the question: what drives economic growth, and where does capital stand in growth generation and sustenance.

The Classical Growth Theory

In classical and the Keynesian theory of growth (as represented by Harrod-Domar Model), the emphasis is on role of capital accumulation and the embodiment of the various forms of technical progress associated with it. The Harrod-Domar growth analysis (Domar, 1947; Harrod, 1948) leads to savings and capital-output ratios as determinants of the growth rate. In this analysis, growth is expressed as the product of ratio of investment to GDP and the productivity of investment. This implies slow growth is the product of a low investment ratio/low productivity of capital, perhaps one of the proximate causes of low growth in developing countries, either overall or sectoral (like agriculture). In early growth/development models (Lewis, 1954; 1955; 1958), structural change and capital accumulation (including knowledge and skill) are treated as the key aspects of development in less developed countries. Further, development economists like Rostow (1960) Lewis (1955) Cairncross (1966), Meir (1984) and Johnson (1969) have considered investment as the most important single factor in the growth process. For example, Johnson (1969) singles out capital accumulation as the distinguishing characteristics of development, and describes structural transformation of economies as a generalised process of capital formation. The condition of being 'developed' consists of having accumulated, and having established efficient social and economic mechanisms for maintaining and increasing large stock of capital per head in the various forms. Similarly, the condition of being underdeveloped is characterised by the possession of relatively small stock of various kinds of capital. In fact, the basic factor sustaining the high rate of growth in Japanese economy over the pre- and post-war period was a constantly maintained capital formation (Koichi, n.d.). It is concluded (Gill, 1976) that capital formation and incremental capital output ratio (ICOR) would account for variations in GDP growth rate across countries.

The Neoclassical Theory of Growth

The growth theory pioneered by Solow (1956; 1957) and Swan (1956) disaggregates the sources of growth into contribution of labour, capital, technical progress and any other variable included in the growth accounting exercise. According to this theory, the thrust for economic growth has to come from outside the system, mainly from technological progress which is obviously treated as exogeneous. But the fundamental question of why labour supply (both quantity and quality), capital accumulation and technical progress grow at different rates in different countries still stays with us. Further, the neoclassical growth theory led by Solow (1954; 1994) predicted convergence of per capital income across countries. But the evidences on sub-Shararan Africa, Latin America and some parts of Asia point towards divergent growth rates across countries, suggesting growth divergence instead of convergence.

The New Growth Theory

The third stream of growth theory called new growth theory (NGT) or exogeneous growth theory was pioneered by Romer (1990; 1986; 1987; 1989; 1994), followed by Rivera-Batiz and Romer (1990), Grossman and Helpman (1991), Aghion and Howitt (1992), Strokey (1991), Young (1991; 1993), Pack (1994), Lucas (2002) and many others. Irrespective of refinements and elaborations of NGT, some of the major tenets are examined.

First, NGT is one of the major attempts to answer the question why do growth rates differ greatly across countries during the same period of time. In the neoclassical theory of growth, growth is exogeneous, beyond the control of economic agents. But in NGT growth is endogeneous, an important departure from the neoclassical theory. Growth arises from intentional action of economic agents and the government.

Second, the NGT believes that increasing returns to scale is made possible by sustained increase in capital (both human and physical). This would create a permanent increase in the growth rate of the economy.

Third, in the NGT, an important role is given to human capital. An increase in the rate of accumulation of human capital—stock of useful knowledge as an engine of growth—enhances the productivity of both human labour and physical capital (Lucas, 1998; 1990; Barro and Becker, 1989). Human capital would help in preventing physical capital from diminishing returns. For example, the fast growth of the economy (improvement in productivity of both agriculture and industry), in Republic of Korea is attributed to human capital, coupled with other forms of capital accumulation (Young, 1995; Nelson and Pack,1999). In fact it is argued that differences in the productivity of nations are due to differences in the skill level and ability to handle technology by workers across countries. Solow (1994) while commenting on NGT observes that treating learning by doing as one mode of productivity increase (Young, 1993) is in order.

Fourth, the NGT lays emphasis on the 'idea gap' between the developed and developing countries (Mazumdar, 2005), which has made the former to grow at a higher rate than the latter. The NGT is suggestive of the inference that globalisation would give rise to capital and technology inflows to developing countries so as to bridge the 'idea gap'. In fact, innovation in technology is an important explanatory factor to the growth rate in any economy (Grossman and Helpman 1991). In other words, it views economic growth from the point of view of creative destruction (an elaboration of this concept in Schumpeter, 1934), and introduction of new technology would help countries to climb up in the 'quality ladder' of technology which in turn would lead to higher growth rate of the economy (see Mazumdar, 2005 for the relationship or lack of it between capital inflows and economic growth in India).

The implications of NGT are profound, with messages for designing policies to increase growth. For example, the externalities associated with human capital suggest that any underinvestment in education and other forms of human capital should be addressed by policy initiatives such as subsidies, because such investment would increase the rate of growth. The NGT also opens up avenues for getting into the 'black box of productivity' and understanding its origin. The main message of NGT is that the role of various forms of capital, among others, is quite crucial as engines of growth.

Growth Accounting through Growth Regressions

Even though there are many growth accounting empirical exercises, only some are examined in this study to answer questions. What factors would account for variations in growth performance of different countries? What is the relative importance of physical and human capital and TFP in growth performance across countries? What are the cross-country differences in TFP? What factors would determine TFP growth? Why output per worker varies enormously across countries? Could there be growth convergences?

In the growth accounting exercise performed by Senhadji (2000) for 88 countries with data for over 30 years (1960-1994), the major inference is that capital accumulation cannot sustain long-run growth, while TFP can. Then, what are the determinants of TFP growth? Why the differences in TFP? TFP is a function of human capital, physical and natural capital, social capital, governance, equity and policies, knowledge development and diffusion (R&D) and economic integration with outside world (Hughes *et al.*, 2008).

Temple (1999) in his study of 'New Growth Evidences' concludes that the key reason for cross-country variation in growth is macroeconomic management. The three proximate causes of growth identified are physical capital, human capital and R&D. The wider influences of growth are population growth, openness to trade, financial intermediation (banking system and stock exchange), Government spending on infrastructure, social and political arrangements and so on. Kanbur (2004) in his study 'Development of Development Thinking', provided insights into the role of economic, social and political factors in influencing growth performance in different countries (See Stern, 1989 for some of the 'grand issues' of development).

The issue of variations in output per worker across countries is yet another area of growth accounting exercise (Hall and Jones 1999). In 1988, output per worker in the US was more than 35 times higher than output per worker in Niger. In just over 10 days, the average worker in US produced as much as an average worker in Niger produced in an entire year. According to the analysis (Mankiw *et al.*, 1992; Dougherty and Jorgenson, 1996), based on aggregate production function, growth differences among countries could be attributed to differences in human capital, physical capital and productivity. It is true that countries produce high level of output per worker, because they achieve higher rates of investment in physical and human capital, and because they use these inputs with a high level of productivity. But, why would some countries achieve these, and others cannot? Hall and Jones (1999) has argued that success on each of these fronts is driven by the institutions and policies (called social infrastructure) that make up the economic environment within which the economic agents make investments, create and transfer ideas and produce goods and services. The results of this study indicate that differences in social infrastructure account for much of the differences in long growth performance throughout the world as measured by output per worker. The index of social infrastructure and output per worker varies directly. For example, Switzerland, US and Canada represent the countries with highest level of social infrastructure and highest level of output per worker, whereas Zaire, Haiti and Bangladesh represent lowest level of social infrastructure and lowest level of output per worker.

Recent empirical evidences suggest that technical progress, human capital accumulation, increasing returns to R&D and government policies might have better explanatory power in determining variations in income across countries (Barro and Sala-i-Martin, 1995). In fact, this is one of the central themes of NGT.

Yet another issue is how growth convergence could occur in some countries. Wolff (1991) in his study on growth catch-up among the 'Group Seven (G7)' developed countries (US, UK, Japan, Germany, Italy, France and Canada) between 1870 and 1979, comes out with the following inferences:

- Between 1950 and 1979, there was a strong convergence in TFP, labour productivity and capital intensity among the G7 countries. TFP catch-up is found to be positively associated with capital–labour ratio growth, and strongest when growth of capital intensity is found to be quite strong. In brief, the rates of capital formation are found to have positive impact on TFP growth. Further, the convergence of labour productivity levels has been due to narrowing of differences in factor intensities (capital–labour ratios) among industrialised countries.
- Positive correlation of 0.79 was found between the rate of TFP growth and that of capital–labour ratio. This supports the existence of positive interaction between technological advance and capital accumulation and TFP catch-up.
- It follows that sustained capital accumulation is necessary to put new inventions into practice and to effect their widespread employment. This association is referred to as the 'embodiment effect', since at least some technological innovation is embodied in capital.
- It is also consistent with the 'vintage effect' which states that new capital is more productive than old capital per (constant) dollar of expenditure.
- The investment growth may lead to growth in demand and thereby to the maintenance of favourable climate for investment—called Vendoorn or Kaldor effect.

- The introduction of new capital may lead to a better organisation, management and the like and facilitate 'learning by doing'. Thus, the testing of 'catch-up' hypothesis in case of G7 developed countries brings out the convergence of labour productivity, narrowing of differences in factor intensities (capital–labour ratios) and convergence of TFP. The positive impact of capital formation on TFP, positive interactions between capital accumulation and technology advance, improvement in organisation and management with the introduction of technological advances as well as opportunities for 'learning by doing' (all these leading to growth convergence) are the lessons for developing countries to reduce the 'idea gap' and thereby to move towards growth convergence recorded in G7 countries.

Capital and Growth: Lessons for Developing Countries

This section recapitulates some of the major conclusions, inferences on the concept of capital, role of capital in the matrix of deep drivers of growth and in growth/development theories, growth accounting through growth regressions, growth convergence, and to derive lessons/messages for developing countries.

Compared to its early usage, the concept of capital has been broadened and deepened so as to include physical capital, human capital, social capital, natural capital, institutional capital, infrastructure capital and so on. Further, three broad deep drivers of growth are labour, capital (in the broad sense) and TFP.

There are three broad waves of growth/development theory which graft capital into the matrix of deep drivers of growth—the classical theory of growth, the neoclassical and the new growth theory (NGT). The classical growth theory (represented by Harrod-Domar Growth Model) places emphasis on capital accumulation and the embodiment of various forms of technical progress. Further, early development economists have also considered the investment as the most important single factor in the growth process as well as structural transformation of the economy of a country. The neoclassical theory of growth disaggregates the sources of growth mainly into labour, capital and technical progress. Further, the thrust for economic growth has come from outside the system, mainly from technological progress which is treated as exogeneous. The NGT treats growth as endogeneous, arising from intentional actions of economic agents and government. Sustained increase in growth rate is to be achieved through sustained increase in capital (both physical and human). Human capital would augment the productivity of both labour input and physical capital. The concept of 'idea gap' is quite a useful one to support the inflow of capital and technology to developing countries so as to bridge the 'idea gap' necessary for higher growth.

The empirical works on growth accounting through growth regressions have identified physical capital, human capital and TFP as factors to account for variations in growth performance across countries. Further, physical and human capital are also identified as explanatory factors for differences in TFP across countries. Added to these, the key reason for cross-country variations in growth is identified to be macroeconomic management. Yet, cross-country variations in output per worker, even though explained in terms of investments in physical and human capital and in R&D, are explained in terms of social infrastructure (institutions and policies) that would constitute the economic environment for economic agents to decide on investment, creation and transfer of ideas, and production of goods and services. Social infrastructure and output per worker across countries are found to vary directly. Further, the testing of catch-up hypothesis with data from seven developed countries with time series data for over 100 years has identified the convergence of capital intensity, labour productivity and TFP. The bridging of 'idea gap' to experience high growth rates is found to have been accomplished in G7 countries through convergence of capital formation, positive interaction between capital accumulation and technology/management advancement and increased labour productivity as well as TFP. These growth convergence experiences are critical lessons for developing countries. Added to all these is the argument (Mazumdar, 2005) that considerable emphasis was placed on capital accumulation as a means to faster growth; but a new body of evidence (Easterly, 2001) suggests that it is not the change in the level of capital stock alone, but change in TFP that promotes growth.

From the examination of growth/development experiences across the countries, capital accumulation (in the broader sense of the term) stands out as one of the major deep drivers of growth, and all these would require investment. The growth accounting regression study across broad groups of developing countries would illustrate the importance of capital *vis-à-vis* other drivers of growth (Senhadji, 2000).

Table 2.1

Sources of Output Growth by Region of the World: 1960-1994

	Region	*Annual Output Growth (%)*	*Contribution of*			
			Capital	*Labour*	*Human Capital*	*TFC*
1.	South Asia	4.66	2.87	0.99	0.25	0.55
2.	East Asia	6.49	4.50	1.27	0.44	0.28
3.	Sub-Saharan Africa	2.83	1.79	1.39	0.22	-0.56
4.	Middle East and North Africa	5.05	3.99	0.84	0.25	-0.03
5.	Latin America	3.42	2.31	1.22	0.28	-0.39

Source: Senhadji (2000).

It could be seen from Table 2.1 that:

- Capital accumulation is by far the most important contributor to measured growth in output in all the regions. The study on South Asia, East Asia, and Latin America for the years 1960-1987 by the World Bank (1991) had also come to the same conclusion.
- Yet another study by Hu and Khan (1997) by investigating the sources of growth in China for the period 1953-1994, confirmed the dominant role of capital and productivity. Perhaps for this reason Collins and Bosworth (1996) argues that the marginal product of physical capital is higher in developing countries.
- The negative contribution of TFC in three study regions for output growth is a disturbing trend. However, the results of this study are to be considered with caution, due to problems of measurement of inputs, consistency/reliability of time series data, and pooling of data across countries to develop region-wise data set. But the role of capital as a major deep driver of growth needs to be recognised.

The developing countries are to get the message that all types of capital could contribute for increased output and productivity. All these would require investment by different economic agents. Capital accumulation is not only important in its own right, it is the major conduit for advances in knowledge, which in turn are major determinants of productivity and output growth. In fact, capital is the main vehicle for the introduction of technical progress in the productive system. The embodiment effect, the vintage effect and the Kaldor effect of investment would reinforce this argument.

Capital formation and structural transformation of an economic system (Fisher, 1939; Johnson, 1969) tend to move together. Structural transformation is one of the major indicators of the development status of a country.

In developing countries with low capital-output ratio, the very act of capital deepening (giving each worker a little more capital to work with), may make a substantial difference to output growth, and productivity (both partial and total). Details on this issue will be elaborated in later pages.

Capital accumulation is considered as an escape from the 'vicious circle of poverty'—a circle of low productivity leading to a low level of capital accumulation per head, leading to low productivity. Low productivity is considered as the source of 'vicious circle of poverty', where the circle must be broken by capital accumulation and its efficient use.

In the context of investment in capital, World Bank (1994) emphasises both increases in quantity of infrastructure (transport, power, irrigation, sanitation and so on) in developing countries, but also the quality of infrastructure.

Apart from the issue of capital formation and its efficient use, development economists have also brought out other obstacles to development such as dualistic structure of development, circular and cumulative causation (Myrdal, 1957, 1963), geographic determinism (Krugman, 1995), and many other obstacles. In addition to all these, the problem of 'idea gap' in promotion and sustainability of growth should be addressed by developing countries, as done successfully by Japan, and being addressed effectively by China.

Nexus between Growth and Poverty

Since 1970s, one of the 'grand issues' of development has been poverty in developing countries, and since 1990s the slowdown in poverty reduction, in spite of unprecedented high growth rates in some of the major developing countries; has intensified the global concern for persistent poverty in some developing countries. This concern is much more reinforced by UN Millennium Development Goal for poverty reduction, among other goals.

Given this backdrop, the need for examining the nexus between growth and poverty is imperative. The proximate drivers of poverty are said to be growth, inequality and population. Growth and distribution inequality determine the rate of poverty, population then determines the number in poverty. In fact, inequality (the distribution of income), growth and poverty form the three vertices of a 'triangle' arithmetically connected in a fairly straight forward way (Bourguignon, 2003). For details on Kuznets inverted U-relationship between growth and inequality, see Kuznets (1955; 1963).

Do benefits of economic growth diffuse automatically to the poor? An important premise of early development theory was that the benefits of economic growth would trickle down to the poor automatically. This was the dominant development thinking in the 1950s and 1960s. But by the early 1970s, the trickle down theory lost some of its relevance, and it has been agreed that growth is a necessary condition, but not a sufficient condition for poverty reduction (details later). A study by Adelman and Morris (1973) was one of the first major studies to question the automaticity of the relationship between economic growth and benefits to the poor. And then came the influential contribution by Chenery *et al.* (1974), focussing on the importance of redistribution alongside economic growth. Ahluwalia *et al.* (1979) have examined the relationship between growth and poverty in developing countries. Although the output of the world economy had expanded at an unpredicted rate since the middle of 1950s for about a quarter century, and developing countries were also partners in increasing global economic growth, the benefits percolated to the poor were very limited. Further, this failure was because the distributional pattern of past growth had left the poorest groups outside the sphere of economic expansion and material improvement. The study also concluded that there is mounting evidence that the growth processes underway in most developing countries are such that incomes of the poorer groups increase more slowly than the average. Perhaps, this observation is also relevant for the period of economic reforms in globalisation syndrome across developing countries.

Recent Evidences on the Nexus: Some Empirical Evidences and Typologies

The first step in examining recent evidences on the nexus between growth and poverty is to discuss three studies (Datt and Ravallion, 1992; Kakwani and Pernia, 2000; Kakwani *et al.*, 2000; Kakwani, 2000), relating to the methodology of analysing the impact of growth on poverty. Datt and Ravallion (1992) propose a methodology of decomposing change in poverty into growth effect and distribution effect. The growth effect refers to change in poverty due to change in mean income alone (controlling income distribution effect), and the income distribution effect refers to change in poverty due to income distribution alone, controlling growth effect. This methodology would answer the question: how much of any observed change in poverty can be attributed to changes in distribution of income, as distinct from growth in average incomes. This also implies that the increase in average incomes reduces poverty and the increase in income distribution inequality increases poverty. The magnitudes of two components provide the relative sensitivity of poverty reduction to growth and distribution inequality. If the growth component dominates over the distribution inequality component, then growth maximising policies and strategies may be adequate in achieving a rapid reduction in poverty. If the distribution inequality component dominates, then policies and strategies should be one of pro-poor growth. Further, it is also argued (Kakwani, 2000) that low initial inequality will have a greater poverty reduction effect of growth, whereas countries with high initial inequality will have a greater poverty reduction effect from pro-poor growth policies/strategies. These are illustrated below with typologies of experiences:

First, Thailand is said to be a country with high distribution inequality and rapid economic growth. Consequently, the rate of poverty reduction has been much slower. Hence, growth-maximising policies and strategies alone will not be sufficient to achieve rapid reduction in poverty.

Second, Republic of Korea (even Lao PDR) is a nation with high economic growth and low distribution inequality. In this case, growth-enhancing policies and strategies may be adequate to reduce poverty.

Third, the Philippines is a country with lower economic growth and higher distribution inequality. A situation like this needs an appropriate mixture of growth-maximising and pro-poor-growth policies and strategies.

All these three typologies of experience leads to the major development lesson that the impact of growth on poverty depends on levels of distribution inequalities in assets and income. Ravallion (1997) has found that lower the poverty elasticity of growth, the higher the initial level of distribution inequality. Thus, initial distribution inequality is one of the very important factors in explaining differences in poverty reduction in different countries. That is why Deininger and Squire (1998) concludes that initial distribution inequality hurts mainly the poor, but not the rich.

Yet another way of looking at the issue of nexus between growth and poverty is who (the poor or rich) stands to gain more from growth. The study by ESCAP (2008) of the case of Thailand answers this question, but not for generalisation. Thailand's almost 10 per cent GDP growth rate per year during 1988-1992 did not proportionately benefit the poor. During the financial crisis years of 1996-2000, the worst affected were the poor. Poverty increased sharply from 11.4 per cent in 1966 to 16.2 per cent in 2000 (Son, 2003).

The study by Islam (2004) also suggests different combinations of growth and poverty reductions. Indonesia, Vietnam and Uganda represent a case of high GDP growth rates and high rates in poverty reduction, Bolivia: medium growth rates and high rates of poverty reduction, India: high growth rate and low rates of poverty reduction and Bangladesh: medium growth rate and low rate of poverty reduction. These different experiences are due to choice of sectoral pattern of growth, initial distribution inequalities, employment generation effects of growth pattern and so on. Kanbur (2004) has examined the variability of performance of different systems (statist model and market model) in growth and poverty reduction during the last decade, and concludes that a key factor underlying this variation in performance in growth and poverty reduction is the performance of institutions, broadly defined political, social and economic institutions.

Reinstatement of Growth-Maximisation Approach to Poverty Reduction

Recent cross-country studies argue that growth and poverty reduction are positively related. It is argued that growth tends to reduce absolute poverty (World Bank, 1990; Ravallion and Shaohua, 1997; Fields, 2001; Karry, 2004). Yet in another study by Ravallion (2000), it is inferred that the elasticity of poverty to growth is negative, impliying an increase in growth rate would reduce poverty in the headcount index of poverty. But there are also voices of caution (Cline, 2004; Khan and Weiss, 2006), indicating weaker-than-expected response of poverty levels to growth.

A stronger version of the positive relationship between growth and poverty reduction (via income distribution) is by Dollar and Kraay (2002); the study with an empirical examination of the relationship between growth and income distribution across 80 countries over 40 years has found that income of the poor (the bottom 20 per cent of the population) rises one-to-one with overall growth, and the relation is no different in poor countries than in rich countries. In other words, growth seems to benefit the poor as much as the rich so that relative inequality (the Gini ratio) stays the same. But the absolute inequality still widens, because the same growth of income gives more dollars to a rich than a poor person.

Naqvi (1995), based on the study of 40 developing countries, tends to come to the conclusion that high growth rates and distributive justice move together. These lines of arguments would provide a strong case for growth-maximising policies and strategies, and governments may not follow pro-poor growth policies. This argument that governments need not follow pro-poor growth policies appears to ignore the problem of absolute poverty in developing countries which very much warrants pro-poor growth policies and strategies (Eastwood and Lipton, 2000). It is also not clear whether cross-country studies by pooling data of different countries with varied socio-economic-political matrix would cloud the relationship between growth and poverty.

Counter to Growth-Maximising Alone Approach

If there is one-to-one correspondence between growth and poverty, how one would account for the persistence of high incidence of poverty despite unprecedented growth in developing countries like India. The growth-poverty inverse relationship definitely exists, but it is not perfect (Majid, 2004). There are studies (e.g. Fields, 1999) to indicate that the poor gain proportionately less than the average individual. These results are at odds with results of Dollar and Kraay (2002) study. The study by Foster and Szekely (2000), using social welfare approach casts doubts on the result that the income of the poor rises one-for-one with overall growth. Perhaps growth is good for the poor, but it is decidedly better for other segments of the society. This supports the concept of pro-poor growth and the concept of 'growth plus interventions' approach (Weiss and Khan, 2006), because benefits of growth do not percolate automatically to the poor. This argument is relevant for translating growth into development. Development without growth is not conceivable, but growth is possible without development.

In the context of counter to the arguments of Dollars and Kraay (2002) and others, it is also relevant to consider two general conclusions of the study by Fields (1999). First, 'nearly always economic growth has reduced poverty'. Second, 'when poverty has not fallen, it is usually because economic growth has not taken place'. Both the conclusions are somehow contrary to growth/development experiences of some of the developing countries like India.

The Growth–Poverty Relation Debate: Inconclusive

Different methodologies have led to different inferences on the relationship between poverty and growth. But this debate supports both growth-maximising and targetted poverty-reducing policies and strategies for developing countries. But a fine balance of combinations of both is needed, with a proper choice of pattern of growth keeping in view sectoral and social distribution of poverty (details in the following Section). This is absolutely needed as a part of pro-poor growth framework, and this framework is supported, among others, both by Asian Development Bank and UN Millennium Development Project 2005 (Hughes *et al.*, 2008). It is because economic growth is no longer treated synonymous with economic development, as it was upto 1970s. When the 'inadequacy' of growth alone for reducing absolute poverty is recognised, attempts are to be directed towards pro-poor growth and human development through pro-poor growth strategies.

The International Futures, a large scale integrated global modelling system (Hughes *et al.*, 2008) representing 182 countries, emphasises, among others, that humans as individuals should be able to develop their capabilities, attaining literacy, securing nutrition and health care, and gaining access to basic level of economic resources (similar to livelihood security concept in Bisaliah, 2009b). In this perspective, pro-poor growth is to be recognised as one of the pillars of sustainable human development. The goal is to move beyond income poverty and look much more broadly to capabilities-based measures.

In this quest for elements of pro-poor growth, Islam (2004) places emphasis on augmenting productivity of labour force in developing countries by providing more capital for labour to work with. Employment mediates between growth and poverty, and the following virtuous circle illustrates these relationships.

Figure 2.1

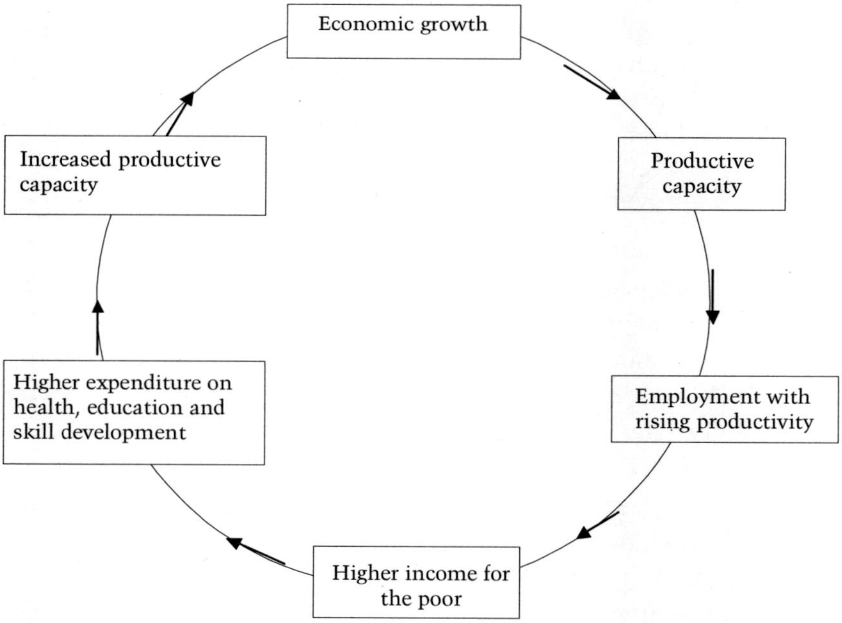

That explains why generation of employment is argued to be put at the centre of development agenda (Bhaduri, 2008). Jobless growth will not forge the positive relation between growth and poverty reduction, and the case in point is organised sector of India, and to some extent China also.

Capital Formation, Agricultural Growth and Poverty Alleviation

Recapitulation of results/inferences on capital and growth (Section II) and the nexus between growth and poverty (Section V) is in order, before the analytical and empirical issues related to capital formation and agricultural growth, and agricultural growth and poverty alleviation are outlined.

- First, a search for sources of growth both in theoretical and empirical studies has led to the conclusion that the capital (a broad concept) is one of the critical factors for growth. In all the three waves of growth theory—classical, neoclassical and new growth theory (endogeneous growth theory), the role of capital has turned out to be crucial for growth. Among other forms of capital, human, knowledge, physical and institutional would form a set of crucial forms of capital for growth.
- Second, growth accounting through growth regression studies have also concluded that capital is crucial for 'catch-up' in growth path and for growth convergence. Failure to 'catch-up' through capital accumulation and technological advancement (investment is needed for 'catch-up'), growth divergence, labour productivity divergence and divergence of TFP across countries would persist. Hence, investment in capital is needed for 'embodiment, 'vintage' and Kaldor effect to take place in growth process. Further 'idea gap' continues to persist between countries leading to growth divergence, in the absence of adequate amount of capital accumulation.
- Third, developing countries are to realise that capital accumulation is by far the most important contributor to measured growth of output in South Asia, East Asia and Latin America, as identified in a region-wise study of sources of output growth. Capital accumulation is important in its own right for these countries, but it is the major conduit for advances in knowledge/technology, which in turn are major determinant of productivity (both partial and total) and

output growth. Capital deepening (giving each worker a little more capital to work with) would make a substantial difference to productivity and output growth. Added to all these, capital accumulation is considered as an escape from the 'vicious circle of poverty'.

- Fourth, a study of debate on the nexus between growth and poverty suggests that the benefits of economic growth generally do not trickle down automatically to the poor. The decomposition analysis of change in poverty into growth effect and distribution effect suggests that the impact of growth on poverty depends on relative strength of these two effects. Dominance of growth effect over distribution effect would lead to rapid reduction of poverty, but the dominance of distribution effect over growth effect would lead to slowdown in poverty reduction. This would suggest that pro-poor growth policies and strategies will have a greater poverty reduction effect. Hence, the empirical evidences are mixed in the sense that different combinations of growth and poverty reduction are observed across different developing countries. The emergence of different combinations is due to choice of sectoral pattern of growth, initial distribution inequalities and employment generation. However, inadequacy of growth alone for poverty reduction is recognised, and 'growth plus intervention' strategy is suggested. In the quest for elements of pro-growth, productivity-augmentation of labour force in developing countries by providing more capital to work with in agricultural sector is important in view of the fact that poverty is dominantly a rural phenomenon.

Agriculture as a Leading Sector in Development Agenda

The imperatives for reinstating agriculture/rural sector at the centre of development agenda of developing countries could be examined from many perspectives:

First is the spatial and social distribution of poverty (Bisaliah, 2009). In regard to spatial distribution of poverty at the global level, South Asia and Sub-Saharan Africa are the hunger spots. Further, poverty is dominantly a rural phenomenon in these regions. It is estimated that 70 per cent of the people of food insecured regions are in rural areas. With respect to social distribution, small holders, landless labour and women and children would form a bulk of food-deprived people.

Second, in view of 'parking of' bulk of the poor in rural areas, growth of agro-rural sector is crucial for poverty alleviation. Since agro-rural sector is the predominant provider of employment for the rural people, and about 60 per cent employment generated in developing world is from the agricultural sector, agricultural production/productivity is likely to have a significant impact on poverty (Majid, 2004). If there is any sector that helps in achieving maximum poverty reduction goal directly, it ought to be agriculture sector. In fact, one of the major development experiences of India is recent emergence of service-led growth and decelerated growth of rural sector; as a result India is not in a position to 'honour' Millennium Development Goal of halving the number of poor people by 2015. In this regard, a disportionately high share of the service sector in GDP in many countries such as those in South Asia is considered a cause for some concern (Tisdell, 1999).

Third, high growth performance of agriculture sector is likely to trigger rural non-farm (RNF) activities which could lower rural unemployment and rural poverty (Lanjouw and Lanjouw 1995; Saith, 1992). This is the development multiplier effect of agricultural growth. Rural non-farm activities are not just outside the agricultural sector in a sectoral sense, but typically form part of rural households.

Fourth, in the Lewis Model (1954; 1955; 1958) there is an explicit treatment of the interaction and complementarity between agriculture and industry in terms of 'release of labour' to industry and demand expansion from rural sector as a stimulous to industrial growth. Further, agriculture should not be seen as static and its change has been a major factor in the long-run process of economic growth/development (Mellor, 1976; Lipton, 1988).

Fifth, higher productivity growth leading to higher food grain output (or any other food product) results in lower food prices benefitting the poor (Hayami and Herolt, 1977; Alauddin and Hossain 2001). In fact, a greater availability of food output is indicative of a better potential position of the rural poor than a lower availability. More recent literature provides ample evidence of the poverty reducing effect of higher agricultural growth resulting from higher productivity growth (Datt and Ravallion, 1999; Fan *et al.*, 2001). Further it is convincingly argued that agricultural productivity growth generates higher income for poorer farmer (Hayami and Ruttan, 1985; Lipton, 1977).

Sixth, no developed economy became so without agricultural sector recording substantial productivity gains. There is some historical evidence that agricultural revolution preceded industrial revolution in countries like Japan. It has been tracked that pre-war agricultural growth supported the post-war industrialisation of Taiwan and South Korea (Correa, 2008). Cross-country studies (Correa, 2008) which seek to track the sectoral sources of growth have concluded that dynamic agriculture has the strongest linkage to growth in other sectors and aggregate growth. Many developing countries have a long way to go in this type of transition (see Bose (2007) about India's problem of transition). Perhaps some developing countries are passing through 'grand tension' towards the right track of growth transition.

Seventh, a recent study by ESCAP (2008) has brought out clearly the critical role of agriculture for rural development and poverty reduction in ESCAP region. But decelerated agricultural growth has undermined the capacity of the region to reduce poverty and inequalities which are the major development policy goals.

Eighth, there is a deeper link between agricultural labour productivity and poverty reduction. Further, labour productivity and capital deepening are directly related (details later).

Ninth it is true that faster economic growth is one avenue for reducing poverty. But growth-maximising development policy may not always lead to maximisation of poverty reduction. Instead it is growth pattern and sectoral composition of aggregate output growth which would contribute for a higher rate of poverty reduction (Ravallion, 2000); because poverty has both spatial and social dimension. Hence, growth efforts need to be directed to areas where the poor people live, sectors in which poor people work, to the factors of production they possess, and to the products they consume. Because majority of the poor live and work in rural areas, have little education, provide unskilled labour and consume mostly basic necessities such as food, rural growth becomes the nodal strategy to promote this pro-poor growth. The argument of Warr (2000) that overall rate of growth is overwhelmingly an important determinant of poverty reduction and sectoral composition of growth may be less important will have to be subjected to further research scrutiny which he himself admits. Hence, for developing countries agriculture is conceded, in general, as a pro-poor growth sector, and hence to be treated as a leading sector for poverty reduction and for reducing growing distribution inequalities. Agricultural productivity growth is more poverty alleviating than non-agricultural productivity-led growth.

Agricultural Growth and Poverty Reduction: Cross-Country Experiences

The preceding section has argued for treating agriculture as a leading pro-poor sector, and for increasing productivity and production in this sector. This section examines some of the inferences drawn in empirical cross-country studies:

In developing countries, there has been a general decline in agricultural productivity and labour productivity and slowdown in poverty reduction since early 1990s. There is likely to be a deeper link between agricultural/labour productivity and poverty reduction. How else China could experience a concomitant maintenance of high labour productivity in agriculture and continued poverty reduction beyond early 1990s. Further, China's development experience suggests that growth in TFP in agriculture and high level of labour productivity are both crucial for poverty reduction (Majid, 2004). In fact, the growth performance of agriculture in China has matched with general growth performance of the economy. On the other hand, Sub-Saharan Africa has registered worst growth performance in both agricultural labour productivity and TFP in agriculture. This has generated a development experience typology of low labour productivity and low TFP and stagnant trend increases in poverty in Sub-Saharan Africa. This cross-country experience suggests that growth in both labour productivity and TFP would lead agriculture to positively impact poverty reduction. However, it is difficult to generalise; because the impact is negative in Latin America, and extremely weak in South Asia.

There is a body of growth accounting literature on agriculture that is devoted to systematically accounting for growth in labour productivity, capital intensity, human capital, land quality and other factors. The studies by Craig *et al.* (1997) and Thirtle *et al.* (2002) have attempted to measure the influence of agriculture R&D expenditure on growth in productivity. In a fairly comprehensive and influential study, Hayami and Ruttan (1985), while elaborating the role of agriculture in development, have provided estimates of land and labour productivity for a large number of countries and then have explored the causes of productivity differentials across countries. Much of their analysis has focussed on labour productivity and its determinants in the form of changing land-labour ratios, the use of fertilisers and tractors in agriculture production. Hayami (2002) has reinforced the importance of these sources of growth in agriculture. Cross-country labour productivity differentials are also examined (Kawagoe and Hayami, 1985; Lau and Yotopoulos, 1989) in terms of farm scale, education and research.

Instead of focussing only on labour productivity in agriculture there is a need for focussing on growth of TFP also. Some of the major findings from cross-country studies are as follows:

- Labour productivity and TFP in agriculture together could impact poverty reduction. Poverty reduction will be more when both labour productivity and TFP in agriculture increase. TFP alone will not lead to high level of poverty reduction (Majid, 2004). In fact an increase in labour productivity has a more direct effect on poverty reduction. However, labour productivity itself depends on TFP.
- What factors would influence TFP?
  - Craig *et al.* (1997) have investigated the role of input quality, infrastructure and research in explaining TFP growth. Improvements in skills of agriculture labour, better quality fertilisers, tractors with greater horse power and better seed varieties are examples of technical input quality that have direct bearing on TFP.
  - Majid (2004) has examined TFP augmentation by considering institutional, policy and structural factors. This seeks to explain variations in TFP in agriculture across 52 countries by considering a number of economic, geographical and institutional factors—effects of macroeconomic policy,

education, quality of governance, geography and so on (details in Majid, 2004). The study has identified the negative impact of wrong government policy, illiteracy and prevalence of deadly diseases (like malaria) and geographic isolation on TFP. The areas that are identified to increase TFP are investment in human capital through increased outlay on education and health, improvement in physical infrastructure for rural sector, implying more of public investment. Since agriculture labour productivity is negatively related to poverty, augmentation of labour productivity through increased TFP (or otherwise) is crucial.

- The study by Prasada Rao *et al.* (2004) has focussed on agricultural productivity growth, employment and poverty in developing countries, drawing data (for a period of over three decades 1961-2000) from 111 countries covering more than 95 per cent of global agricultural output and 98 per cent of the world population (see Prasada Rao *et al.*, 2004 for details on data, definition and measurement of variables and methods of analysis). The major relevant findings of the study are as below:
  - The agricultural productivity variable, both partial productivity ratios and TFP, exerts a significant ameliorating influence on incidence of poverty. Further, percentage of rural population and institutional factors such as policy and corruption also exert significant influence on poverty.
  - In view of dominant influence of TFP on agricultural productivity, what factors would affect TFP? The regression results suggest that irrigation, government expenditure and export (export as a percentage of GDP), a proxy variable for 'openness', are found to have significant positive influence on TFP. The countries with 'openness' in their economic policies have higher TFP levels in agriculture, perhaps due to more of technology transfer under 'openness' regime. The negative impact of illiteracy on TFP is very well observed. Land quality and geographical distance are also found to have bearing on TFP.
  - In case of Asia, Africa and Latin America, institutional, political and macroeconomic variables are also found to have strong

influence on TFP in agriculture. For example, TFP is adversely influenced by underdevelopment of human capital.

- A comparison of TFP growth in China and India between two periods of time (1970 *versus* 2000) would be quite contrasting compared to USA with 1.00. The TFP in Chinese agriculture increased from 0.29 in 1970 to 0.45 in 2000, whereas in India TFP had deteriorated from 0.32 to 0.25 during the same period, implying that growth in TFP in India has not kept pace with that of USA. However large gap in TFP between USA and these two countries is quite evident. China with a very average performance until the mid-1980s, suddenly gathered momentum in TFP growth acceleration, in addition to efficiency change and technical change.
- Developing countries are advised to increase TFP in agriculture by increasing investment in human capital and investment in improved physical infrastructure. Investment in agriculture R&D, by promoting greater foreign trade and by attracting foreign direct investment for rural sector, of course, by enforcing appropriate regulatory guidelines.

Both in China and Vietnam, agricultural growth has reduced poverty. Emphasis on agricultural growth did not sacrifice growth; on the other hand it drove growth. Rural growth spurred farm and non-farm enterprises that boosted employment and incomes, creating virtuous cycle of growth and poverty reduction. However, there are evidences on growth performance of China (Pasha, 2002) to suggest that during the early 1980s China's agriculture-led development strategy was highly pro-poor, but when China shifted its strategy towards exports and foreign direct investment, growth became less pro-poor and poverty reduction slowed (ESCAP, 2008). In case of Vietnam, with the introduction of land reforms (dismantling collective farms) and abolition of price controls, there was a spectacular growth in the 1990s, reducing poverty (Kakwani *et al.*, 2004). This leads to the development experience that it is not only the overall growth that determines how much poverty is reduced, it is also pattern of growth.

ESCAP study (2008) has brought out some useful development experiences relating to agricultural growth and poverty reduction.

First, the share of agriculture GDP in overall GDP has declined since 1990s in ESCAP region due to low productivity of agriculture, leading to lower employment and income opportunities for the poor. On the other hand, the number of people depending on agriculture has not declined as rapidly as the share of agriculture GDP especially in countries like India (Timmer, 2005).

Second, declining labour productivity in agriculture is yet another development experience of the region since 1990s. Raising average agricultural labour productivity in the region to that in Thailand could take 218 million people out of poverty. Agricultural labour productivity growth of 2.5 per cent in 1980s dropped to 1 per cent during 2000-2002. The main reason for this decline in labour productivity was stagnation of productivity growth in agriculture. It is estimated by ESCAP (2008) that 1 per cent increase in agriculture labour productivity would reduce the number of poor by 2.37 million in ESCAP region.

Third, the potential gains from higher productivity in agriculture are large. For example, a percentage point of additional growth in agricultural GDP per capita in South Asia would reduce poverty headcount 3.85 times more than an additional percentage growth outside agriculture in the region. Further ESCAP (2008) has estimated that raising agricultural productivity to the level of Thailand could reduce inequality measured by the Gini coefficient by 6 per cent.

Fourth, to emphasise the importance of agriculture labour productivity on poverty reduction, ESCAP (2008) estimates would provide additional evidence. It is estimated that 1 per cent increase in agricultural labour productivity would lead to a 0.37 per cent drop in poverty in the region. For example, it is estimated (Fan *et al.*, 2003) that the agricultural labour productivity elasticity of poverty is -0.417 for Thailand.

Fifth, agriculture sector could be a powerful engine for reducing poverty and ensuring social equity. Then what is holding back agriculture in the region? Structural constraints like inequality in land ownership, lack of human capital development, inadequate rural infrastructure, policy constraints such as anti-macroeconomic policies, failures in agricultural credit system and lack of adequate investment in R&D and extension services? In fact, agriculture R&D, education of the rural people and rural infrastructure, particularly, electricity and roads are key determinants of productivity in agriculture and have a major impact on poverty reduction (Fan *et al.*, 2003). To make agriculture socially and economically viable, and to promote inclusive growth, capital investment is needed for developing markets, human capital, augmenting R&D capacity, irrigation and water management and development of rural growth centres to provide non-farm employment and income opportunities so as to diversify their income sources and insure against shocks to their agricultural incomes (McCullockh *et al.*, 2007).

Capital Formation: A Major Driver of Agricultural Productivity and Growth

It is recalled from earlier sections that:

- Aggregate economic growth is far from adequate to address the development problems like poverty, inequalities and unemployment in developing countries. Agriculture/rural growth could be 'remedy' for some of these problems, because agriculture/rural growth is treated as pro-poor, and poverty is dominantly a rural phenomenon.
- Cross-country agricultural growth and poverty reduction studies suggest closer link between decelerated agricultural output/ productivity growth and slowdown in poverty reduction.
- Growth in agricultural labour productivity and augmentation of TFP could have larger impact on poverty reduction. For example, a rise in the average agricultural labour productivity by 1 per cent in the ESCAP region to the level of Thailand could take 218 million people out of poverty in the region.
- The determinants of TFP are irrigation, government expenditure on agriculture, rural infrastructure, human capital, agriculture R&D and so on. All these determinants would need capital formation in/for agriculture. Further investment for the development of non-farm sector in rural sector would be equally important for increasing and diversifying employment and income opportunities for the poor in developing world. Hence, capital (in the broader sense) is one of the major drivers of agricultural productivity/growth, and thereby poverty reduction. Capital formation, structural and policy constraints need to be addressed to achieve the development policy goals.

Debate on the Concept of Capital in Agriculture

The United Nations concept of capital includes tangible reproducible assets destined to be used in future production (Hooley, 1967). Agricultural implements and machinery, land improvements, laying of new orchards and plantations, irrigation and other constructions, and so on perhaps could be included as forms of capital formation in agriculture. Based on a study of capital formation in agriculture of 62 countries, Larson *et al.* (2000) have considered fixed capital in agriculture, capital in orchards (tree stock), and capital in livestock as components of capital formation in agriculture. These components account for most of agricultural capital. However National Accounts usually report fixed capital investment, which does not wholly include livestock and tree stock. Further, while estimating agriculture capital stock, the issue whether agricultural land be included (as discussed in Wilcox (1943), or investment in improving the productivity of land alone be included is being debated. One of the major issues in capital formation is compositional shifts in capital formation with structural transformation of the economy. To illustrate this point, some of the results of the study by Larson *et al.* (2000) could be used. Ratio of livestock and tree capital to fixed capital in agriculture in a study of 62 countries could be one of the ways to gauge compositional difference in capital formation broadly between two groups of countries.

Table 2.2

The Ratio of Tree Stock and Livestock to Agricultural Fixed Capital (Averages over 1967-1992)

Country	*Tree Stock*	*Livestock*
Canada	0.009	0.140
France	0.263	0.245
Japan	0.078	0.013
USA	0.055	0.223
New Zealand	0.033	1.011
India	0.208	1.758
Indonesia	5.569	3.014
Kenya	0.909	3.876
Pakistan	0.295	1.587

Source: See Larson *et al.* (2000) for methodology of constructing fixed capital, tree and livestock capital series.

One major observation on the results in Table 2.2 is related to compositional difference in capital formation between developed and developing countries. The capital accumulation from fixed capital (machinery, irrigation, building etc.) is found to be more important than capital of agricultural origin such as livestock and tree stock in developed countries. In view of declining importance of livestock and tree stock *vis-à-vis* fixed capital, agriculture has become more capital intensive in these countries. In developing countries, livestock capital is found to be still more important *vis-à-vis* fixed capital, and tree stock capital in countries like Indonesia is more important than fixed capital, and tree stock capital in Kenya is at least as important as fixed capital. This may also imply low fixed capital base for agriculture in developing countries. The relationship between fixed capital stock and productivity of agriculture in different countries will be discussed later. Three more results from Larson *et al.* (2000) are important. First, agriculture has become more capital intensive in most of the countries, even though total agricultural capital stock—including livestock and orchards—have declined in about 30 per cent of study countries. Second, the composition of agricultural capital has also changed in most of the countries. Within the agricultural sector of developed countries, the growth of fixed capital generally exceeds that of total capital in agriculture, indicating smaller growth rate of livestock and freestock. Third, in developing countries in general, capital of agriculture origin is found to be more important than fixed capital.

It is also appropriate to examine the shifting composition of agricultural capital historically, based on an important study by Tostlebe (1957) on USA. The study has considered growth of real farm capital measured under four major categories *viz.*, land and buildings, machinery, livestock and stored crops. The study on the capital growth centers on the inter-relationships among three variables—farm capital, labour and output. A few of the results of this study are relevant in the context of the present study:

- First, demand for capital replacement and addition is a function of increasing stock of knowledge, leading to change in composition of capital stock, and growing purchase of capital from industrial sector.
- Second, the percentage share of implements and machinery in total capital stock increased from 4 per cent between 1870 and 1910 to

37 per cent between 1910 and 1950. Further, the historical study also infers that land became less important and machinery and power somewhat more important in the whole of physical farm capital. During the Second World War, the need for increased output coincided with an acute labour shortage on farm; as a result farmers added to their stocks of machinery at unpreceded rate. As a result of these, with mechanical technological innovations, farmers could produce farm output at an increasing rate, even though there was a decline in factors of production such as labour.

- Third, output per unit of capital increased slowly until 1920. Then the increase accelerated so that by 1950 output per unit of capital was 40 per cent higher than in 1920. Further, productivity of labour (output per person engaged in agriculture) was upward throughout the study period of 80 years due to capital deepening in agriculture. The chief factor that accounted for the persistent rise in output per agricultural worker was due to simultaneous rise in capital per worker.

  The lesson from the examination of this historical study is quite obvious for developing countries. The large and continuing importance of capital as a determinant of productivity of labour is to be recognised in the perspective that one of the avenues to address the problem of poverty in rural areas is to increase the productivity of labour engaged in agriculture. The developing countries have to realise that the physical capital assumes meaning only with a given technological and institutional framework. A study by Easterly and Levine (1997) has found that the conventional factors of growth alone do not fully explain Africa's experience, and hence institutional factors like agrarian structure, land distribution etc., are also relevant. Hence, the role of capital formation in agriculture growth has to be examined in its totality, including technological and institutional factors.

- Fourth, the prospective trends derived from the study such as increase in output per unit of capital, rise in capital stock per person engaged in agriculture, and gradual modification to composition of total capital stock are good lessons for developing countries.

There are three major stages identified with respect to capital formation in agriculture (Perkins and Witt, 1961), which are pertinent messages for developing countries:

First, there is a large subsistence segment in agriculture with less of market orientation with a scarce capital supply coupled with unused land and labour resources; the development situation would call for investment of surplus labour in capital creating projects.

Second, social overhead capital becomes exceedingly important, when development environment is dotted with less of unused natural and labour resources. This environment would need the support of social overhead capital in the form of education, training programmes, research and extension efforts so as to 'produce' and use land-saving technological resources for increasing the level of agricultural productivity. That would also create better climate for private investment in agriculture. Japanese model of agricultural growth by developing and using land-saving technologies like investment in irrigation, and biochemical inputs could be good examples. To overcome the scarcity of land, investment in land substitutes like irrigation and production of biochemical inputs becomes relevant.

Third, this is a stage of developed agriculture in which wage rates are increasing, and capital has to be substituted for labour in the form of 'labour-saving' technologies in the form of mechanical technologies. In this development stage, capital deepening takes place. The American agriculture growth path may illustrate this situation.

But in developing countries, combinations of all these three stages may co-exist, with consequent differences in capital formation pattern requiring proper investment decisions.

Capital Deepening for Agricultural Growth

It is recapitulated from earlier discussion that growth in agricultural labour productivity and augmentation of TFP could have a larger significant impact on poverty reduction. But the growth of both labour productivity and TFP would need capital deepening, in the sense more capital is needed to accomplish growth at both fronts and thereby to experience higher growth of agricultural output. But low level of capital accumulation (in the broader issue) in agriculture is one of the distinguishing characteristics of developing countries.

The following data illustrates less of capital deepening in agriculture– less of capital items like agriculture machinery (tractor as a proxy for agriculture machinery) in developing countries *vis-à-vis* developed countries.

Table 2.3

Capital Deepening and Productivity of Agriculture Workers

	Country	*Tractors per Thousand Agricultural Workers (1995-1997)*	*Agricultural Productivity per Agricultural Worker (1996-1998 in USD)*
1.	Bangladesh	-	276
2.	India	6	406
3.	Brazil	57	4081
4.	Japan	637	31094
5.	Germany	991	22759
6.	Italy	913	20031

Source: World Development Report (2000).

It follows from the data that capital intensity and labour productivity in agriculture generally vary directly. It is realised that labour productivity in agriculture depends not only on agriculture machinery, but also on human capital, social capital, institutional capital, natural capital and so on. Further, the determinants of TFP (which may have bearing on labour productivity) are irrigation, government expenditure on agriculture, rural infrastructure, human capital and agriculture R&D. As discussed earlier, all these would need capital formation in/for agriculture; added to this is the need for capital investment to support non-farm sector development in rural areas to diversify and enlarge employment and income opportunities for the poor.

To support this reasoning, empirical results from Table 2.1 could be recalled. The aggregate growth accounting regressions across broad groups of countries would illustrate the importance of capital *vis-à-vis* other drivers of growth. Capital accumulation is by far the most important contributor to measure growth in output in all the countries. The country studies of Israel (Sadan, 1968) and on China (Chow, 1993) would also illustrate the importance of capital in the matrix of deep drivers of growth.

Agricultural Capital Stock, Labour Productivity and Prevalence of Hunger in Developing Countries

It is appropriate to state major results of three studies FAO (2001), Stephan *et al.* (2009) and Schmidhuber *et al.* (2009) on agricultural capital stock (ACS) productivity of labour engaged in agriculture, and prevalence of hunger in developing countries. This is to establish the relationship between ASC, productivity of labour and hunger in developing countries.

These results would reinforce the argument that ACS tends to have positive impact on productivity of labour in agriculture and thereby negative impact on prevalence of hunger in developing countries.

- A study (Stephan *et al.,* 2009), covering the period between 1975-2007, has inferred that since the early 1990s, rates of ACS growth in developing countries have remained positive, but continue to fall.
- It is found that there is a tendency for low ACS per worker, low labour productivity and high prevalence of undernourished population to 'co-exist'. Further, the regions with the lowest prevalence of chronic undernourishment—Latin America, Near East and North Africa—are found to have a much higher ACS per agriculture worker. In other words, the level of capital intensity is found to be the highest in regions with lowest prevalence of hunger.
- The regions with low capital intensity per agriculture worker showed a low productivity per worker.
- The value added per worker in the group of countries with the lowest per cent of the population undernourishment was 2.0 times higher than in the group of countries with highest level of undernourishment.
- Between 1975-2007, the average annual growth rates in ACS was 1.33 per cent in Latin America and Caribbean, -0.26 per cent in South Asia and -0.44 per cent in Sub-Saharan Africa. Further, the rate of growth of ACS per worker was 2.76 per cent in least hunger category of countries, -0.30 per cent in highest hunger category. China had recorded 0.74 per cent growth rate. In brief, the ACS had

grown the least in countries with the highest prevalence and depth of hunger. In several of the least developed countries, in particular, in Sub-Saharan Africa and South Asia, capital deepening has declined.

- TFP growth rate in agriculture between 1975-2007 was the highest (2.1%) in China, lowest (0.9%) in Sub-Saharan Africa and 1 per cent in Latin America. (Details on decomposition of TFP into efficiency and technical change components in Stephan *et al.*, 2009).
- Factors having positive impact on TFP are found to be irrigation development, political regime index, government expenditure on agriculture and FDI under some institutional environment like lack of corruption and democratic political structures.
- The outlook study of Schmidhuber *et al.* (2009) for a period of 44 years (2005/06-2050) has provided some more details on the importance of capital stock in agriculture.
- The cumulative gross investment requirements for developing countries would come to US $9.2 trillion (component-wise break-up in the outlook study), during 2005/06-2050. About 60 per cent of the total would be required to replace the existing capital stock, the next 40 per cent to add to the existing capital stock to increase output (nearly double) and raise productivity. Further, primary agriculture would account for US $5.2 trillion of the total and US $4 trillion for downstream needs (processing, transportation, storage and so on).
  - Growth accounting analysis suggests that overall growth will be characterised by a growing substitution of labour with capital and moderate TFP growth. However, in Latin America, growth will be capital intensive, and in Sub-Saharan Africa, growth will be heavily labour and moderately capital based.
  - A farmer in Latin America, on an average, has 10 times more capital available than his counterpart in Sub-Saharan Africa.
  - An important factor that explains difference in output per worker is capital stock per worker. (See Schmidhuber *et al.*, 2009 for other reasons for differences in productivity).

- It is also argued that incremental capital-output ratio (ICOR) could be the basis for deciding where more capital should go. For example, the lowest (3.1) ICOR is for Sub-Saharan Africa (average over 2005/06–2050). This is also suggestive of higher returns on investment made in this region. This is consistent with the argument that marginal productivity of capital is high in capital deficient developing countries.

It is obvious that any country that has experienced productivity growth—both partial and total—in agriculture has done so through capital deepening among other supportive measures. But one of the fundamental obstacles to growth/development of agriculture in developing countries is low capital accumulation as well as its efficient use. Given a limited amount of investment resources, the development merit of a sector is to be judged by how much the sector would contribute for addressing the development problems like poverty, unemployment and inequalities, and by how much of development multiplier it would give rise to inducement effects. Agriculture tends to emerge as a deserving candidate on both the counts of merit. Further, the agriculture sector of developing countries is passing though what Hirschman (1960) called 'grand tension' in their development process and development disequilibrium. Low productivity of labour force in many of the developing countries due to capital deficiency, among others, has sharpened this 'grand tension' in the form of high prevalence of hunger.

3 Capital Formation, Agriculture Growth and Poverty in India

Macro Evidences and Analysis

It has been concluded in the preceding chapter that the most important contributor to measured growth in agriculture is capital formation, among others like TFP. Further, the relationship between agriculture capital stock (ACS), productivity of labour engaged in agriculture and prevalence and depth of hunger in developing countries have also been examined. The major conclusion of this analysis is that high capital intensity (capital deepening) has positive impact on productivity of labour in agriculture, and high productivity of labour leads to low prevalence and depth of hunger in developing countries. In this chapter, the focus is on case study of India, one of the hot spots of poverty from the angle of both spatial and social distribution of poverty, and where poverty is dominantly a rural phenomenon with over 60 per cent depending on agriculture for employment and income opportunities. Further, India has entered into high growth trajectory, and this has been accomplished mainly through service sector-led growth. The present chapter is designed to focus mainly on complexity and concerns of Indian agriculture sector, concepts and coverage of ACS, growth of capital stock and its composition, investment behaviour of public and private sector (determinants of capital formation), complementarity between public and private sector capital formation, the relationship between capital formation and productivity/output growth in agriculture and the impact of agricultural growth on poverty.

The Context, Complexity and Concerns of Agricultural Sector

An analysis of complexity and concerns of agriculture sector would form a backdrop to the theme of this chapter. Further, there are many imperatives for placing agriculture at the centre of the development agenda of the country. The imperatives are large segment of the population depending on agriculture for livelihood, positive relationship between agricultural growth and poverty reduction (discussed in global perspective in Chapter 2), key to higher GDP growth rate through supply and demand routes, widening and deepening rural-urban development divide, increasing food insecurity and so on. Keeping these imperatives, the following facets of the context, complexity and concerns of agricultural sector are outlined to search for drivers and directions of agricultural growth (Bisaliah, 2009):

- The complexity of agriculture growth is enhanced by the large number of holdings and their small size. As per Agricultural Census of 2000-01, there were 120 million holdings of which 83 per cent were marginal and small (100 million holdings). The average size of land holdings had declined from 2.28 hectare in 1970-71 to 1.3 hectare in 2000-01.
- The share of agriculture GDP (AGDP) in national GDP has decreased from 55 per cent in 1950-51 to about 16 per cent in 2008-09. But there has been less of a structural transformation, because about two-third of the country's work force continues to depend on agriculture for their livelihood. A recent study by Broadberry and Gupta (2009) has clearly brought out the low labour productivity in Indian agriculture *vis-à-vis* that of UK. While identifying the great divergence of productivity and living standards between UK and India, the study has convincingly argued that productivity divergence is largely due to low labour productivity performance in Indian agricultural sector. This is the only sector where India has continued to fall farther and farther behind UK, whereas in service sector there has been an upward trend in labour productivity. Hence, India needs to drastically increase agricultural labour productivity if it is to improve its overall productivity performance and to accelerate the 'catching-up' process in growth performance.
- Added to low agricultural labour productivity is the productivity (measured in terms of productivity per unit of land) fatigue and agricultural technology fatigue in India and falling TFP which in turn have strong bearing in output growth performance. To put in brief, since the period of economic reforms from 1991 as a part of

structural adjustment programme (SAP), there has been a decelerated output growth in agriculture sector, accelerated growth in service sector and stagnant/marginally improved growth in industrial sector (Bisaliah, 2006). Growth rate of agriculture GDP (from agriculture and allied sectors) has declined from 3.6 per cent during 1984-85 and 1995-96 to 1.8 per cent during 1995-96 and 2004-05 and to 1.6 per cent in 2008-09. In a land-constraint country where productivity-led growth has to be the major driver of agriculture output growth, productivity fatigue/decrease is bound to give rise to decelerated agriculture growth. In fact, international comparisons reveal that average productivity of land in Indian agriculture is generally 30 per cent to 50 per cent of the highest average yield in the world.

- As a result of dismal performance of agriculture in both output and employment growth in rural sector (Bisaliah, 2006), rural poverty is still high (Dev *et al.*, 2008a). A re-estimate of poverty in India suggests that about 28 per cent of rural people are below the poverty line when only expenditure on food is considered and the estimate comes to 36 per cent, if minimum level of private expenditure on health and education is also included. This is comparable with Tendulkar Committee Report of 2009 (Bisaliah, 2010a) which has reported percentage of people below the poverty line, as 37 per cent, and of rural 42 per cent. This explains why Report of Expert Group on Agriculture Indebtedness 2007 (Bisaliah, 2010a) observes that India is passing through an agrarian crisis, one of the symptoms is that about 200,000 farmers had committed suicide between 1997 and 2008.
- Depletion and degradation of natural resource base (land and water) giving rise to biological disequilibrium is yet another concern that needs to be addressed to restore the productivity of agriculture.
- Polarised growth instead of broad-based virtuous growth has given rise to growth enclaves, bypassing a large segmentation of agriculture. The outcome of this polarised growth is agricultural segmentation with the rural affluent elite, dynamic farmers with roots in agriculture, and footloose farmers waiting for the 'opportunity' to leave agriculture. It is estimated that about 60 per

cent of the farmers are struck in agriculture, not because they have found agriculture 'profitable', but because they do not have alternative avenues for their livelihood. This implies failure to shift 'surplus' labour force from agriculture at least to rural non-farm sector by diversifying livelihood options.

- The low rate of poverty reduction from 3.1 per cent per annum during 1983 and 1990-91 to 1 per cent and less per annum during 1990s is another concern. Even in 1990s, there was a considerable decline in urban poverty, but rural poverty reduction rate was almost close to zero, and there are no signs of improvement in rural poverty reduction rates. Why productivity fatigue and technology fatigue and why impasse in growth performance of Indian agriculture? What are the search areas (drivers) for agricultural growth (details in Bisaliah, 2009c)? To place agriculture on high growth trajectory, there are many areas such as rebuilding natural resource base, augmenting rural human capital by improving its quality, energising agricultural R&D domain, improvement in irrigation, markets, roads, adequate emphasis on non-price factors of agricultural growth in addition to price interventions (setting the prices right), rural electrification development of non-farm sector and so on.

All these growth promoting agents require investment in agriculture. But one of the most disquieting developments in the agricultural sector during the last decade has been the neglect of capital formation in agriculture, especially in public sector. Which ever the research reports and policy documents one reviews, the development experience of Indian agriculture has seen fall in public investment in agriculture giving rise to dismal productivity/production performance of Indian agriculture, falling TFP (Ranjita and Mruthyunjaya 2005) and so on. The experience of China shows that high rate of investment in agriculture can ensure big spurt in agricultural output (Rao and Gulati, 1994). Many of the problems of agriculture sector *viz.*, low productivity, low employment opportunities, high intensity of poverty, and inadequate infrastructure are attributed to inadequate and progressive decline in public investment in physical capital (irrigation, rural electrification, roads, markets etc.), human capital (health, education and training) and development of non-farm sector. These arguments are reinforced by a recent report by UN World Food Programme

(UNWFP) and MSSRF (2009) which recommends more public investment in agriculture, among others, to prevent further fall in agricultural productivity and to ensure a food-secured India.

Concepts and Data Base on Capital Formation: Three Bouts of Research

To analyse the impact of capital formation on agricultural growth, and of agricultural growth on poverty, there is a need for analysing the trends and composition of capital formation in/for agriculture. Before that, the concepts of data base on capital formation would be essential, because what should constitute capital formation has been one of the methodological controversies debated by researchers. The controversy has been sharpened by the distinction which Dantwala (1986) has drawn between capital formation in and for agriculture.

The first major attempt has been made by Shukla (1965) in her pioneering work on 'Capital Formation in Indian Agriculture during 1920-1921 and 1960-61'. The study was conducted at a time when there was no unanimity of opinion regarding the items to be included in the capital stock; of course this methodological issue is still alive. Starting with a broad definition of capital consisting of physical durable assets, the working capital and the resources invested in human capital, the study has confined to the definition of capital stock to include capital invested in land, capital in the form of housing, farm equipment such as tractors, ploughs, carts, oil engines and electric pump sets for private irrigation, sugarcane crushers, work animals (only bullocks), and investment in irrigation. The definition has been constructed, in view of data availability on these assets in physical units, and on valuation problems for aggregation to arrive at total capital stock. In broad terms, the difference between land substituting capital like irrigation, and labour (human and bullock) substituting capital like tractors is still relevant, because the process of agricultural growth is the process of finding substitutes especially for scarce inputs. This is actually the theme of 'induced invocation' model of agricultural growth (Hayami and Herdt 1985). It is not out of place to state a few major conclusions of this study with data for a period of 40 years between 1920-1921 and 1960-1961, and Indian agriculture was yet to escape from the trap of low level of equilibrium. Perhaps some of the underdeveloped/

developing countries like Sub-Saharan Africa are still placed in this situation. First, accumulation of the stock of capital has barely kept pace with the increasing labour supply. Following this, capital/labour and capital/output ratios were nearly constant during 40 years of study. Lack of technological improvement over the period of study would imply a somewhat rigid relationship of complementarity between labour and capital (i.e., almost constant capital/labour ratio). This theory leads to conclude that capital stock would rise with technological improvements in agriculture. Further, constant capital/output ratio also represents lack of technological change. Second, lack of technological change and relationship of complementarity between capital and labour leads to the explanation why major portion of capital investment is devoted to traditional forms of capital when investment rate is low. Hence, the only major 'route' to break the long-term low level of equilibrium of Indian agriculture was technological change in agriculture, which started occurring from the middle of 1960s in the form of mainly biochemical technology.

The second stream of research has been with the data compiled by Central Statistical Organisation (CSO) as a part of National Accounts Statistics (NAS) in accordance with the concepts and definitions in the System of National Accounts (SNA) of United Nations (Recommendations of SNA-1993 in Report of the Committee on Capital Formation in Agriculture, 2003 for enlarging the accounts of sub-sectors). CSO has compiled estimates of capital formation in agriculture with break-up of public and private investments as a part of NAS. CSO estimate of public sector investment includes investment in irrigation schemes and plantations in the forestry sector. Irrigation alone would account for more than 90 per cent of the gross public capital accumulation in agriculture. In the scheme of estimation of capital formation considered are: assets created by construction like irrigation, machinery and equipment and change in stocks (inventories). Among others, one of the limitations of CSO estimate of household sector capital formation is that it does not take into account change in the stocks of supplies and materials and work in progress during the accounting year. All it does is to estimate the inventories relating to livestock. This implies that change in capital stock in household sector is under estimated (Mishra, 1996a). For this reason and many other reasons stated in the Report of the Committee on Capital formation in Agriculture (GoI, 2003), the data set provided by CSO is termed as 'narrow data series'.

Private sector investment includes investments made by farm households and private corporates. The household sector investment comprises investment on farm equipment, machinery, irrigation, land reclamation and land improvement. Household investment alone would account for over 90 per cent share in private sector investment. The household data is developed, using the data generated by Reserve Bank of India under All India Debt and Investment surveys (AIDIS) conducted once in 10 years.

The private corporate sector investment under construction includes expenditure on tea, coffee and rubber plantations. It also includes investments made by cooperative entities like sugar and milk cooperatives as discussed earlier in Chapter 1.

Two concepts of capital formation used by CSO also need to be placed in the perspective of examining trends in capital formation in the next section. The concept of fixed capital formation refers to a set of assets produced as outputs from the process of production that are themselves used repeatedly or continuously in other process of production for more than one year. Fixed capital gets 'consumed' in the process of production. The extent of loss of its productive potential is known as consumption of fixed capital (CFC). Fixed capital formation computed without netting for CFC is known as gross fixed capital formation (GFCF). The term gross capital formation (GCF) refers to the sum of GFCF and change in inventories, as stated in Chapter 1.

The second major bout of interest in this area of research (based on 'narrow data set') was in late 1980s and early 1990s, bringing out the issue of fall in public investment in agriculture during 1980s, echoing the neglect of agriculture in public resource allocation and its adverse impact on private investment (in the context of complementarity issues between these two types of investment) as well as agricultural growth and equity concerns of development policy of the country. These concerns and controversies have given rise to third bout of research which further has deepened and broadened the concerns and controversies. These concerns and controversies centre around declining public sector investment in agriculture, confirming/refuting complementarity hypothesis between public and private investment, compositional shifts in capital stock, determinants of public and private investment behaviour, interstate (regional) disparities in capital stock and its implication for transfer of resources from Central (Federal) government to state government, impart of capital formation on agriculture growth, impact of agriculture growth on poverty, efficiency in capital use, and the needed policy directions for matching growth in rate of capital stock with targetted output growth.

The third bout of research is based mainly on what is called 'broad data series' as against 'narrow data series', provided by CSO (See HLC, 2009: Chapter IX for coverage and methods of estimation of capital formation in India). The main reason for developing the 'broad series' is to re-examine the issue of falling agriculture output due to falling/stagnant public investment in agriculture since 1980s as argued by researchers using CSO data set (Rath, 1989; Mitra, 1996; Rao, 1997 and many others), since these conclusions are based on CSO data base with its concept, coverage and estimation procedure. Further, the reasons for falling public sector investment have been attributed to rising subsidies, growing opposition to big irrigation dams and so on (Rao, 1997; Mitra, 1996; Gulati *et al.*, 1997; Dhawan 1998). All these methodological controversies have warranted research efforts for redefining the concept of capital formation in public sector and to re-estimate it.

The argument of Dantwala (1986) to draw the distinction between capital formation in agriculture and capital formation for agriculture has provided the logical foundation for the third bout of research. To monitor agricultural growth and its drivers, it is necessary to have a broader measure of agricultural capital formation that includes capital formation in activities such as production of fertilisers and pesticides, development of agricultural markets, rural roads and communication, agricultural education, research and development of agricultural technology, rural electrification and so on which can be called capital formation for agriculture in comparison with capital formation in agriculture being compiled by CSO as a part of National Accounts Statistics. Many significant attempts (Chand, 2000; 2001; Roy, 2001b; Gulati *et al.*, 2002; GoI, 2003) have been made to redefine the concept of public investment in/

for agriculture and to develop 'broad data series' relating to public investment as against 'narrow data series' of CSO.

First, Chand (2000; 2001) using the data available in financial accounts of Union (Federal) and state (regional) governments for 23 years (1974-75 and 1996-97) has developed investment series called 'broad series' (Bisaliah, 2004). This 'broad series' cover capital expenditure in public sector under 23 heads, including the ones in CSO series and investment in fertiliser industry, rural roads and so on. Further, Chand (2000) has also developed time series data on private investment at the state level, using data generated once in 10 years by Reserve Bank of India under All India Debt and Investment Surveys (AIDIS), data generated by National Sample Survey Organisation (NSSO) under household capital expenditure, and the national level private investment data compiled by CSO. Second, Roy (2001b) has broadened the 'broad data series' on public investment by considering capital expenditure under 21 heads (including the ones in CSO 'narrow series'), and 50 per cent of revenue expenditure on rural development, agricultural research and education. He has also constructed time series national level data on private investment by using the CSO data. Further, by using CSO data, generated by Reserve Bank of India under AIDIS, and by NSSO under household capital expenditure, he has also developed time series state level data on private investment. Third, Gulati *et al.* (2002) have re-examined the major issues of declining public investment in 1980s, complementarity hypothesis and impact of capital formation on productivity growth, using three concepts of public investment, *viz.*, Concept I as made available by CSO covering basically Government investment in irrigation schemes and plantations in the forestry sector; Concept II comprising components of Concept I of CSO plus part of the investment in power sector that goes to agriculture, as reported by Central Electricity Authority/Planning Commission; Concept III comprising components Concept II plus investment in agriculture and allied sectors under 11 items of expenditure, as per budgetary classification under centrally sponsored schemes. However, the efforts made by Chand (2000; 2001) and by Roy (2001b) and Gulati *et al.* (2002) in developing 'broad data series' are mainly in relation to their personal research works, but not for the publication of 'broad data series' on public sector investment in agriculture as a time series data set continuously.

The Report of the Committee on Capital Formation in Agriculture (GoI, 2003) has further sharpened the data base for analysing public investment for agriculture. The Committee has argued for broader investment series, keeping in view the difference between capital formation in/for agriculture. Information needs of agricultural development managers extend beyond farm production activity. They need information from sectors such as agriculture & allied industry (agricultural machinery, fertilisers and pesticides), electricity and water supply, construction (irrigation structures, rural roads, agricultural markets etc.), trade, railways/shipping/airways/roads, storage, communication, banking and insurance, capital expenditure on rural development, crop husbandry, soil and water conservation, preservation of wildlife and environments and so on. We need three data series to construct broad data series for agricultural development managers:

First, capital formation for agriculture obtained by regrouping the CSO estimates. Second, capital formation for agriculture through investment in agricultural education, research and extension. Third, expenditure on conservation of forest (including wildlife) and environment also qualify for inclusion as capital formation for agriculture. But all these would go beyond the confines of SNA. However, any attempt to expand the data set for including expenditure on education as investment in human capital may also invite suggestions for including public expenditure on health, housing, as investment in human capital. Hence, too much broadening of the capital formation will raise the methodological controversy of benefit gestation period, and apportion of expenditure towards consumption and production components for assessing the impact on agricultural growth. But data on these items under three data subsets may be of help for monitoring supportive and sustaining factors for agricultural development. The following rough and provisional estimate of proportion of expenditure to be allotted to agriculture suggested by the Committee (GoI, 2003) may provide some insights into the role of different sectors in capital formation for agriculture.

Table 3.1

Proportion of GFCF Meant for Agriculture

Sl. No.	*Sector*	*Proportion of GFCF Meant for Agriculture*
1.	Agriculture & allied	1.0
2.	Agricultural machinery	1.0
3.	Fertilisers & pesticides	0.96
4.	Electricity/gas & water supply	0.09
5.	Construction	0.09
6.	Trade	0.25
7.	Railways	0.07
8.	Storage	0.69
9.	Communication	0.09
10.	Banking & insurance	0.05

Added to this apportionment of proportion is the percentage share contribution of different sectors to GFCF for agriculture during 2001-02 at 1993-94 prices.

Table 3.2

Percentage Share in GFCF for Agriculture

Sl. No.	*Sector*	*Percentage Share in GFCF for Agriculture*
1.	Agriculture	68.95
2.	Agricultural machinery	0.86
3.	Fertilisers & pesticides	9.16
4.	Electricity/gas & water supply	6.69
5.	Construction	1.20
6.	Trade	4.82
7.	Railways	1.05
8.	Storage	0.50
9.	Communication	3.20
10.	Banking & insurance	0.42
11.	Public administration and defence	3.15
	Total GFCF for agriculture	100.00

It is obvious that three sectors alone *viz.*, agriculture, fertilisers and pesticide industry, electricity, gas & water supply sector would form about 85 per cent of capital formation for agriculture. Among other recommendations of this Committee, one important recommendation about data on capital formation needs serious condition. That is, the System of Economic Accounts for Food and Agriculture (SEAFA) designed by FAO may be adopted by the Ministry of Agriculture for implementation. The major sources of data for SEAFA are input survey, livestock census, agricultural census and livestock and landholding survey conducted by NSSO.

One more data set developed by FAO recently on agricultural capital stock for 237 countries (including India) along with region-wise classification needs critical examination *vis-à-vis* agricultural capital stock data estimated by NAS of India and some other countries in accordance with the concepts and definitions in the SNA of United Nations. This is beyond the scope of present study.

Investment Behaviour in Indian Agriculture

The level as well as the growth rate of capital stock in agriculture, both in public and private sector (farm household sector), would depend on the investment behaviour of decision-makers. Before the growth analysis of capital formation and the shifts in its composition, an analysis of investment behaviour of both the sectors focussing on determinants of investment is in order. Any policy/programme designs will have to depend on causal factors governing investment behaviour of public and private sectors. If agricultural sector is 'starved' of capital stock with its negative impact on agricultural growth which in turn adversely affects the rate of poverty reduction, an understanding of investment behaviour becomes crucial. Answer to the issues of falling public investment and the regime of incentives to which private sector would respond positively may have to be attempted through the study of investment behaviour. This section draws heavily from a study by Bisaliah (2004). Investment behaviour is a complex economic relationship which may not be amenable for dissection. Hence, there is a large gap between theory of investment behaviour and the study of investment behaviour in developing countries (Gandhi, 1990; 1996). In the absence of a strong relevant theoretical foundation to develop postulates, one may have to depend on empirical hunches. Hence, there is still some room for empirical enquiry into the magnitudes and directions of movements under given conditions.

In macromodelling literature, investment in Indian agriculture has been considered in two ways (Dhawan and Yadav 1997): while a behavioural investment function is specified for private fixed farm investment, public investment is deemed to be exogenously determined. Further, behaviour of public investment is largely determined by agricultural problems and policies of the time (details in Bisaliah, 2004). An examination of public sector investment behaviour appears to have been dictated mainly by food situation of the country and agricultural policies governed by political economy of the time (Mishra, 1996; Roy, 2001; Gulati *et al.*, 2002). It is possible to identify four broad epochs in this regard.

First, the food deficit after independence was strong enough to pilot more public investment towards the development of irrigation system.

Second, the food crisis of 1960s was compulsive enough to accelerate public investment in agriculture R&D, irrigation, and other rural infrastructure like roads, markets and so on. This really escalated public sector investment growth rate at a trend rate of about 8 per cent per annum during 1970s (Details in the next section).

The third epoch has been since 1980s when decline in public investment has been strongly voiced. The irony is that the success of Green Revolution itself has led to the emergence of some political economy compulsions which continue to persist. The emergence of 'surplus' produce in agriculture sector had given rise to the formation of politically powerful farmer groups, which have become rather powerful to 'dictate' priority setting for public expenditure in agriculture. The first priority has been to meet the demand for production subsidies to meet which Government budgetary resources have to be diverted from capital account to current account. The next important priority has been to finance private sector capital formation by institutional loans and capital subsidies.

The fourth epoch is the one that has been in vogue since the dawn of economic reforms. Given the 'dictates' of economic reforms for 'setting the prices right' by eliminating subsidies, and for encouraging private sector to crowd into increase its investment in agriculture and for the public policies to create an incentive regime for private investment, especially corporate investment, the prescription has been to effect reforms in agriculture sector. However, political economy compulsions again appear to tone down the 'dictates' especially on subsidies. Further, a set of 'demands' such as to prevent declining TFP in agriculture, to focus on the development of dryland agriculture, to increase investment in agriculture R&D and extension to meet the challenges of liberalised trade regime, to make investment for value addition to agriculture and horticulture products, and to increase investment in irrigation and renovation of water bodies are putting pressures on government to increase its investment in agriculture as a part of 'non-price interventions' for agriculture growth. With all these, the major empirical determinants of public investment are subsidies, opposition to major and medium irrigation systems by environment groups, interstate disputes on water sharing, and so on (see Bathla and Thorat, 2006 for details on determinants of public investment).

In the context of public investment in agriculture, determinants of public investment at state level are equally important. The level and composition of public investment at state level are postulated to depend on rural literacy level, population growth, state agriculture GDP, farm subsidies and grant-in-aid from Federal government. An important state level study (Roy, 2001b) has concluded that rural literacy, population, agriculture GDP, and grant-in-aid from Federal government have positive impact on public investment, whereas farm subsidies crowd out public investment as suggested by negative relationship between farm subsidies and public investment.

Modelling of private investment behaviour could be straight forward, if prospective profitability of investment (rate of return on investment) is known; but there are many uncertainties and risks. The yield and price risks and low-risk bearing ability of farmers would make the decision-making by farmers on investment very complicated. Any study of farmers' investment behaviour has to be undertaken in multivariate and simultaneous equation framework, with relevant price and non-price determinants as explanatory variables and with proper lag structure. For this reason, the modelling of private investment function has considered various explanatory variables such as price factors like terms of trade (Misra, 1998; Mishra *et al.*, 1996b; Chand, 2000) farm interest rate, farm wage rate (Gandhi, 1996) and non-price factors like technology (Gandhi, 1990, 1996; Mishra *et al.*, 1996b) institutional (eg. institutional credit, see

Gandhi, 1996; Karmakar, 1998; Chand, 2000), landholdings size, tenancy etc., infrastructural variables like rural roads and electrification by public sector, other public sector investment items like watershed development programme, irrigation works, regulated markets, value of agricultural output, private capital stock in the preceding year and rural savings (Gandhi, 1996). Choice of explanatory variables to explain the variations in private investment and their measurement, and the choice of equations for estimation and data period would have bearing on the direction and magnitude of elasticity of private investment with respect to explanatory variables.

Results from a couple of studies could illustrate the choice of methodology for identifying the determinants of private investment. Chand (2000) in his study of determinants of investment during 1980-81 and 1996-97 has concluded that terms of trade for agriculture and institutional credit to farmers have positive and significant impact on private capital formation at national level, but a study of state level private investment behaviour has led to the inference that both public investment and institutional credit have exerted a positive significant impact on private capital formation in agriculture. In yet another study by Chand and Kumar (2004), rate of return to private investment (which in turn depends on terms of trade and technology) is found to be the most important determinant of private capital formation. The second most important determinant of private investment is the addition of new farm holdings. Institutional credit and subsidies are found to have positive impact on private capital formation. There is asymmetry in the impact of increasing and decreasing public investment on private investment. An increase in public investment definitely impacts positively private investment, while decline in public investment forces farmers to cope with the adverse impact of decreased public investment by increasing private investment. This kind of asymmetry needs to be interpreted carefully, because the composition of public and private investment would not be the same, excepting perhaps in case of irrigation.

Roy (2001), in a major study using data of 17 states from 1970-71 to 1988-89, and estimates made with simultaneous equation model, has attempted to explain variations in private investment in agriculture. This study has identified public investment (as per broad data series), terms of trade, rural road density and subsidy as the major determinants of private investment with positive impact. The positive impact of subsidy on private investment runs against the well-articulated stand that agricultural subsidies are 'bad', and subsidies would reduce public investment. However, it is difficult to be conclusive that positive gain in private investment due to subsidy would compensate the 'loss' due to decreased public investment. The incidence of rural poverty is also found to have negative impact on private capital formation. Further, the negative and significant impact of percentage area under marginal holdings is suggestive of landholding size constraint on investment in farm assets, and it is also suggestive of the need for more public investment in agriculture to support and sustain the viability of marginal holdings.

Another approach (Gulati *et al.*, 2002) to identification of determinants of private investment is to measure public investment in both physical and monetary terms with appropriate lags to find out the impact of institutional credit and index of terms of trade (lag one year). Performing the analysis in a multiple regression framework with data for the years 1980-81 and 1998-99, Gulati *et al.* (2002) have inferred that public sector investment in agriculture (measured in terms of canal irrigation and power supplies to agriculture in cumulative form), terms of trade and institutional credit have positive influence (inducement effect) on private investment. It is also argued that any neglect of these variables in Government investment programmes would have an adverse impact on private sector investment and growth.

It is obvious from the discussion preceded that studies on determinants of private investment have been conducted using data for different periods of time, using CSO data set and broad data series, using state level and national level data, and with different estimation procedures. Hence studies have identified different determinants of private investment, but also have indicated varying importance of same determinants in influencing private investment. The signs and sizes of the coefficients of determinants appear to hinge on period of study, choice and measurement of variables, and the choice of estimation procedure. Most of the studies have concluded that public investment is an important determinant of private investment (call it as complementary effect or inducement effect). However, the magnitude of the influence of public investment on private investment may vary depending on model specification, period of study, stage of technological and agricultural development and policy environment. Further, there is some validity in the argument that if public investment is measured with broad data series, and if appropriate lags are incorporated (to account for response of private investment to public investment), then public investment tends to have a strong impact on private investment. The issue of which public investments would induce more private investment, which ones reduce private investment, and which of private investment are unaffected by public investment is still a matter of further research, and the results of which will be quite valuable in policymaking on public investment resource allocation. Hence the topic of the impact of public investment on private investment is still debated, and it forms the theme for further discussion.

One could also analyse the determinants of aggregate capital formation in/for agriculture ignoring the difference between public and private investment. In the aggregative analysis, it is possible to postulate that agriculture GDP, public investment and private investment, terms of trade, subsidy, rural literacy level (a proxy for human capital), share of marginal holdings, population growth, institutional credit, modern input use (high yielding varieties, chemical fertilisers etc.), density of rural roads and markets, irrigation intensity and so on will have impact on capital formation. In brief, socioeconomic, political, institutional, infrastructural, technological and agro-ecological variables could be postulated to impact capital formation.

The discussions preceded has brought out three major dimensions of research on capital formation and related issues. First, is the choice of data set and timeframe of the study. There are three major data sets used by researchers for testing the hypotheses on various aspects of capital formation—the Central Statistical Organisation (CSO) investment data set (called narrow data series), broad data series developed by individual researchers, by using data available in Financial Accounts of Central and state government on major heads relevant to investment in agriculture, and the methodology suggested by Bhattacharya Committee 2003 in Bisaliah, 2004 for regrouping CSO data series into a comprehensive data set on capital formation in/for agriculture. Second, serious research attempts have been made with respect to complementarity issue and its implications for the role of public and private investment in formulating agricultural development policy. Third, use of multivariate technique instead of simple explanatory approach, and simultaneous equation approach instead of single equation approach have been employed to resolve the controversies as well as to generate new methodological controversies. The choices of analytical devices have been made with respect to determinants of capital formation, agricultural production/productivity and poverty alleviation.

Capital Formation: Investment Growth Cycle and Shifts in Composition

This section draws heavily from a detailed study conducted by Bisaliah (2004; 2010a) on the theme of investment growth cycle in agriculture and compositional shifts in capital formation. An identification of investment growth cycle is meant to identify the period of growth, the period of deceleration and of marginal recovery, and the direction of change in public and private investment. This analysis is performed with both CSO data series and broad data series. The shifting composition analysis is directed to answer the questions: whether the relative share of public and private investment has changed over a period of time, what trends could be observed in relative share of agriculture and allied sectors *vis-à-vis* the share of forestry and fishery sectors, whether the share of investment made by departmental commercial undertakings (DCU) under public sector investment has altered in relation to the share of investment by non-departmental commercial undertakings (NDCU), and what kind of compositional shifts have occurred in farm household capital expenditure in agriculture.

Investment Growth Cycle

Since 1989, the research studies on trends in capital formation in Indian agriculture have given rise to many concerns and controversies. CSO investment series-based studies have identified a kind of growth cycle in capital formation. This growth cycle encompasses rising trend during sixties, relatively subdued phase during the first half of seventies, momentum of peak phase during second half of eighties, and a persistent decline thereafter. This persistent loss of momentum is considered as a disquieting development, with implications for agricultural growth. Further, while analysing the growth rate of public and private investment, the low positive growth rates of private investment has been not enough to compensate the negative growth rates in public investment, leading to a loss of momentum in total GFCF in agriculture.

Given the above broad concerns, the growth-deceleration syndrome could be gauged from different angles. First, what have been the trends in agriculture GFCF *vis-à-vis* aggregate GFCF? Second, how different are the temporal shares of aggregate GFCF in GDP and of agriculture GFCF? Third, whether the share of agriculture GFCF in agriculture GDP has altered over a period of time? Fourth, how comparables are the annual growth rates of public and private investment in agriculture? Fifth, whether the conclusions derived from CSO investment series analysis different from those of broad investment series analysis? The subsequent sections examine the evidences on these as well as related issues. Further, the recent trends in growth rates and compositional shifts will be analysed.

One of the ways to identify investment growth-deceleration epoch is to analyse the aggregate growth rates of GFCF and of agriculture GFCF. Two broad results on this could be extracted from Table 3.3(a).

Table 3.3(a)

Distinct Growth Epochs in Aggregate and Agriculture GFCF in India at 1993-94 Prices

Period	*Annual Compound Growth Rates (%) (CSO Series-based)*		
	Aggregate	*Agriculture & Allied Sectors*	*Agriculture*
A. *Broad periods*			
1960-61 to 1980-81	4.35	6.20	6.34
1980-81 to 1999-2000	5.85	1.83	1.38
B. *Decade*			
1960s	4.43	6.39	6.48
1970s	5.14	6.08	6.06
1980s	4.86	-0.40	-0.96
1990s	5.99	2.64	2.05

Source: Bisaliah (2004).

- The annual compound growth rates of aggregate GFCF increased from 4.35 per cent during 1960-61 to 1980-81 to 5.85 per cent during 1980-81 to 1999-2000. Whereas the corresponding growth rates in agriculture and allied sector decreased from 6.2 per cent to 1.83 per cent. In case of agriculture alone, the decline was still more.

- Table 3.3(b) illustrates recent trends in the share of agriculture in total GCF. It could be observed from these trends between 1999-2000 and 2006-07, that there has been a decline in the share of agriculture in national GCF.

Table 3.3(b)

Share of Agriculture in Total GCF at 1999-2000 Prices

Year	*% Share*
1999–2000	8.6
2000–2001	8.0
2001–2002	10.2
2002–2003	8.4
2003–2004	6.7
2004–2005	6.2
2005–2006	5.8
2006–2007	5.8

Source: HLC (2009).

These broad conclusions are further reinforced by decadal growth rates. In case of agriculture and allied sectors, and agriculture alone, the growth pattern experienced negative growth in 1980s, and a reversal to positive growth in 1990s, but far lower than that of the growth rates of sixties and seventies.

Growth-deceleration pattern could also be analysed with shares of aggregate GFCF in GDP and of agriculture and allied sectors in GDP. As observed from Table 3.4(a), the decadal averages of aggregate GFCF as a percentage of GDP increased from 17.4 per cent in 1960s to 22.1 per cent in 1990s. In case of agriculture and allied sectors, the share had declined from 2.5 per cent to 1.7 per cent during the same decade. An examination of results reported in Bhattacharya Committee Report 2003 in Bisaliah (2004) would reinforce this conclusion. As per cent to GDP, GFCF in agriculture had declined from 3.4 per cent in 1980-81 to 1.6 per cent in 2001-02. The corresponding share of GFCF for agriculture had decreased from 4.3 per cent to 2.3 per cent. Further, the share of public sector GFCF in agriculture in relation to GDP had declined from 1.8 per cent in 1980-81 to 0.4 per cent in 1999-2000. The share for agriculture had declined from 2.5 per cent to 0.9 per cent during the same period.

Table 3.4(a)

Decadal Averages of Capital Formation as Percentage to GDP at 1993-94 Prices

Decade	*CSO Series-based*		
	Aggregate GFCF	*Agriculture & Allied Sectors GFCF*	*Agriculture GFCF*
1960s	17.4	2.5	2.3
1970s	18.6	2.7	2.5
1980s	21.2	2.5	2.3
1990s	22.1	1.7	1.5

Source: Bisaliah (2004).

In this perspective of declining trends in capital formation, an examination of share of agriculture GDP in aggregate GDP is in order. It could be seen from Table 3.4(b) that the share of agriculture GDP in aggregate GDP had declined sharply between 1960s and 1990s. (Recent trends will be discussed in later pages. It is not clear whether this is a part of structural transformation in growth process, and part of that could be attributed to declining investment in and for agriculture.

Table 3.4(b)

Decadal Averages of Agriculture GDP as a Percentage of Aggregate GDP at 1993-94 Prices

Decade	*% Share of Agriculture GDP in Aggregate GDP*	
	Agriculture & Allied Sectors	*Agriculture*
1960s	47.8	42.0
1970s	42.8	37.7
1980s	36.4	33.1
1990s	29.1	26.4

Source: Bisaliah (2004).

An examination of results in Table 3.5 would further reinforce the argument that the share of agriculture and allied sectors in total GFCF had been halved between 1960s and 1990s. The share of agriculture and allied sectors (agriculture alone) experienced drastic decline from 14.4 per cent (13.5%) to 7.8 per cent (6.9%) between 1960s and 1990s.

Table 3.5

Decadal Averages of Share of Agriculture in Aggregate Capital Formation at 1993-94 Prices

Decade	*Per cent to Aggregate GFCF*	
	Agriculture & Allied Sectors	*Agriculture*
1960s	14.4	13.5
1970s	14.4	13.6
1980s	11.6	10.7
1990s	7.8	6.9

Source: Bisaliah (2004).

What have been the trends in agriculture GFCF as percentage of agriculture GDP? It could be observed from Table 3.6, that the percentage share of agriculture GFCF in agriculture GDP was lower in 1990s than either in 1970s or 1980s, but marginally a little higher than in 1960s. Hence, the growth of GFCF in agriculture experienced decline in momentum in 1990s, with implications for agriculture growth subsequently.

Table 3.6

Decadal Averages of Agriculture GFCF as Percentage of Agriculture GDP at 1993-94 Prices

Decade	*GFCF*	
	Agriculture & Allied Sectors	*Agriculture*
1960s	5.8	6.1
1970s	6.9	7.4
1980s	7.4	7.5
1990s	6.5	6.2

Source: Bisaliah (2004).

The growth-deceleration syndrome could also be examined with annual growth rates of public and private investment. It follows from Table 3.7, that public sector investment growth rates, which were quite high during 1970s, became negative during 1980s, and negative growth rates continued during 1990s. Private sector investment growth rates were positive althrough 1960s and 1990s; but lower rates were experienced during 1980s and 1990s, even though there was some improvement in 1990s over 1980s. Further, with regard to private sector growth rates, the increase in growth rates in 1990s over 1980s was higher in agriculture and allied sector than in agriculture proper, implying some degree of diversification of investment portfolio in farm sector.

Table 3.7

Trends in Compound Rates (Per cent) of GCF in Agriculture as between Public and Private Sector at 1993-94 Prices

Decade	Growth Rates (%)			
	Agriculture & Allied		Agriculture	
	Public Sector	Private Sector	Public Sector	Private Sector
1960s	2.62	9.55	2.54	9.81
1970s	9.50	7.81	9.60	7.90
1980s	-3.89	2.62	-4.38	2.08
1990s	-0.11	3.73	-0.16	3.04

Source: Bisaliah (2004).

A closer look at the investment growth rate performance of public and private sector during eighties and nineties would provide yet another perspective into deceleration syndrome. As evident from Table 3.8, during the period of 1982-1992, the negative growth rate in public sector was compensated by high growth rate in private sector, giving rise to less than 2 per cent positive growth in investment. Further, weak performance of public sector in nineties was somehow offset by respectable growth rates in private investment during the period of 1992-1999 and 1992-1997 so as to

Table 3.8

Trends in Public and Private Sector Growth Rates of GFCF in Agriculture

Period	Growth Rates (%)		
	Public	Private	Total
1982-1992	-2.5	5.2	1.6
1992-1999	0.8	3.5	2.3
1992-1997	1.5	4.2	2.8
1997-1999	-1.1	1.8	1.1

Source: Adopted from Gulati *et al.* (2002).

generate an overall investment growth of over 2 per cent. But during the period of 1997-1999, the negative growth rate experienced in public sector investment could not be offset enough by positive but low growth rate in private investment, so as to maintain the tempo of 1992-1999 and 1992-1997. Since, private sector investment accounts for over 70 per cent of investment in agriculture, any slowdown in private investment will have implications for growth of agricultural sector. Further, any weak performance of public sector investment would imply decline in investment in surface irrigation system.

The declining trend in public sector investment in agriculture could also be examined under three concepts of public investment developed by Gulati and Bathla (2002). The results for the period 1974-75 to 1998-99 are presented in Table 3.9. First, the absolute volume of investment increases as we move from one concept to another. The differences were quite substantial (almost double) as between C-I and C-III in 1974-75. The differences were narrowed down by the year 1998-99. Second, percentage change in volume of public investment in 1984-85 over 1974-75 was both positive and substantial. But the percentage change in 1994-95 over 1984-1985 was negative under all three concepts, implying declining public investment in agriculture. However, the decline is found to be less in 1998-1999 under C-I and C-III. Third, public sector investment in real terms, whatever the concept used, declined after 1980s, even though the decline was less during the later part of 1990s. In a state level study, using broad investment series concept, Roy (2001) has reported declining trend of public investment in real terms across the board in most of the states since mid-1980s.

Table 3.9

Trends in Public Sector GCF in Agriculture at 1993-94 Prices

(Rs Billion)

Year	*C-I*	*C-II*	*C-III*	*% Change since 1974-75*		
				C-I	*C-II*	*C-III*
1974-75	34.49	39.49	75.23	-	-	-
1984-85	69.21	81.25	125.85	100.0	105.7	67.30
1994-95	53.97	78.78	89.27	-22.1	-3.3	-29.1
1998-99	48.18	67.72	69.65	-10.8	-14.0	-22.0

Source: Computed drawing data from Gulati and Bathla (2002).

Analysis of Compositional Shifts

It is recalled from previous Section that the share of private sector in capital formation has been increasing over time. This requires further analysis from the direction of shifts in the share of public and private sector in total investment over a period of time. Table 3.10 and 3.11 would provide some useful insights into this question. It could be seen from Table 3.10 (CSO series-based analysis) that the share of public sector had declined from about 46 per cent in 1960-61 to about 24 per cent in 2002-2003, and correspondingly the share of private sector had increased from about 54 per cent to 76 per cent. Part of this could be explained in terms of

Table 3.10

Percentage Share of Public and Private Sector in GCF in Agriculture and Allied Sectors at 1993-94 Prices (CSO Series-based)

Years	*Share (%) in GCF in Agriculture and Allied Sectors*	
	Public Sector	*Private Sector*
1960-61	45.6	54.4
1970-71	37.5	62.5
1980-81	51.3	48.7
1985-86	44.0	56.0
1990-91	28.9	71.1
2002-03	24.3	75.7

Source: Adopted from Thulasamma (2003). CSO, New Delhi.

Table 3.11

Percentage Share of Public Sector in GCF in Agriculture under Three Concepts of Public Sector Investment at 1993-94 Prices

Year	*% Share of Public Investment*		
	Concept-I	*Concept-II*	*Concept-III*
1980-81	51.30	54.64	64.49
1985-86	43.96	48.29	56.15
1990-91	30.41	38.33	41.46
1995-96	30.23	36.53	39.66
1998-99	25.34	32.30	32.92

Source: Adopted from Gulati and Bathla (2002).

changing role of public sector in development process and the ability of private sector to augment its share by utilising the initial infrastructural facilities (like irrigation, power, storage structures, etc.) created under public sector. In case of declining share of public sector investment in total investment, part of that could also be explained in terms of changing political economy compulsions.

The declining share of public investment could also be analysed (Table 3.11) with three data concepts suggested by Gulati and Bathla (2002). Barring a few exceptions, the share of public sector in GCF in agriculture and allied sectors is found to have declined over a period of time. The decline between 1980-81 to1998-99 is much more visible under Concept-III and Concept-I. Perhaps this shared variation during different years could be due to shifting priorities assigned in public investment for irrigation (Concept-I), irrigation plus power (Concept-II), and irrigation plus power plus 11 other items of capital expenditure under public sector.

The compositional change in public sector investment could also be examined with results in Table 3.12. Out of the total public investment made in agriculture and allied sectors, forestry and fishery, the share of fishery sector is very negligible, but also there was a decline in its share between 1983 TE and 1998 TE, whereas, forestry sector is found to have increased its share between 1983 TE and 1998 TE. It is agriculture and allied sector, which accounts for over 90 per cent of the share of public investment. However, its share was 94 per cent in 1980s, decreased to 89 per cent by mid-1990s, and increased to about 91 per cent thereafter.

Table 3.12

Distribution of Public Investment in Agriculture by Enterprise Category at 1993-94 Prices

TE	*% Share*			
	Agriculture & Allied	*Forestry*	*Fishery*	*Total*
1983	94.22	5.73	0.05	100.00
1993	88.75	11.19	0.06	100.00
1998	90.50	9.48	0.02	100.00

Source: Adopted from Gulati and Bathla (2002).

Yet another way of examining the compositional shift is to analyse the expenditure share of DCU and NDCU in total capital expenditure under public sector for agriculture and allied sector. As could be seen from Table 3.13, in the total public sector investment in this sector, the share of investment made through DCU is the most dominant, even though declining share is observed as between 1983 (91%) and 1998 (79%). The most important item of capital expenditure incurred through DCU is irrigation. Hence, the trend in declining public investment refers basically to decline in public investment in major and medium irrigation schemes.

Table 3.13

*Distribution of Public Expenditure on Agriculture and Allied Sectors by Government Departments**

(in Percentage)

TE	*Total Share (%) of Agriculture & Allied Sectors*	*% Share of*	
		DCU	*NDCU*
1983	94.22	91.43	2.79
1993	88.75	87.55	1.20
1998	90.51	79.14	11.37

Note: * Departmental Commercial Undertaking (DCU) and Non-Departmental Commercial Undertaking (NDCU).

Source: Adopted from Gulati and Bathla (2002).

Compositional shifts in public investment could also be examined with a broad investment series framework developed by Chand (2000). A few important observations could be made with the results presented in Table 3.14. First, the real annual investment in public sector had drastically declined from Rs 4,396 crore during the Fifth Plan period to Rs 2,566 crore during the Eighth Plan period. Second, public investment in irrigation schemes continued to be the most dominant item, followed by investment in food and storage, even though there was a decline in annual investment in these two items between Fifth and Eighth plans. However, these two items alone accounted for around 65 per cent of public capital investment in agriculture. Third, even though public investment in roads continued to maintain and increase its importance, crop husbandry, fertiliser industry and cooperation are found to have their relative importance lowered.

The results derived on compositional shifts in public investment portfolio by Roy (2001) considering 21 items of public investment could also be placed in this perspective of shifting composition. During the period between TE 1967-68 and TE 1998-99, even though the irrigation schemes continued to enjoy dominant share in public investment, its share came down from more than 43 per cent during early period to 28 per cent during nineties. But minor irrigation schemes, agricultural research and education, infrastructural items (like storage, market, road, electrification and credit institutions) claimed the second largest share in total public investment. The share of rural development programmes increased from a little more than 10 per cent of total public investment to about 24 per cent during 1990s.

Table 3.14

Compositional Distribution of Public Investment in Agriculture at 1980-81 Prices, as per Broad Investment Series

(Rs Crore)

Investment Item	*Plan Period Annual Expenditure*			
	Vth Plan	*VIth Plan*	*VIIth Plan*	*VIIIth Plan*
Crop husbandry	688	251	91	24
Food & storage	1266	1040	675	720
Irrigation	1493	1458	1247	1081
Fertiliser industry	266	130	71	19
Cooperation	216	187	101	60
Roads	168	251	233	200
Total-I	4097	3313	2418	2104
Total-II: Other 16 investment items	299	319	338	462
Grand total	4396	3632	2755	2566

Source: Developed from data reported in Chand (2000).

It is recalled from Table 3.10 that the private sector had increased its share in GCF in agriculture from about 54 per cent in 1960-61 to about 76 per cent in 2002-03. In this context an examination of changing structure of private investment in this sector is in order. Private sector investment consists of investment by corporate sector and household sector. The investment by corporate sector could be in organised corporate sector like big plantation firms, and in unorganised corporate sector like sugar and milk cooperatives. Since this definition of corporate sector accounts for less than 5 per cent of private investment (Gulati and Bathla, 2002), the dominant share is that of household sector which partially owns the share of unorganised corporate sector. The data on composition of capital expenditure incurred by household sector are provided once in 10 years by Reserve Bank of India through its *All India Debt and Investment Survey* (AIDIS). Table 3.15 provides results on composition of household capital expenditure in agriculture at a point in time, and compositional shifts over a period of 20 years.

Table 3.15

Percentage Distribution of Fixed Capital Expenditure of Households in Agriculture: All-India Estimates

Capital Asset	*% Share*		
	1971-72	*1981-82*	*1991-92*
Machinery and equipment	43.20	51.95	47.80
Wells and other irrigation structures	26.80	20.45	24.70
Land improvement	16.50	15.25	12.91
Farm houses and animal sheds	10.50	4.55	3.67
Orchards and plantations	1.80	2.80	5.08
Other capital assets	1.20	5.00	6.26

Source: Gulati and Bathla (2002).

It is observed that agricultural implements, machinery and transport equipment would form the most important item of capital expenditure, followed by well and other irrigation structures. These two items alone would form a little over 70 per cent of capital expenditure incurred by household sector in agriculture during the 20-year period of study. Almost the same composition of household sector investment in agriculture is also observed at state level for 1991-92, as per AIDIS (Gulati and Bathla, 2002). It is understandable that composition of capital expenditure varies with growth/development stage of the sector, and the development incentives provided by Government. But agricultural machinery/equipment/transport and wells/other irrigation structures are likely to maintain their dominant position for years to come, even though capital expenditures for land improvement, development of orchards and plantations, and construction of animal sheds (with increased role of dairy) are likely to increase their share. For the year 2001-02, it is reported (Personal communications from S. Mahendra Dev, Director, Indira Gandhi Institute of Development Research, Mumbai) that wells and other irrigation resources (33.1%) and machinery equipment and transport (22.1%) would form 55.2 per cent of fixed capital expenditure incurred by farm households in India. There has been a decline in percentage share of expenditure on land improvements, and substantial increase on farm houses and animal sheds.

An analysis of changes in aggregate GCF and agriculture GCF (AGCF) as well as changing relative importance of public and private sector during post-reform period *vis-à-vis* pre-reform period is in order. Table 3.16 would provide such insights into annual percentage change in aggregate GCF and AGCF during pre-reform period of 10 years (1981-82–1990-91) and post-reform period of 10 years (1991-92–2000-01).

Table 3.16

Changes in Total GCF and AGCF during Pre-Reform and Post-Reform Decade

Decade/Year	*Total GCF (Rs Crore)*	*% Change*	*AGCF (Rs Crore)*	*% Change*
Pre-Reform Decade				
1981-82	125859	-	14079	-
1982-83	114461	-9.0	14529	+3.2
1983-84	105581	-8.0	14725	+1.35
1984-85	128063	+21.0	14948	+1.51
1985-86	144777	+13.0	14132	-5.46
1986-87	143533	-1.0	13708	-3.00
1987-88	122274	-15.0	14294	+4.27
1988-89	158291	+29.0	14762	+3.27
1989-90	159512	+0.77	13424	-9.06
1990-91	166077	+4.11	16416	+22.29
Post-Reform Decade				
1991-92	172863	-	14965	-
1992-93	178248	+3.11	16141	+7.86
1993-94	181133	+1.62	15249	-5.53
1994-95	229879	+26.91	16785	+10.07
1995-96	284557	+23.78	17689	+5.38
1996-97	252555	-11.25	18326	+3.60
1997-98	261541	+3.56	18305	-0.11
1998-99	240672	-7.98	18964	+3.60
1999-2000	268527	+11.57	21388	+12.78
2000-01	274917	+2.38	19451	-9.06

Source: National Accounts Statistics, EPW Research Foundation, July 2002.

- In broad terms, the annual positive change in aggregate GCF was greater during post-reform period than pre-reform period. The same inference could be drawn with respect to AGCF during post-reform period. This is in fact a measure of recovery (however marginal it is) in GCF in agricultural sector during post-reform period.

- However, the annual rate of change in aggregate GCF has been found to be higher than those of AGCF. It is understandable in view of shifting sector priorities of post-reform period, impacting the growth rate of capital stock.

The next issue is whether there has been a shifting importance of public and private sector during the post-reform period *vis-à-vis* during the pre-reform period. As could be seen from Table 3.17:

Table 3.17

Trends in Percentage Share of Public and Private Sector in Total AGCF during Pre-Reform and Post-Reform Decade

Decade/Year	*% Share in Total AGCF*	
	Public Sector	*Private Sector*
Pre-Reform Decade		
1981-82	50.6	49.4
1982-83	48.8	51.2
1983-84	48.9	51.1
1984-85	46.3	53.7
1985-86	44.0	56.0
1986-87	42.8	57.2
1987-88	42.3	57.7
1988-89	38.6	61.4
1989-90	37.0	63.0
1990-91	29.6	70.4
Post-Reform Decade		
1991-92	28.9	71.1
1992-93	28.1	71.9
1993-94	33.0	67.0
1994-95	33.0	67.0
1995-96	30.9	69.1
1996-97	28.9	71.1
1997-98	25.0	75.0
1998-99	26.0	74.0
1999-2000	24.4	75.6
2000-01	23.2	76.8

Source: 1. *National Accounts Statistics*, EPW Research Foundation, 2002.
2. *Economic Survey: 2003-04*, Government of India.

- During the pre-reform decade, public sector investment recorded a decline in its share from about 51 per cent to 30 per cent; whereas during the post-reform decade, the decline was from about 29 per cent to 23 per cent. Hence, the decline was sharper during the pre-reform decade than during the post-reform decade.
- In case of the share of private sector in total AGCF, the increase registered was from about 49 per cent to 70 per cent during pre-reform period; whereas, during the post-reform period, the increase was from about 71 per cent to 77 per cent. Hence, the increase in the share of private sector was more during pre-reform period.

A few broad observations could be made with the preceded analysis of investment growth cycle in agriculture and compositional shifts in such investment. First, investment growth cycle has been analysed from different angles like growth rate trends in agriculture GFCF *vis-à-vis* aggregate GFCF, shifting shares of aggregate GFCF and of agriculture GFCF in GDP, shifting share of agriculture GFCF in agriculture GDP, and trends in the annual growth rates of public and private investment in agriculture in relation to trends in overall investment growth. This analysis has led to a few inferences: (a) the investment growth cycle encompasses rising trend, subdued phase, peak phase, persistent deceleration, and only marginal recovery; (b) the annual growth rates of aggregate GFCF are found to have increased between 1960s and 1990s, whereas agriculture GFCF had suffered deceleration during the same period; (c) the share of aggregate GFCF as a per cent of GDP had increased between 1960s and 1990s, whereas the agriculture GFCF as a per cent of GDP had declined; (d) the percentage of agriculture GFCF in total GFCF had halved between 1960s and 1990s; (e) the percentage share of agriculture GFCF in agriculture GDP was lower in 1990s than in 1970s or 1980s; (f) public sector investment growth rates were quite high during 1970s, became negative during 1980s, and there has been a decline in growth rate deceleration during 1990s. This kind of decelerating growth of public sector investment could not be compensated by respectable investment growth rates in private sector, leading to a loss of momentum in total GFCF (in real terms) in agriculture. Analysis with broad investment series has confirmed deceleration in public investment both at national and state level; (g) a decadal analysis of pre-reform and post-reform period suggests that in case of aggregate GCF as well as AGCF, the positive changes were greater during post-reform period, and the rates of change were greater in case of aggregate GCF than in the case of AGCF and (h) decline in the percentage share of public sector in AGCF was greater during pre-reform period, and obviously the increase in the share of private sector was more during pre-reform period.

Second, the analysis of compositional shifts in capital formation has provided a few useful insights: (a) in general, during early years (of the period 1967-68 to 1998-99) the share of public and private sectors in total investment was almost equal during early phase, and there has been a steady rise in the share of private investment since eighties. For example, the share of public sector investment in total investment had declined from 46 per cent in 1960-61 to 24 per cent in 2002-03, leading to a corresponding increase in private investment; (b) out of the total investment in agriculture and allied sectors, forestry and fishery, the share of agriculture and allied sector has been over 90 per cent; (c) out of the total investment made in public sector, the investment carried through departmental commercial unit (DCU) has been the most dominant one, even though the share had declined from 91 per cent in 1983 to 79 per cent in 1998. The most important item of capital expenditure incurred through DCU is irrigation. Hence, any decline in public investment refers basically to declining public investment in major and medium irrigation schemes; (d) analysis of compositional shifts in public capital expenditure in agriculture with broad investment series suggests that investment in irrigation schemes and food and storage would form around 65 per cent of the total investment. Even though public investment in roads continued to maintain its importance, crop husbandry, fertiliser industry and cooperation are found to have experienced declining share over a period of time. The rural development programmes have experienced hike in their share; (e) with respect to composition of farm household investment, agricultural implements, machinery, equipment and well/other irrigation structures alone would account for over 70 per cent of capital expenditure incurred by household sector in agriculture. Almost the same composition is observed both at national and state level. It is likely that capital expenditure for land improvement, orchards and plantations and dairy sheds would increase their share in course of time, even though the dominance of agriculture machinery/equipment/transport and well/other irrigation structures would continue.

State-wise Analysis of Investment Intensity and Investment Growth

Three approaches are followed to analyse the investment intensity of different states. First, capital expenditure per hectare of net sown area (NSA) at constant prices could be analysed across states. This could be coupled with trend rate (%) of growth analysis for the same states. Second, both public and private investment intensity of states could be analysed, along with investment growth rate (%) of public and private sector. Third, analysis of public-private sector investment as a per cent of AGDP could be yet another way of examining investment intensity across states (See HLC, 2009 Chapter X for possible approaches for estimating capital formation at regional level and its importance for regional planning).

Table 3.18 provides state-wise statistical profile with respect to capital expenditure per hectare and trend rate of growth across states during the period 1974-75 to 1996-97.

- With respect to 17 major states, only 6 states (Jammu & Kashmir, Punjab, Maharashtra, Himachal Pradesh, Uttar Pradesh and Kerala) are found to have registered above national average (Rs 239) of per hectare capital expenditure per annum. In fact, Madhya Pradesh, Rajasthan and Tamil Nadu had experienced per hectare capital expenditure intensity of less than Rs 100/ha/annum.
- The small-sized northeastern states and Goa are found to have recorded far above the national average. The range is between Rs 500 per hectare (Meghalaya) to Rs 1,554 (Goa, Daman and Diu). The notion that northeastern states have not been given adequate importance in development resource allocation stands dispelled at least with respect to agricultural sector. There may be other development issues.
- For the country as a whole, the trend rate of growth of capital expenditure per hectare was negative (-3.16) during the study period. All the 17 major states had experienced negative growth rates of capital expenditure. The states with high negative growth rates (over 2.5 per cent) are Punjab, Bihar, West Bengal, Tamil Nadu, Himachal Pradesh, Madhya Pradesh, Orissa and Uttar Pradesh.

- In case of smaller States, only Nagaland, Goa and Manipur are found to have experienced negative growth rates of capital expenditure.

Table 3.18

State-wise Analysis of Capital Expenditure and Trend Growth Rates of Capital Expenditure during 1974-75 to 1996-97 (At 1980-81 Prices)

States	*Average Per Hectare Expenditure/ Annum (Rs)*	*Trend Rate of Growth (%)*
Andhra Pradesh	160	-0.78
Assam	172	-0.98
Bihar	182	-4.78
Gujarat	186	-1.16
Haryana	198	-2.05
Himachal Pradesh	323	-2.99
Jammu & Kashmir	1242	-1.17
Karnataka	146	-1.66
Kerala	295	-1.56
Madhya Pradesh	99	-2.57
Maharashtra	323	-1.87
Orissa	185	-2.57
Punjab	616	-5.39
Rajasthan	76	-1.22
Tamil Nadu	97	-3.25
Uttar Pradesh	299	-2.80
West Bengal	119	-3.39
Goa, Daman and Diu	1554	-0.90
Arunachal Pradesh	1148	4.57
Manipur	1295	-0.61
Meghalaya	500	2.94
Mizoram	1606	0.21
Nagaland	702	-6.90
Sikkim	537	0.42
Tripura	1043	0.31
Union Government	29	-11.16
All India	239	-3.16

Source: Adopted from Chand (2001).

Table 3.19 presents an analysis of public and private sector investment intensity across states as well as investment growth rates of public and private sector.

- Based on investment intensity (Rs /ha), the states could be clustered into four groups:
  - High public and low private investment: Assam, Jammu & Kashmir, Orissa and northeastern states.
  - Low public and high private investment: Haryana, Karnataka, Madhya Pradesh, Rajasthan and Tamil Nadu.
  - High public and high private investment: Uttar Pradesh, Punjab, Maharashtra, Kerala and Himachal Pradesh.
  - Low public and low private investment: Andhra Pradesh, Bihar, Gujarat and West Bengal.
- Based on investment growth rates in public and private sectors, the states could also be clustered into typologies:
  - High public and low private investment growth: None.
  - Low public and high private investment growth: Andhra Pradesh, Gujarat, Himachal Pradesh, Jammu & Kashmir, Kerala, Madhya Pradesh, Maharashtra, Rajasthan, Tamil Nadu, northeastern states and All-India.
  - High public and high private investment growth: Haryana, Karnataka and Punjab.
  - Low public and low private investment growth: Assam, Bihar, Orissa and West Bengal.

One major observation could be made on the results presented in Table 3.18 and 3.19.

- The clusters developed from the results of both the tables do not tally converge, because the results of Table 3.18 would provide insights into intensity of public and private investment in average terms per annum, whereas Table 3.19 provides results on estimated investment growth rates between 1987-1999.

Table 3.19

Public-Private Investment Intensity and Investment Growth in Agriculture: State-wise Analysis–1987-1999 (At 1980-81 Prices)

States	Investment Intensity (Rs/ha)		Investment Growth Rate (%)	
	Public Sector	Private Sector	Public Sector	Private Sector
Andhra Pradesh	240	216	0.48	6.10
Assam	216	59	-6.18	1.66
Bihar	200	86	-11.00	2.65
Gujarat	244	-	1.56	5.56
Haryana	238	407	3.01	8.97
Himachal Pradesh	408	531	0.00	6.87
Jammu & Kashmir	1369	146	0.88	7.43
Karnataka	165	409	5.28	6.18
Kerala	340	591	2.36	5.85
Madhya Pradesh	119	313	-4.95	10.82
Maharashtra	367	311	1.39	8.93
Orissa	207	49	-1.68	2.77
Punjab	543	397	10.89	9.45
Rajasthan	109	272	2.91	10.06
Tamil Nadu	174	564	0.64	7.22
Uttar Pradesh	325	337	0.11	5.18
West Bengal	206	147	0.76	7.06
Northeastern States	1132	229	-1.08	6.91
Union Territories	1007	1034	-2.36	2.9
Union Government	21	-	-0.95	-
All India	265	288	0.43	7.44

Source: Adopted from Roy (2001b).

Yet another way of examining investment intensity across the states is to examine public and private investments as per cent of AGDP. Table 3.20 would provide results on this issue:

- High public and low private investment: Jammu & Kashmir, Orissa and northeastern states.
- Low public and high private investment: Haryana, Himachal Pradesh, Karnataka, Kerala, Madhya Pradesh, Punjab, Rajasthan and Tamil Nadu.
- High public and high private investment: Andhra Pradesh, Gujarat, Maharashtra and Uttar Pradesh.

– Low public and low private investment: Assam, Bihar and West Bengal.

Table 3.20

Public-Private Investment and AGDP during 1987-1999: State-wise Analysis (At 1980-81 Prices)

States	Investment as Per cent of AGDP	
	Public Investment	Private Investment
Andhra Pradesh	5.06	5.85
Assam	3.84	2.34
Bihar	3.30	2.31
Gujarat	7.46	9.12
Haryana	2.73	7.00
Himachal Pradesh	4.99	7.70
Jammu & Kashmir	19.08	4.36
Karnataka	4.70	12.67
Kerala	3.60	7.41
Madhya Pradesh	4.23	10.28
Maharashtra	9.78	9.87
Orissa	6.20	1.97
Punjab	4.97	8.97
Rajasthan	4.16	10.04
Tamil Nadu	3.10	10.57
Uttar Pradesh	5.26	6.72
West Bengal	2.08	2.04
Northeastern States	18.44	4.20
Union Territories	10.87	11.70
All India	5.13	6.75

Source: Adopted from Roy and Pal (2002).

Trends in Capital Use Efficiency

It is realised that it is not enough to analyse only trends in the level of investment, but it is equally important to assess efficiency of investment made. Efficiency of investment is usually assessed by incremental capital output ratio (ICOR) and the inverse of that being marginal efficiency of investment (MEI). ICOR is both a measure of capital intensity and measure of efficiency in its use. It is a useful device for determining sectoral allocation of capital resources, and also to estimate the level of investment required to achieve a targetted output level and growth. Further, it could also be used for deriving output growth rate, once capital resource position is known.

A review of estimates on ICOR and MEI is suggestive of variations across estimates derived, depending mainly on choice of time period, deflator base year, and the choice of time lag used for determining the flow of capital services. The estimates (Table 3.21) of ICOR by Misra and Hazell (1996) for the period 1952-53 to 1991-92 are suggestive of improved efficiency of capital use in Indian agriculture during late 1980s, as ICOR decreased from 4.37 to 3.32 during the 1978-79 to 1986-87 to 1987-88 to 1991-92. This is also reflected in the increased MEI during late 1980s. This improved efficiency could be partly due to increased private investment during late 1980s, and also to enhanced use of yield increasing inputs and improved market support.

Table 3.21

Estimates of ICOR and MEI in Indian Agriculture during 1952-53 to 1991-92

Period	*ICOR*	*MEI*
1952-53 to 1964-65	3.47	0.29
1967-68 to 1977-78	4.17	0.24
1978-79 to 1986-87	4.37	0.23
1987-88 to 1991-92	3.32	0.30

Source: Misra *et al.* (1996).

Chand (2000) has estimated (Table 3.22) ICOR for a period of 20 years from 1974-75 to 1994-95, using both the CSO investment series and broad investment series developed by him. Three major observations could be made on these estimates. First, during the first two periods of study, there was a considerable difference in ICOR as well as MEI based on CSO and broad series for the obvious reason of same value of incremental output used in case of both the series, whereas the incremental total capital in case of broad series was considerably higher than the one computed with CSO series. Second, the ICOR based on broad series declined sharply with effect from second period, and the difference in ICOR narrowed down over time. Third, compared to first period, there was an improvement in the capital efficiency in agriculture as reflected in MEI of both CSO and broad series, even through symptoms of marginal deterioration in efficiency is observed for fourth period compared to third period. However, a broad conclusion that could be drawn from the analysis is that there has been an improvement in capital use efficiency in Indian agriculture since the beginning of 1980s.

Table 3.22

Estimates of ICOR and MEI in Indian Agriculture: 1974-75 to 1994-95 at 1981-82 Prices

Period	ICOR		MEI	
	CSO Series	Broad Series	CSO Series	Broad Series
I. 1974-75 to 1978-79	3.77	6.52	0.27	0.15
II. 1980-81 to 1984-85	2.95	4.05	0.34	0.25
III. 1985-86 to 1989-90	2.22	2.82	0.45	0.35
IV. 1990-91 to 1994-95	2.75	3.44	0.36	0.29

Source: Adapted from Chand (2000). Estimates based on total investment of both public and private sectors.

The study by Roy (2001), using data for the period of 1969-70 to 1996-97, has indicated that the lowest ICOR was found in case of Fourth Plan period (1969-1974). Even though it increased during Fifth Plan period, it started declining after and got reverted to Fourth Plan level by the end of Eighth Plan. The possible reasons for the lowest level of ICOR (or the highest level of capital use efficiency) during the Fourth Plan period could be attributed to impressive output growth during the first phase of Green Revolution, and the increased flow of services from capital investments made on major irrigation projects. The study has also indicated, barring variations in ICOR across states, that most of the states have experienced an improvement in efficiency of capital use in agriculture.

In yet another recent study, Gulati and Bathla (2002) have estimated ICOR and MEI (Table 3.23) at 1993-94 prices. Since ICORs varies annually mainly due to fluctuations in output, ICOR is estimated on the basis of three-yearly moving averages of GDPA and GFCFA. The pattern of behaviour of ICOR over the Five Year Plan periods (Fourth Plan to Eighth Plan) suggests an improvement in the efficiency of investment in agriculture from Fourth Plan period to Eighth Plan period, with some variations in between. The MEI, which was 0.207 during Fourth Plan period increased to 0.511 during Eighth Plan. This improvement in capital use efficiency is found to have taken place, even though there was a reduction in the ratio of GFCF in agriculture to incremental GDPA from 7.58 in mid-eighties to 6.56 in mid-nineties.

Table 3.23

Plan Period Estimates of ICOR and MEI in Indian Agriculture at 1993-94 Prices

Plan	*Plan Years*	*ICOR*	*MEI*
Fourth plan	1969-1974	4.81	0.207
Fifth plan	1974-1978	3.09	0.323
Sixth plan	1980-1985	1.64	0.606
Seventh plan	1985-1990	2.14	0.465
Annual plan	1990-1991	3.35	0.298
Eighth plan	1992-1997	1.95	0.511

Source: Gulati *et al.* (2002).

An examination of state-wise analysis of ICOR in agriculture during 1992-1997 (Table 3.24) suggests the following broad inference:

- Barring a few states, the values of ICOR are found to be quite low in eastern and southern states as compared to northern states. Perhaps this could be attributed to less capital intensive agricultural production system and to efficient use of capital resources in these two groups of states.

Table 3.24

Estimates of ICOR in Agriculture: A State-wise Analysis-1992-1997 (At 1980-81 prices)

ICOR Range	*Cluster of States*
< 2.0	West Bengal (1.81)
2.0–3.0	Andhra Pradesh (2.97), Gujarat (2.56), Orissa (2.01), Rajasthan (2.56) and Tamil Nadu (2.16)
3.0–4.0	Bihar (3.10), Haryana (3.71), Kerala (3.51), Maharashtra (3.34) and Punjab (3.38)
4.0–5.0	Assam (4.50), Karnataka (4.44) and Madhya Pradesh (4.41)
5.0–8.0	Himachal Pradesh (5.55), Uttar Pradesh (5.58) and Union Territories (7.57)
> 8.0	Jammu & Kashmir (8.77) and Northeastern States (8.28)
All India	3.66

Note: Figures in parentheses are the respective state ICORs.

Source: Adopted from Roy (2001b).

One broad observation that would follow from all these analysis is that there has been visible improvement in capital use efficiency in agriculture. Further, the state level analyses of ICORs are suggestive of variations in these values across states. The question that needs examination is whether the use of one value of ICOR for all states in resource allocation for agriculture is appropriate and does it not alter the normative allocation of resources for agriculture across states.

Some Recent Trends in Investment Growth and Compositional Shifts

An examination of recent trends in agricultural investment and the compositional shifts would add to our understanding of investment growth cycle *vis-à-vis* earlier trends. While doing this analysis, one has to keep in view the methodological issue surrounding whether one should use the measure of GCF or GFCF. One view is that one has to look at GFCF rather than GCF, because of the fluctuations in the stocks (Alagh, 1994; 1997; Mishra *et al.*, 1995). Counter to this view is that the trends in public sector GFCF would be similar to those of GCF with minor differences (Dev, 1997). An examination of trends in the percentage share in agriculture (Table 3.25) suggests that the share of public and private sector was almost

Table 3.25

Percentage Share of Public and Private Investment in Agriculture

Period	*Public Sector*	*Private Sector*
	At 1993-94 Prices	
1960s	43	57
1980s	45	55
1990s	28	72
	At 1999-2000 Prices	
2000-01	18.5	81.5
2001-02	18.6	81.4
2002-03	17.0	83.0
2003-04	20.8	79.2
2004-05	21.1	78.9
2005-06	24.2	75.8

Source: Golait (2008) and *Economic Survey, 2007*, Government of India.

the same during 1960s and 1980s; but the share of private sector increased to 72 per cent and that of public sector decreased to 28 per cent. Between 2000-01 and 2003-04; the share of private sector was almost 80 per cent, and of late there has been a marginal increase in the share of public sector (24 per cent in 2005-06).

Yet another way is to examine the percentage share of agriculture and allied sectors in national GDP (Table 3.26(a)). It is obvious from these results that the percentage share of the sector has been over 2 per cent of GDP between 2004-05–2007-08, with a marginal increase in the year 2008-2009. The overwhelming dominance of private sector stands out with 2.6 per cent of GDP and 0.5 per cent in case of public sector during 2008-2009. Added to this, one could also analyse the GFCF in/for agriculture as a percentage of national GDP. It could be observed from the results of Table 3.26(b) that compared to 1980-81, the total share of the sector has been on

Table 3.26(a)

Percentage Share of Public and Private Sector Investment in Agriculture and Allied Sectors as a Per cent of Total GDP (At 2004-05 Prices)

Year	*Percentage Share of*		
	Public Sector	*Private Sector*	*Total*
2004–05	0.5	1.9	2.4
2005–06	0.6	2.1	2.6
2006–07	0.6	1.8	2.4
2007–08	0.5	2.0	2.6
2008–09	0.5	2.6	3.1

Source: Central Statistical Organisation, Government of India, New Delhi.

Table 3.26(b)

GFCF in/for Agriculture as Percentage of National GDP: At 1993-94 Prices

Year	*In Agriculture*	*For Agriculture*	*Total*
1980/81	3.4	4.3	7.7
1990/91	2.3	3.1	5.4
2000-01	1.5	2.3	3.8
2001-02	1.6	2.3	3.9

Source: Datt (2006).

the decline till the beginning of the present decade. Further, the decline is found to be much more evident in case of GFCF share (%) in agriculture than for agriculture; but in both the cases, the share of GFCF in national GDP has halved between 1980-81 and 2001-02.

How are the trends in the percentage share of GCF in agriculture and allied sectors in the GDP originating in this sector? It could be observed from Table 3.27 that starting with about 11 per cent in 1999-2000, the share is found to have increased to about 14 per cent in 2007-08. The issue could also be examined with broad trends in percentage share of GCF in/for agriculture in agriculture GDP between 1980s and 1990s (Table 3.28). Two observations could be made on these results. First, the percentage share of

Table 3.27

Percentage Share of GCF in Agriculture and Allied Sectors in AGDP at 1999-2000 Prices

Year	*% Share*
1999-2000	11.20
2000-01	10.20
2001-02	12.00
2002-03	12.68
2003-04	11.09
2004-05	11.98
2005-06	12.93
2006-07	13.15
2007-08	13.88

Source: Central Statistical Organisation, Government of India, New Delhi.

Table 3.28

Percentage Share of GCF in/for Agriculture in Agriculture GDP

Period	*GCF in Agriculture*	*GCF for Agriculture*	*Total*
1981-1983 (Avg.)	8.3	10.7	19.0
1991-1993 (Avg.)	6.8	9.5	16.3
1996-1998 (Avg.)	6.4	9.4	15.8
1998-2000 (Avg.)	6.1	9.1	15.3

Source: GoI (2003).

GCF for agriculture in AGDP was higher than that of GCF in agriculture. This justifies the need for considering 'broad data series' for investment analysis. Second compared to 1981-1983, average percentage share of total AGCF in AGDP, the percentage share is found to have declined during two decades. This reinforces the earlier argument of loss of momentum in agricultural capital formation.

What have been the trends in the percentage share of agriculture and allied sectors in total GCF? As could be seen from Table 3.29 that the share of agriculture and allied sectors declined from 23.5 per cent in 1952-1953 to between 20 per cent to 14 per cent during 1953-54 and 1983-84, to 9.9 per cent in 1990-91 to 6.2 per cent in 1995-96 and to 9.0 per cent in 2002-03. With all the marginal recovery during the recent years, the share of agriculture and allied sectors in total GCF has been on the decline during the last 50 years in India. One more approach to examine this issue is to discuss the trends in the percentage share of public sector and private sector in the total share of agriculture and allied sectors in total GCF for the economy (Table 3.30) during the last 15 years or so. It is also obvious from these results that the percentage share of the sector has been declining all along, even though there has been a decline in the share of private sector in total GCF of the economy and some increase in the share of public sector. Further, the GFCF for the economy out of national GDP had increased from about 23 per cent in 1980-81 to 26 per cent in 2001-2002, whereas the share of agriculture had decreased from 7.7 per cent to 3.9 per cent (Datt, 2006).

Table 3.29

Percentage Share of Agriculture and Allied Sector in National GCF

Period	*% Share*
1952-53	23.5
1953–1983-84	20 to 14
1990-91	9.9
1995-96	6.2
2000-01	7.6
2000-02	8.1
2002-03	9.0

Source: Bisaliah (2010a).

Table 3.30

Percentage Share of Agriculture and Allied Sectors in National GCF: 1999-2000 Prices

Year	*% Share of*		*Total*
	Public Sector	*Private Sector*	
1999-2000	6.0	11.9	10.2
2000-01	5.8	11.3	9.7
2001-02	6.7	13.7	11.7
2002-03	6.5	11.5	10.3
2003-04	7.4	9.2	8.8
2004-05	7.8	7.7	7.7
2005-06	7.9	7.1	7.2
2006-07	8.2	6.6	7.0

Source: Bisaliah (2010a).

Data generated by Report of the Committee on Capital Formation in Agriculture (GoI, 2003) could also be analysed to find out the shifting contribution of 10 specific sectors to GFCF for agriculture during 1991-92 and 2001-02 (Table 3.31). In the framework of 'broad data series' also, the capital expenditure under agriculture and allied sector continued to be over

Table 3.31

Percentage Contribution of Heads of Capital Expenditure for GFCF for Agriculture at 1993-94 Prices

Heads	*1991-92*	*2001-02*
1. Agriculture and allied sectors	69.8	69.0
2. Agriculture machinery	0.5	0.9
3. Fertilisers and pesticides	5.0	9.2
4. Electricity, gas and water supply	9.2	6.7
5. Construction	0.8	1.2
6. Trade	4.5	4.8
7. Railways	1.2	1.0
8. Storage	0.2	0.5
9. Communication	1.8	3.2
10. Banking & insurance	1.4	0.4
11. Others	5.6	3.1
Total	100.0	100.0

Source: Bisaliah (2010a).

two-third of total capital expenditure under 11 heads, followed by other heads like fertilisers or pesticides, trade, communication and so on. Further, the share of heads like agriculture machinery, fertiliser and pesticides, communication had experienced considerable increase, whereas the heads like electricity, gas and water supply and banking and insurance have registered considerable decline.

It is also appropriate to analyse the trend growth rates in capital stock, technology, electricity use, gross irrigated area and cropping intensity in agriculture (Table 3.32). The analysis of trends in growth rates for about a quarter century would provide broad insights into investment in agriculture, development of technology, gross irrigated area, electricity use in agriculture and cropping intensity which have a strong bearing on agricultural productivity and output growth. It could be seen from these results that the growth rates of total fixed capital stock in agriculture had declined from 2 per cent to 1.28 per cent between first period and third period. This has been mainly due to decline in rate of growth of public sector net fixed capital stock from 3.86 per cent per annum to 1.42 per cent during these two periods, and partly due to decline in the rate of growth of private sector net fixed capital stock from 2.17 per cent to 1.17 per cent between second period and third period. Coupled with this growth rate

Table 3.32

Trend Growth Rates in Net Fixed Capital Stock, Technology, Electricity Use, Gross Irrigated Area and Cropping Intensity in Agriculture: 1980-81 to 2005-06

Item	*1980-81 to 1990-91*	*1990-91 to 1996-97*	*1996-97 to 2005-06*
Public sector net fixed capital stock	3.86	1.92	1.42*
Private sector net fixed capital stock	0.56	2.17	1.17*
Total net fixed capital stock	2.00	2.06	1.28*
Technology	3.3	2.81	0.00
Gross irrigated area	2.28	2.62	0.51*
Electricity use in agriculture	14.07	9.44	-0.53**
Cropping intensity	0.51	0.39	0.12

Note: * upto 2003-04

* upto 2004-05

Sources: Dev (2008) and Kapila (2009).

deceleration in capital stock in agriculture have been decelerations in the growth rates of technology development (agricultural productivity as a proxy), irrigation, electricity use and cropping intensity—all proximate causes, of agricultural growth. All these decelerated growth rates tend to impact adversely growth performance of agriculture and tempo of poverty reduction.

What could be the broad substantive conclusions therefore? First, capital formation in agriculture as a proportion of total GDP and total capital formation in the economy and in terms of capital stock growth rates in agriculture since 1980s, has experienced deceleration. This has been mainly due to fall in public investment in agriculture. Although some increase in private investment has been recorded, as discussed already public and private investment cannot be treated as substitutes. Their compositions are different. For example, public investment is mainly in medium and major irrigation work, while private investment is mainly in minor irrigation, mechanisation and land development (Sawant *et al.*, 2002). Second, apart from difference in composition, public investment affects directly growth performance of agriculture sector, and indirectly through its inducement effect on private sector investment. Third, agriculture is basically a private activity and public investment has a critical role to play in creating the infrastructure in terms of irrigation, roads, markets, storage facilities, rural electrification and technology development, besides rural health and education (Thamarajakshi, 1999). Fourth, both public and private investment in agriculture and agri-business are crucial, but both have remained weak since the early 1990s, despite accelerating growth in the overall economy and a large domestic market for agricultural products; Growth in farm output has slowed down since the early 1990s, mainly due to inadequate infrastructure for the sector (Thorat, *et al.*, 2003; Landes, 2008). It has been very well articulated (Blarcom *et al.*, 1993; Alagh, 1997) that the level of public investment (meant for infrastructural development for augmenting productivity capacity in the agricultural sector) is crucial for growth of agricultural output and for addressing other items of development policy agenda like unemployment and poverty. Further, this decline in public investment in agriculture with its adverse impact on growth performance of this sector would contribute for economy-wise slowdown (Chand, 2004) through supply and demand routes and lower development multiplier. The crucial role of public investment for development of infrastructure to support agriculture is very well recognised. But what is needed is to review of policies which have led to the diversion of scarce resources away from the creation of productive assets, by better targetting of subsidies. Because, during the past two decades, Government expenditure control (to ensure fiscal discipline as part of Economic Reform Agenda) have led to cut-back on agricultural investment, but not on subsidies especially on fertiliser, power and irrigation water.

Debate on Complementarity between Public and Private Investment in Agriculture

This section is almost a reproduction of the analysis performed by Bisaliah (2004), excepting some deletions and additions.

It is recalled from earlier sections that all-India trend analysis of public and private capital formation indicates the movement of both investment series in the same direction between 1960s and mid-1980s, and a divergent movement of these series since mid-1980s with public sector investment falling and that of private sector rising steadily. This decline in the momentum of public sector investment was considered as a disquieting development in India. Further, public investment is one of the major determinants of private investment. And any neglect of public investment in resource allocation by both Central and state governments would adversely affect agricultural growth and policy concerns like poverty alleviation. However, the relationship between public and private sector investment has become a matter of great debate with its implications for policy directions so as to influence capital formation in Indian agriculture. The argument has been sharpened by the studies by Rath (1989), Shetty (1990), Gandhi (1990; 1996), Rao (1994; 1997) and Dhawan (1996 and 1998), Storm (1993), Mitra (1996), Misra and Hazell (1996; 1998), Mishra *et al.* (1995), Chand (2000), Roy (2001b), Gulati *et al.* (2002) and Chand *et al.* (2004). An examination of these studies would lead to five major inferences.

- There is a crowding in or positive inducement effect of public investment on private investment due to strong complementarity between public and private investment.
- There is only weak complementarity between these two types of investment.
- There is a strong relationship between two types of investment at micro level like canal-irrigated areas. Complementarity at macro level may not show up due to aggregation problem of treating all public investments alike with respect to impact.
- There is no apparent complementarity. Private investment may be partly induced by public investment and partly autonomous.
- State level analysis of trends and proper definition and measurement of public investment variables support a strong case for complementarity both at national and state level.

Given these inferences drawn by different researchers, the estimated elasticities of private investment with respect to public investment have turned out to be different. For example, the value of elasticity coefficient is found to be 0.62 in a study by Chakravarthy (1987) for the period 1970-71 to 1982-83, 0.66 in a study by Shetty (1990) for the period 1960-61 to 1986-87, 0.66 by Storm (1993), 0.25 by Dhawan (January-June, 1996) with respect to canal irrigation ratio (treated as a proxy for public investment), -0.50 by Mishra *et al.* (1995), 1.55 for the period 1960-1970, 0.69 for the period 1970-1980 and –0.31 for the period 1980-1990 by Misra and Hazell (1996), and 0.50 by Saibaba (1996).

Differences in inferences derived on complementarity between public and private investment and in the estimated elasticities of private investment with respect to public investment could be attributed to many reasons such as different data sets used, data period, failure to see differences between instantaneous and cumulative effects of public investment on private investment, different lag structures used to find out the response of private sector investment to public sector investment, use of different terminologies such as complementarity, inducement effect and crowding in/out effects, failure to include relevant variables to assess the net effect of public investment, failure to recognise lagged response from farmers and lagged impact of public investment, failure to differentiate between movement of trend series and causal relationships, use of physical and financial variables, different evidences from macro and micro level studies, and treating public investment in irrigation on par with other variables like investment in roads.

With all the differences in inferences derived and elasticities estimated, the debate has been quite useful to understand and unearth the complexities of relationship between public and private investment. A brief presentation of methodologies and results of a few studies would illustrate the nature of the controversy and complexity in confirming or rejecting complementarity hypothesis.

Based on increasing trend in the CSO estimates of both private and public investment in Indian agriculture till 1980-81, there are many studies which have confirmed the proposition on complementarity. The studies by Rath (1989), Shetty (1990), Storm (1993), Rao (1994; 1997), Gandhi (1990; 1996), Dhawan (1996; 1998) have confirmed complementarity between public and private investment. Arguments of some of these studies could be placed in the proper perspective. Rao (1994; 1997), while confirming the complementarity proposition, has argued that if public investments made in agriculture are properly accounted for including the excluded items like rural electrification, rural roads, storage, etc., the complementarity between public and private investments stands out prominently. Dhawan (1996; 1998), another supporter of complementarity proposition, has treated public canal irrigation intensity as a relevant explanatory variable instead of total public investment in agriculture for explaining variations in private investment. The rationale is that public canal irrigation accounts for a major share of total public investment in agriculture. Hence, the positive and significant impact of canal irrigation intensity on private investment both with macro and micro level data establishes the veracity of complementarity hypothesis. Infact macro and micro level evidences are found to lend support to the complementarity proposition that public sector investment in canal irrigation stimulates private investment, including private means of irrigation.

The distinct trends have been observed with CSO data upto the end of 1980s. First, the movement of investment series of both public and private sector till 1980-81 has led to the emergence of complementarity proposition. Second, after 1980-81 both the series started moving in opposite direction (declining trend in public sector investment, but continuous increase in private investment). This movement of both the investment series in the opposite direction has been the basis for questioning the validity of complementarity hypothesis by Chand *et al.* (2004). Yet another line of argument has been that though aggregate series of public and private investment do not support the complementarity hypothesis, project-specific public sector investment, especially in irrigation, induced the investment in agriculture on private account does (Mitra, 1996). This partial acceptance of complementarity proposition gives credence to the argument that complementarity hypothesis should be tested at the level of investment projects, and could be more prominent in the construction of assets like irrigation.

A redefinition and re-estimation of public investment in agriculture (broad investment series) has led to conflicting/confirming inferences on complementarity issue. For example, Chand (2000) has found negative and non-significant impact of public sector investment on private investment. This result is suggestive of lack of complementarity. But Chand (2000), using state level cross-section study for the year 1981-82 to 1991-92, has led to the inference that broad public investment series bears a positive and significant impact on private investment in 1981-82, and positive but insignificant impact in 1991-92. So his state level study with broad investment series suggests the conclusion that there is a partial complementarity depending on the type of public investment in different regional settings. Yet in a recent study by Chand *et al.* (2004), it has been established that there is asymmetry in the impact of public investment on private investment. An increase in public investment is found to have positive impact on private investment, but a decline in public investment is found to have increased private investment as a part of coping strategies of private investors.

Redefinition and re-estimation of public investment data to derive broad investment series, and appropriate measurement of investment components, appropriate lags incorporated (to account for response of private investment to public investment), and the modelling of relationship between public and private sector investment in a simultaneous equation framework may lead to different conclusion. Roy (2001), using this methodological structure, has derived the inference that public investment has a strong impact on private investment, and there is a strong case for complementarity proposition at national and state level.

It is recalled from earlier section that irrigation accounts for more than 90 per cent of public sector investment in agriculture. Further, public sector investment in power sector is required for pumping water. But these items of capital expenditures have a long gestation period of public investment in these two sectors. Hence, it is not rationale to visualise a strong complementarity. Further, the farmers' response to public sector investment in irrigation and power supplies cannot be instantaneous, and it is likely to be stretched over years. Hence expecting strict complementarity in such a situation is not warranted. There are two options to measure public sector investment in these two areas for testing complementarity hypothesis. First, one could use quantity of water and power supplied to agriculture each year. But it is difficult to get data on water supplied each year under canal irrigation system. Second, in the absence of easy availability of data on water supplied each year, one could use cumulative potential created as a proxy variable for the total water supplied. Hence, it is rational to use physical quantity of power supplied to agriculture each year, and cumulative potential of canal irrigation created, and the annual expenditure incurred in public sector under 11 heads (Gulati *et al.*, 2002) to test the impact of public investment on private investment in agriculture. Measurement of cumulative investment in canal irrigation could be both in physical and financial terms. Gulati *et al.* (2002) have performed this kind of analysis, using data from 1980-81 to 1998-99, and concluded that it is hard to reconcile with the argument of no inducement effect or weak complementarity between public and private investments as stated by Chand (2000) and others. The analysis performed by Gulati *et al.* (2002) has led to the inference that there is a significant positive impact of public investment (if properly measured and lagged) on private investment, whether the public investment is measured in physical or financial terms.

On summing up the results on complementarity hypothesis, there appears to be more evidence to confirm the complementarity hypothesis without ignoring other determinants of private investment. However, the magnitude of elasticity of private investment with public investment is bound to vary with the period of study, choice of variables on public sector investment and their measurement, construction of appropriate lags to impact and to respond, and specification of structural equations.

While arguing with narrow data set that private sector investment may increase even under the situation of declining public sector investment, one has to keep in view the compositional differences as between public and private sector investment, and the difference in their investment objective function. Public sector investment portfolio is expected to be a part of broader development agenda like equity, conservation of environment, poverty alleviation, enhancing competitive capacity of Indian agriculture both in domestic and international markets, and the like. The enabling investments in rural link roads, big irrigation projects, rural power supply, storage structures and market yards may have to be handled under public sector investment to induce private sector investment. Any entry of corporate sector to these lines of investment to induce farm household sector investment may be unimaginable for the time being, and certain types of public sector investments are necessary even to induce corporate sector to invest for agriculture. Hence, the challenge is to identify the sectors/areas where public sector investment is likely to have strong complementarity, weak complementarity, and where there is lack of complementarity, so as to decide public investment portfolio. Hence, from the viewpoint of long-term agricultural growth, lack of complementarity or weak complementarity should not underestimate the importance of public sector investment. The challenge lies in identifying right priorities for public investment by keeping in view the varying priorities depending on stage of agricultural growth/development, broader development agenda, and more inducement effect on private farm household and private corporate sector investment.

Yet one more methodological issue relating to the analysis of time series data needs examination. Modelling of complementarity in a single equation ordinary least square (OLS) framework may give rise to spurious relationship between public and private investment, if the assumption of stationarity of series is violated (Granger *et al.*, 1974; 1977; Nelson *et al.*, 1999; Maddala, 1992; Murray *et al.*, 2000). To test the time series data on public and private investment for their stationarity, Augmented Dicky–

Fuller Test (ADF) can be applied. Once the results show that raw time series data is not stationary, use of cointegration technique to establish the relationship between public and private investment is appropriate, known as two-step procedure in estimation. But most of the studies (Dhawan, 1996; Dhawan *et al.*, 1997; Mitra, 1996; Rath, 1989; Rao, 1997 and many others) have used raw time series data to test the existence of complementarity or otherwise.

Capital Formation, Agriculture Growth and Poverty Alleviation

This section is concerned with the assessment of relationship between capital formation and agriculture growth and poverty alleviation in India. A recall of some of the major conclusions/inferences from the preceding sections is in order, as that would provide a logical farmework for analysing the experience of India.

First, a search for sources of growth both in theoretical and empirical studies has led to the inference that capital (in a broad sense) is one of the major critical drivers of growth.

Second, growth accounting through growth regression studies has concluded that capital is a crucial input for 'catch up' in growth path and growth convergence. Added to this is the premise that 'idea gap' persists between countries leading to growth divergence, in the absence of adequate amount of capital accumulation.

Third, developing countries are to realise that capital accumulation is an escape from the vicious circle of poverty. One of the elements of pro-growth is productivity augmentation of labour force in developing countries by providing more capital to work with (i.e., capital deepening) in agricultural sector, since poverty is dominantly a rural phenomenon.

Fourth, an analysis of growth-poverty nexus is suggestive of the inference that faster economic growth is only one avenue for reducing poverty. But growth maximising development policy may not always lead to maximisation of poverty reduction. Instead it is growth pattern and sectoral composition of aggregate output which would contribute for a higher rate of poverty reduction. Hence, the need for directing growth efforts to areas (rural), sectors (agriculture) in which poor people work, to the factors of production they possess, and to the products they consume. All these would suggest the need for growth of agriculture and rural sector.

Fifth, cross-country experiences on agricultural growth and poverty reduction have led to the inference that labour productivity and TFP together could impact poverty reduction. The determinants of TFP are irrigation, Government expenditure on agriculture, rural infrastructure, human capital, agriculture R&D and so on. Further, investment for the development of non-farm sector in rural areas would be equally important for increasing and diversifying employment and income opportunities for the poor in the developing world. Hence, capital (in the broader sense) is one of the major drivers of agricultural growth and poverty reduction through augmentation of labour productivity and TFP in agriculture.

Sixth, studies by Stephan (2009) and Schmidhuber (2009) have established the relationship between agricultural capital stock (ACS), productivity of labour engaged in agriculture and hunger in developing countries. It is found that low ACS per worker, low labour productivity and high prevalence of undernourished 'co-exist'.

Seventh, given a limited amount of investment resources in developing countries, the development merit of a sector is to be judged by how much the sector would contribute for addressing the development problems like poverty, unemployment and inequalities, and how much of development multiplier it would give rise to through inducement effects. Agriculture emerges as a deserving candidate on both the counts of merit.

Eighth, with respect to Indian experience, there has been a loss of momentum in capital formation in agriculture in 1980s as well as 1990s with implication for agriculture growth and poverty reduction. Capital formation in agriculture as a proportion of total GDP and total capital formation in the economy and in terms of capital stock growth rates in agriculture since 1980s has experienced deceleration. This has been mainly due to fall in public investment in agriculture with implications for agricultural growth and poverty reduction. During 1980-81–1990-91 and 1996-97–2005-06, the country is found to have experienced fall in growth rates of net fixed capital stock in agriculture, stagnation of technology development, fall in growth rates of gross irrigated area, negative growth rate in electricity use in agriculture, and fall in growth rate of cropping intensity. All these proximate drivers of agricultural productivity and production growth would obviously tend to decelerated growth in Indian agriculture.

Agriculture: Bypassed Sector in High Growth Trajectory

Indian economy has entered the high growth trajectory during the last two decades or so, and deserved to be labelled as one of the fastest growing economies of the world. But it is yet to address the problems of 'exclusive growth', leading to bypassing of some regions, some sectors like agriculture and some segments of the society like rural society in the move towards high growth trajectory. The consequence of exclusive growth instead of inclusive growth is reflected in the persistence of poverty, unemployment and too much of development distance. It is evident from Table 3.33 that sectoral (agriculture and allied sector, industry and service sector) growth rates between recent years (2005-06–2007-08) vary among sectors. The sectoral growth rates of industry and service sector are found to be far high *vis-à-vis* growth rates of agriculture.

Table 3.33

Sectoral Growth Rate of GDP at 2004-05 Prices and Sectoral Share

Year	*Sectoral Growth Rates (%)*			*Sectoral Share (%)*		
	A	*I*	*S*	*A*	*I*	*S*
2005–06	5.2	9.3	11.1	18.1	27.9	53.9
2006–07	3.7	12.7	10.2	17.2	28.7	54.2
2007–08	4.7	9.5	10.5	16.4	28.8	54.8
2008–09	1.6	3.9	9.8	15.7	28.0	56.4

Note: A = Agriculture and Allied Sector; I = Industry; S = Services.

Source: Central Statistical Organisation, Government of India, New Delhi.

This is very well reflected in the share of three sectors in GDP. The share of agriculture had declined from 18.1 per cent in 2005-06 to 15.7 per cent in 2008-09, and of industry had remained at 28 per cent, and of service sector at 56.4 per cent. This also reinforces the argument that rate of reduction in poverty has slowed down, since poverty in India is dominantly a rural phenomenon and agriculture has fallen into decelerated growth syndrome. It has been argued in the earlier sections that agriculture is a pro-poor growth sector, but there has been a deceleration in its growth performance reaching less than two per cent growth rate of AGDP. Further, between 1996-97–2004-05, the growth rate of cereals (a major staple food item) was 0.02 per cent. Per capita food grains production per annum declined from over 200 kgs to 186 kgs (Dev, 2008). Growth rate of land productivity of food grains declined from 2.12 per cent between 1985-86 and 1990-91 to 0.52 per cent between 2001-02 and 2005-06. This decline in productivity of land is attributed to decrease in input use and inadequate investment in public infrastructure, among others (Sen *et al.*, 2004). Hence, many of the problems of agriculture sector *viz.*, low productivity, low employment opportunities, low infrastructure (including irrigation), and high intensity of poverty are attributed to progressive decline in capital formation (Thorat, 2003; Majumdar, 2006; Bhatia, 1999; Chadha, 2003).

The experience of China shows that high rate of investment in agriculture can ensure big spurt in agricultural output and thereby poverty reduction. Fan *et a*l. (2000; 2002) have recognised the returns of agricultural public investment in poverty reduction in China and India. There are evidences to suggest that Government development expenditure has positive impact on reducing poverty in India (Sen, 1996; Datt and Ravallion, 1995).

All these evidences are suggestive of the nexus between capital formation, agriculture output growth and poverty. Added to this is the need for realising that employment mediates between growth and poverty, and growth in productivity of labour engaged in agriculture is crucial for poverty reduction. The analysis below also establishes the relationship between the growth rates of per hectare GCF, per hectare agriculture productivity and productivity per agricultural worker (micro level evidences in Chapter 4).

Shown below are the growth rates (%) of per capita productivity of land, labour and capital in agriculture in India at 1993-94 prices:

Period	*Per Unit of GCF*	*Per Hectare*	*Per Agriculture Worker*
1980-81–1990-91	2.9	2.38	2.54
1990-91–1998-99	0.03	1.84	1.05

Source: Reports of Commission for Agricultural Costs and Prices. Department of Agriculture and Cooperation, Government of India.

It is obvious from this analysis that capital formation, productivity of land and productivity of agriculture labour move together. A high rate of growth in capital formation would lead to high growth rate of land and labour productivity, and a low growth rate to low rates of growth in land and labour productivity; and, the decelerated growth rate in capital formation would lead to decelerated growth rates in productivity of land and labour. The decelerated growth in agriculture sector during 1990s has given rise to low productivity of labour (due to less of capital to work with, among others) and decline in poverty reduction rate.

Empirical Constructs and Evidences

The section preceded has brought out the importance of capital formation in growth performance of agriculture, and thereby in productivity of labour engaged in agriculture and the pace of poverty reduction. It is also recalled from earlier section that much of the decline in poverty in India from the mid-1960s to the early 1980s has been attributed to agriculture growth and the associated reduction in food prices (Ahluwalia, 1985; Srinivasan, 1986; Ghose, 1989). Given the above relationship, it is appropriate to discuss the empirical constructs for establishing the relationship between capital formation, agriculture growth and poverty. There are some research attempts (Chand, 2000; Roy, 2001; Gulati *et al.*, 2002; Thorat *et al.*, 2003) to examine the relationships by constructing different empirical frameworks and by using different data sets. Cutting across all these, two empirical constructs are specified *viz.*, agricultural output growth function and rural poverty function. In general, socio-economic, institutional, and agro-economic variables influence agricultural growth and poverty. The agricultural output could be specified as a function of public investment, private investment, rainfall, population growth, rural literacy, marginal holdings, terms of trade, cropping intensity, village electrification, markets, roads, credit, storage capacity and so on. Rural poverty could be specified as a function of AGDP, public investment in agriculture, private investment, population growth, marginal holdings, rural literacy, village electrification, terms of trade, total government expenditure on poverty alleviation, roads, markets, credit and so on. It is obvious from the specification of these two functions that simultaneous equation model, using two stage least square estimation (LSE), would constitute the relevant empirical construct. Some of the empirical evidences are reproduced from earlier studies by Bisaliah (2004; 2009a).

Before the examination of empirical results, it is appropriate to discuss some of the methodological issues involved (Bisaliah, 2004): First, capital investment is a determinant of agricultural growth, but agricultural growth could also be a determinant of capital investment, particularly in case of private investment. Second, the impact of total investment on growth could be different from that of public and private investment separately. Third, two alternative measures of public investment *viz.*, physical and financial terms may give rise to different productivity and output elasticities. Fourth, there are differences in the choice of public capital expenditure heads (recall narrow and broad public investment data series) to assess the impact. Choice of capital expenditure may be in the form of index of agriculture infrastructure, index of transport and communication, research, extension and educational infrastructure, credit infrastructure, and various other definitions and measurement of investment variables. Fifth, what is the time lag between investment and growth response? Does the time lag vary between public and private investment? Sixth, choice of single equation model as against simultaneous equation model may give rise to bias in the assessment of impact of investment on growth performance of agriculture, and thereby difficulties in establishing the causality or otherwise.

With all these methodological issues, there are some studies which have established the relationship between volume and composition of investment on growth performance of agriculture, and the impact of agriculture growth and poverty (Bisaliah, 2004):

A study by Chand (2000), covering the period between 1974-75 and 1996-97 would provide some empirical insights into the causal relationships. First, the impact of public investment alone on both productivity and output growth is found to be positive, but statistically non-significant; but the impact of total of both public and private investment is not merely positive, but also statistically significant. Second, public investment as a determinant of private investment is found to be less important than terms of trade and flow of institutional credit; but the importance of public investment (the composition of which is different) to create infrastructural support and to promote long-term agricultural growth should not be undermined. This supports the need for reversing the declining trend in public sector investment in agriculture with measures to improve the efficiency of public investment and changing the composition of private investment to meet the development needs of post-reform period.

A simultaneous equation model has been employed by Roy (2001) to derive both agricultural productivity equation (to identify the determinants of agricultural productivity) and rural poverty equation (to identify determinants of rural poverty). The analysis has estimated the effects of various economic, agro-climatic and institutional variables on agricultural investment, productivity and rural poverty. With respect to the relationship between agricultural productivity and investment, and between agricultural productivity and other explanatory variables, certain useful results to provide direction for policy reform could be sorted out. First, the impact of per hectare investment on per hectare agriculture GDP is found to be positive and statistically significant. Though agricultural GDP and its growth did not decline as predicted during the later part of 1980s following a decline in public investment, there is no disagreement about the importance of public investment for long-run output growth. Second, the impact of rural literacy, proportion of area under marginal holdings, per hectare storage capacity, cropping intensity, agricultural subsidy, terms of trade, per hectare institutional credit and rainfall on agricultural productivity are found to be both positive and statistically significant. The impact of cropping intensity captures the effect of irrigation and seed-fertiliser technology, and estimated productivity model does not include rural market and electricity consumption because of multi-collinearity problem with storage and rural literacy rates.Third, instability in Government expenditure on agriculture is found to be inversely related to the growth in agricultural sector. Fourth, among other variables, public and private investment in agriculture are found to have positive impact on AGDP and thereby poverty reduction. This establishes the agricultural productivity/production enhancing and poverty reduction effects of investment in agriculture.

It is appropriate to examine details on the results from rural poverty function estimated by Roy (2001). First, while private investment is found to have played significant impact on poverty reduction, public investment does not appear to have direct impact on poverty. But public investment has positive impact on agriculture productivity which in turn contributes for poverty reduction through employment and wages. In fact agriculture investment affects rural poverty directly and indirectly. While indirect effects arise mainly through gain in agriculture productivity, direct effects arise from wage earning opportunities for the poor. Second, there is a positive association between population growth and poverty, implying population growth as a contributory factor for increase in poverty. Third, rural literacy, village electrification, terms of trade, rural roads and credit flow to rural sector are found to have positive impact on poverty reduction. It is quite obvious that decelerated agriculture growth and accelerated growth in service sector alone (which does not generate demand for unskilled rural labour) are bound to give rise to slowdown in poverty reduction. Further, investment in agriculture helps to reduce poverty directly and indirectly through agriculture growth by improving employment and wages in rural sector and reducing the prices of staple food items (Thorat *et al.*, 2003).

In yet another important research study by Gulati *et al.* (2002), the relationship between investment in agriculture and GDPA has been explored, using data for the period 1980-81 to 1998-99 at 1993-94 prices. The analysis with simultaneous equation model in reduced form has provided a major useful inference. The study has observed significant positive impact of both public and private investment on the growth of AGDP. Whatever the concept of public investment used (Concepts I, II and III as discussed earlier), public investment (measured both in physical and financial terms) is found to have positive significant direct impact on AGDP and indirect impact through its inducement effect on private investment in agriculture. Hence, decline in public investment in agriculture would affect agricultural output growth through both direct and induced effects. Further, the positive and significant impact of terms of trade and gross cropped area on agricultural output growth is also evidenced with the analysis.

The relationship between agricultural productivity and infrastructure variables such as transport, power, irrigation, credit, marketing, research, extension, fertiliser, tractor, communication, education and health has been identified by Thorat (2003). Among various infrastructure variables, irrigation, power, research and transport are found to have a great influence on agricultural productivity and output growth. Hence, public investment impacts agricultural productivity/production directly and through its inducement effect on private sector investment in agriculture is very well established.

A recent study (Chand *et al.*, 2004) has attempted to establish the relative importance of public sector investment in agriculture and subsidies in influencing AGDP, among other determinants of AGDP such as terms of trade, net sown area and rainfall. Instant return to one rupee public expenditure on subsidies is found to be much higher (Rs 3.19) than the impact of one rupee increase in capital stocks on AGDP (Rs 0.61). But this is the impact of only one year. But, if one-year impact of capital stock on AGDP is multiplied by the expected life of capital stock, that total impact has turned out to be more than double the impact of subsidies. In view of this, trade-off in public resource allocation between subsidies and public capital investment, the diversion of public resources in a phased manner from subsidies to public investment is suggested. Another study (Jha, 2007) suggests that stagnant/declining agriculture investment, decelerated agriculture growth and slowdown in rural employment would obviously lead to slowdown in poverty reduction.

With all the methodological complexities related to the choice of data set on investment and the measurement of investment, choice of explanatory variables to account for variations in agricultural productivity/production, and the choice of statistical models, a few inferences on the relationship between capital formation and agricultural growth would follow. *First*, capital formation in/for agriculture has positive impact on agricultural productivity and output growth. *Second*, other variables like terms of trade and technology are found to have positive impact on productivity and output growth in agricultural sector. *Third*, public sector investment becomes a crucial factor to impact the growth of agricultural sector, both because of its direct and inducement effects. *Fourth*, the impact of public investment on AGDP is found to be more than double the impact of subsidies. *Fifth*, any policy failure to reverse the declining trend in public sector investment would adversely affect the growth in agricultural sector, which in turn would affect adversely the growth of non-agricultural sector and thereby the growth of general GDP through both supply and demand linkage of agricultural sector with non-agricultural sector—all leading to slowdown in poverty reduction in India with implications for the 'ability' of India to honour Millennium Development Goal (MDG) of halving poverty by 2015. This is also established by the concomitant occurrence of high rate of capital growth in agricultural productivity (of land and labour), and high rate of poverty reduction. This also implies that low rate of growth in capital stock and low rate of growth in agriculture productivity and lower rate of poverty reduction are the development experiences of India.

4 Micro Evidences on Capital Structure

Growth, Composition, Intensity and Productivity

A brief recapitulation of macro level evidences on capital formation, agriculture growth and poverty in India (Chapter 3) could be a backdrop to micro (farm) level evidences on capital structure in agriculture. First, the studies by Bisaliah (2004; 2010a) have identified investment growth cycle in Indian agriculture, encompassing rising trend during 1960s, relatively subdued phase during the first half of 1970s, momentum of peak phase during second half of 1980s, and decline thereafter with marginal recovery during recent years. Second, the investment growth cycle has been analysed from different angles like trends in growth rate in AGFC *vis-à-vis* aggregate GFCF, shifting shares of GFCF and AGFCF in GDP, shifting share of AGFCF in AGDP, and compositional shifts as between share of public and private investment in total investment in/for agriculture. With respect to all these, the percentage share of AGFCF is to found to be on the decline. This would imply, in broad terms, a loss of momentum in capital formation in agriculture in 1980s and 1990s with implications for agriculture growth and poverty reduction during subsequent years. Third, the share of public and private sector in total investment in agriculture which was almost the same during 1960s had given way for dominant share (76%) of private sector (about 95% of which comes from farm households and 90% as per HLC, 2009 estimate), and declining share of public sector (24%). Fourth, trend growth rates in fixed capital stock in agriculture, technology, gross irrigated area, electricity use and cropping intensity between 1980s and 1996/97-2003/04 had reached the phase of deceleration/stagnation. This pattern of decelerated growth trends in supporting factors (to agriculture productivity and production) had contributed for decelerated growth rate of AGDP from 3.5 per cent per annum during 1980-81 to 1996-97 to around 2 per cent during 1997-98 to 2004-05. Fifth, it is documented and validated (Bisaliah 2004; 2009a; 2010a) that there is a positive association between capital formation and agriculture productivity/production, and agricultural growth and poverty reduction. This has been the international experience also (Bisaliah, 2010a). In fact, low rate of growth in capital stock, low rate of growth in agricultural productivity/production and low rate of poverty reduction could be treated, in broad terms, as the development experience of India. Sixth, in view of dominant role of farm households in influencing private capital formation, the key role of millions of farm households in influencing the rate of capital growth and composition of capital stock needs to be recognised, and accordingly the determinants of private investment in agriculture are to be kept in view so as to design appropriate policies and programmes. It is documented (Bisaliah, 2004; 2010a) that investment in private sector is positively impacted by public investment, terms of trade, technology, institutional credit, and negatively impacted by incidence of rural poverty and percentage of area under marginal holdings.

The overwhelmingly dominant role of farm households in determining private investment in agriculture sets the tone for study of farm level capital formation and growth, composition, intensity, productivity and determinants. The need for this kind of study has been reinforced by macro evidences on investment growth cycle, on the positive relationship between capital growth and agriculture growth, and agriculture growth and poverty. The need is much more, when it is realised that there are hardly studies on farm level capital formation. This chapter is based on the study by Bisaliah *et al.* (2010). The specific objectives of this study, on which the present chapter is based, are as detailed below:

- Analyse the trends in growth of capital stock at farm level and the composition of capital stock.
- Examine trends in farm level capital intensity and productivity.
- Analyse the importance of farm level agricultural capital stock *vis-à-vis* other determinants of agricultural output and of productivity of

labour, and identify the factors governing farm level capital formation.

- Provide micro level empirical basis for policy/programme designs so as to create an enabling environment to support farm level capital formation.

Development of Farm Level Data Set

Given the focus of the present chapter, farm level data are required. The Directorate of Economics and Statistics (DES), Ministry of Agriculture, Government of India, has instituted a scheme called 'Comprehensive Cost of Cultivation Scheme' (CCCS), under which farm level data are collected by agricultural universities and other research institutions spread across the country. Data are collected on all principal crops for different seasons and years by field level technical staff of DES from over 8,000 sample farmers spread across the agro-climatic regions of the country. The collection of data is through 39 schedules (or record types) following cost accounting method. Depending on nature of data, the field level technical staff of the CCCS collect data from sample farmers on daily, monthly or yearly basis. The results on cost of cultivation derived from data, are provided to Commission on Agricultural Costs and Prices (CACP), Government of India, so as to facilitate recommendations on minimum support prices (MSPs) on all principal crops. These recommendations are the basis for Government of India to announce MSPs for crops during two major seasons.

The data set on farm households have been developed, drawing data from the general data pool of DES. In the present study, three states, based on the criterion of productivity of land, have been sampled—high productivity state (Punjab), medium productivity state (Andhra Pradesh) and low productivity state (Orissa). From each one of these three sample states, 50 per cent of the samples of DES study for the years 1994-95 and 2007-08 have been selected at random, the randomness being every alternative sample from each *tehsil*. The sample structure of the present study is given in Table 4.1.

Table 4.1

Sample Study

State	Number of Tehsils	Year	Total DES Sample	Total Sample for the Present Study
1. Punjab	30	1994–95	300	150
	30	2007–08	300	150
2. Andhra Pradesh	60	1994–95	600	300
	60	2007–08	600	300
3. Orissa	45	1994–95	450	225
	45	2007–08	450	225
Total sample for two years	2700	1350		

It could be seen that the data set developed for this study consists of 1,350 sample farm households of three sample states for two years. Data from these 1,350 sample farm households on educational level of the respondent, operated landholding (both area and value), area under irrigation, values of animal capital (AC), farm machinery (FM) and irrigation Capital (IC), total labour (both family and hired) employed for farm operations, gross value of output and credit facility availed have been drawn from the general data pool of DES, depending on accessibility. Since the values of land, animal capital, farm machinery and irrigation capital are in present values of the years 1994-95 and 2007-08, they have been deflated into values at constant prices by using the deflators developed by Central Statistical Organisation (CSO) with 1999-2000 as the base.

It is realised that tree capital stock would form an important item of agricultural capital stock (ACS), and its importance varies with the growth stage of the economy (Larson *et al.*, 2000). In view of data constraint, tree capital as an item of farm level ACS could not be considered. Again due to data constraint, farm building structures for animals, and for agricultural implements and machinery also could not be considered. Nor any attempt is made in this study to estimate the value of farm building structures as a function of animals and agricultural implements and machinery as done in the study by Stephan *et al.* (2009). Yet another methodological issue that needs to be considered is whether the value of the land should be treated as an item of capital stock, along with animal capital (AC), farm machinery

(FM) and irrigation capital (IC). In most of the studies, value of investment made for land improvement is considered. In this study, value of land is also considered as a item of capital stock, because its inclusion in capital stock would provide insights into how important is land capital stock *vis-à-vis* other items of capital stock in case of farmers in India.

Analytical Tools

Given the nature of data and items on which data are accessible, the next step is to decide on the tools for analysing the farm level data of three sample states. The choice of tools, obviously, depends on the objective structure of the present chapter.

Compound Growth Rates between 1994-95 and 2007-08

- Growth rates of four items of capital stock:

  Land: measured in hectare,
  AC: measured in Rs and deflated,
  FM: measured in Rs and deflated,
  IM: measured in Rs and deflated.
- Growth rates are estimated for the aggregative data of all the three states, state-wise and farm size-wise.

Shifts in Composition of Capital Stock between 1994-95 and 2007-08

- Aggregative compositional shifts: All the three states and all the farm-size groups.
  - o The percentage share of land, AC, FM and IC in the total value of all the four capital assets (K): Land/K, AC/K, FM/K, IC/K.
  - o The percentage share of AC, FM and IC in the total value of all the three non-land capital assets (C): AC/C, FM/C, IC/C.
- Disaggregative compositional shifts: The percentage shares in both K and C are computed for individual states and for three farm size groups.

The rationale for considering land as one of the capital assets has been stated in previous Section. The rationale for considering non-land capital assets as a group is quite obvious.

Factor Intensity and Factor Productivity: Ratio Analysis

- Land (A) measured in hectare and value measures are employed in case of AC, FM, IC, total of non-land capital assets (C) and in case of gross value of output (GVO), and labour (L) measured in physical units of man-days. Data from National Accounts on GDP from agriculture (GDPA) in current prices and GDPA at constant prices (2004-05 base) are used for deriving the deflator for making adjustments to GVO data used in the present study.
- Factor intensity measures:
  - o Land–capital intensity: (C/A)
  - o Land–(FM+IC) intensity: (FM+IC)/A
  - o Labour–capital intensity: (C/L)
  - o Labour–(FM+IC) intensity: (FM+IC)/L
  - o Land–labour intensity: (L/A)
- Factor productivity measures:
  - o Labour–output ratio: (GVO/L)
  - o Non-land capital–output ratio: (GVO/C)
  - o Land–output ratio: (GVO/A)

The factor intensity and factor productivity analysis for two periods of time (1994-95 *versus* 2007-08) would provide insights into changing capital intensity and productivity of labour, capital and land. It is realised that these measures are partial intensity and partial productivity measures.

The factor intensity and productivity analysis is performed with pooled data of all three sample states and pooled data of all farm size groups (aggregative analysis) and with data for individual states and different farm size groups (disaggregative analysis).

Regression Models

One of the main objective of the proposed regression models is to answer three questions relevant to examination in this chapter. How important is capital *vis-à-vis* other factors in influencing GVO at farm level? Second, since productivity of labour engaged in agriculture has direct bearing on prevalence of hunger and poverty, what factors would explain the variations in productivity of labour at the farm level? and what is the relative importance of capital stock *vis-à-vis* other factors in influencing productivity of labour? Third, what are the major determinants of capital formation at farm level? Following all these, Chapter 6 will focus on what pathways and policy interventions could be derived from the analysis with regression models and other empirical evidences available on capital formation, agricultural growth and poverty alleviation?

To address the issues lined up above, three basic regression models are proposed *viz.*, GVO function, labour productivity function and capital formation function. It needs to be stated that the choice of variables as well as their measurement depends on the accessibility to farm level data.

Before the formulation of proposed three regression models, the definition and measurement of dependent and independent variables used for both aggregative and disaggregative analysis are discussed.

- GVO=gross value of farm level output, measured in Rs, and deflated using data on AGDP at current and constant prices reported in National Income Accounts of Central Statistical Organisation (CSO).
- AC=value of animal capital measured in Rs, and deflated using the deflator developed by CSO.
- FM=value of farm machinery measured in Rs, and deflated using the deflator developed by CSO.
- IC=value of irrigation capital measured in Rs, and deflated using the deflator developed by CSO.
- NLC=non-land capital (AC+FM+IC) measured in Rs, and deflated using the deflator developed by CSO.
- A=area of land measured in hectare.
- L=labour (total of both family and hired/casual labour) measured in physical units of man-days.
- DVL=literacy status expressed in the form of dummy variable (DVL) with a value of 1 if the farmer is literate and 0 (zero) otherwise.
- DVCR=credit status expressed in the form of dummy variable (DVCR) with a value of 1 if credit availed by the farmer and 0 (zero) otherwise.

- DVY=year dummy variable (DVY) with a value of 1 for 2007-08, and 1994-95 is the base with a value of 0 (zero).
- DVS_1=state dummy variable (DVS_1) with a value of 1 for Andhra Pradesh and 0 (zero) for Punjab, where the data of these two states are pooled.
- DVS_2=state dummy variables (DVS_2) for the pooled data analysis of all the three states.
- GVO/L=GVO per physical unit of labour (i.e., productivity of labour). GVO and L as defined and measured earlier.
- AC/A=value of animal capital per hectare measured in Rs.
- FM/A=value of farm machinery per hectare, measured in Rs.
- DVIR=irrigation dummy variable (DVIR) with a value of 1 for presence of irrigation and 0 (zero) otherwise.

With these definitions, three regression functions can be specified. All these regression functions are specified in log form and relevant elasticities are derived from the estimated functions.

GVO Regression Function

Depending on availability/accessibility to farm level data, the major determinants of GVO identified are: animal capital (AC), farm machinery (FM), land area (A), irrigation (DVIR), literacy (DVL), credit availment (DVCR) and year effect and regional effect/state effect, to be captured through dummy variables. Given these determinants, a complete GVO function in logarithmic form (Ln) is specified as follows:

$$\begin{aligned} \text{Ln GVO} = {} & A + a_1 \text{ LnAC} + a_2 \text{ LnFM} + a_3\text{LnA} \\ & + a_4 \text{ DVIR} + a_5 \text{ DVL} + a_6\text{DVCR} \\ & + a_7\text{DVY} + a_8\text{DVS}_1 + u \ \ldots \qquad (1) \end{aligned}$$

Where: A is the constant term, a^s are the regression coefficients/GVO elasticities, and u is the random error term.

Labour Productivity Function

The major determinants of labour productivity at farm level are postulated to be: animal capital per hectare of land (AC/A), farm machinery per hectare of land (FM/A), irrigation (DVIR), literacy (DVL), credit availment (DVCR), and year effect (DVY) and regional/state effects (DVS_1/ DVS_2). A complete model of labour productivity is specified as detailed below:

$$Ln\ (GVO/L) = B+b_1 Ln\ AC/A+b_2 Ln\ FM/A+b_3 DVIR+ b_4 DVL+b_5\ DVCR+b_6\ DVY+b_7\ DVS+u... \quad (2)$$

Where: B is the constant term, b^s are regression coefficients/elasticities and u is the random error term.

Capital Formation Function

This section is concerned with formulation of a capital formation model, wherein the determinants of non-land capital stock (NLC) are specified.

$$LnNLC= C+C_1 LnA+C_2 DVCR+C_3 DVL+C_4 DVY+C_5 DVS+u...(3)$$

Where: C is the constant term, C^s are regression coefficients/ elasticities and u is the random error term.

It is realised that terms of trade and technology are other important determinants of capital formation at farm level. In the absence of data on technological status of individual farms and almost the same value of terms of trade for all the farmers, these two variables could not be incorporated into the farm level capital formation function. However, the importance of these two variables in determining private capital formation will be discussed in Chapter 6, drawing results from state level studies on private capital formation documented (Bisaliah, 2004 and 2010a).

Agro-Economic Features of Sample States

It is recalled from previous section that three states *viz.*, Punjab, Andhra Pradesh and Orissa have been sampled for the analysis, based on productivity of land. A total of 1,350 farm samples have been drawn from the general data pool for the years 1994-95 and 2007-08. Before the results on growth rates, composition of capital stock, capital intensities and productivity of land, labour and capital are analysed, some broad agro–economic features of sample states are analysed.

Certain broad inferences could be derived from the results presented in Table 4.2: First, between 1994-95 and 2007-08, the percentage change in non-land capital stock (animal capital, farm machinery and irrigation capital) was negative in Andhra Pradesh (-35.76%) and in Punjab (-24.3%). There was only a marginal increase in the capital stock in Orissa. The negative change in non-land capital stock in high and medium agricultural productivity performing state is a disturbing trend. Second, the percentage

Table 4.2

Some Broad Agro-Economic Features of Three Sample States

Agro-Economic Features	*Andhra Pradesh*	*Orissa*	*Punjab*
*Land-man ratio in 2008-09	0.12	0.14	0.16
% change in capital stock (C) at (1999-2000 prices) between 1994/95-2007/08	-35.76	1.93	-24.3
Average size of operational holding of land (as in 2000-01)	1.25	1.25	4.03
% area under food crops	67.11 (2007-08)	84.87 (2008-09)**	88.68 (2004-05)
% area under non-food crops	32.89 (2007-08)	15.13 (2008-09)**	11.32 (2004-05)
**% of net irrigated area to net cultivated area for 2006-07	43.9	32.2	94.9
**cropping intensity for 2006-07 (%)	126.3	151.2	188.1
All non-land capital assets/land (ha) in 2007-08	10283	4525	45097
Per hectare productivity of land in 2007-08	28866	17468	72217
All non-land capital assets/ labour in 100 man-days in 2007-08	9025	3053	44246
Productivity of labour per 100 man-days in 2007-08	25333	11783	70855
Intensity of poverty (urban) (headcount ratio in % for 2004-05)	23.4	37.6	18.7
Intensity of poverty (rural) (headcount ratio in % for 2004-05)	32.3	60.8	22.1

Note: * Land-man ratio in 2008-09 = net sown area/population;

** Provisional data; C = Non-land capital stock

area irrigated is found to establish the needed pathway for irrigation development. The relationship between percentage area irrigated and productivity growth performance are found to be positive. To reinforce this, per hectare productivity of land was over Rs 72,000 in Punjab during 2007-2008, whereas it was about Rs 29,000 in Andhra Pradesh and only about Rs 17,000 in Orissa. Third, per hectare non-land capital stock during 2007-08 in Punjab farms was over Rs 45,000, whereas it was a little over Rs 10,000 in Andhra Pradesh and a little over Rs 4,000 in Orissa. Fourth, the productivity of labour was the highest in Punjab, followed by Andhra Pradesh and Orissa. Further productivity of labour and non-land capital intensity are quite positively related. Fifth, the percentage of both rural and urban poverty varies inversely with productivity of land and labour. Added to this is the higher density of poverty in rural areas, related very well to productivity of land and labour, and to intensity of non-land capital stock.

It is recalled from the aggregative study (Chapter 3) by Stephan *et al.* (2009) that ACS and productivity of labour engaged in agriculture are positively related, and productivity of labour and prevalence of poverty and hunger are inversely related. The present study validates this theorem on the relationship among these three parameters, using data of three sample states. Figure 4.1 establishes the negative relationship between capital intensity and rural poverty, Figure 4.2 also validates the negative relationship between productivity of land and rural poverty, and Figure 4.3 also conclusively leads to the inference that there is a negative relation between labour productivity and rural poverty. Figure 4.4 reveals the positive association between capital intensity and productivity of land and Figure 4.5 shows positive association between capital intensity of labour and productivity of labour. In brief, capital formation in/for agriculture is a critical factor for increasing productivity of land, labour and for reducing poverty.

Figure 4.1

Capital Intensity and Rural Poverty

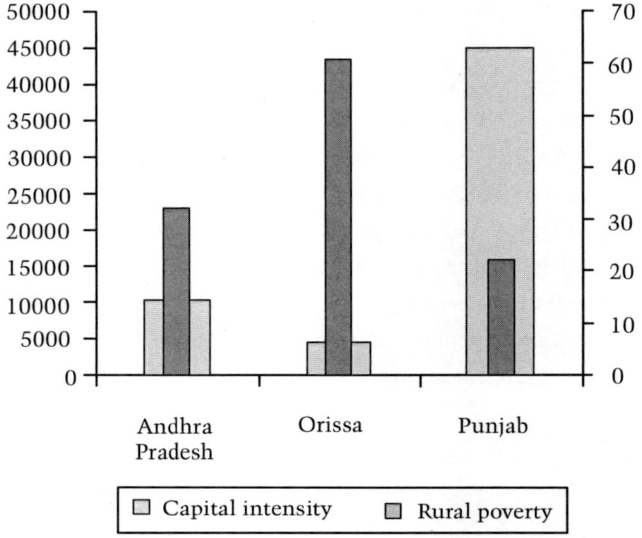

Figure 4.2

Land Productivity and Rural Poverty

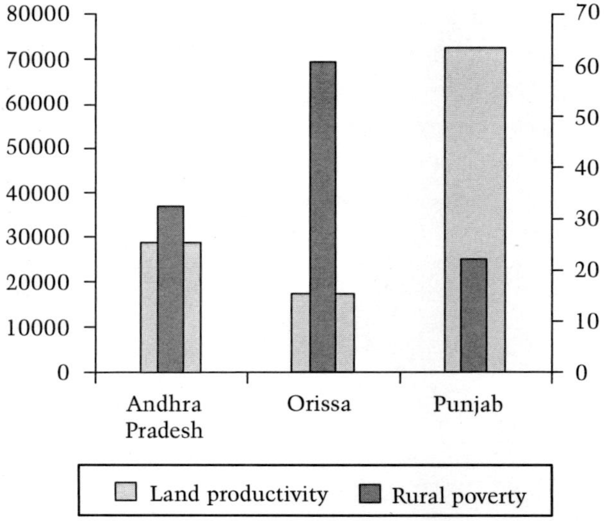

Figure 4.3

Labour Productivity and Rural Poverty

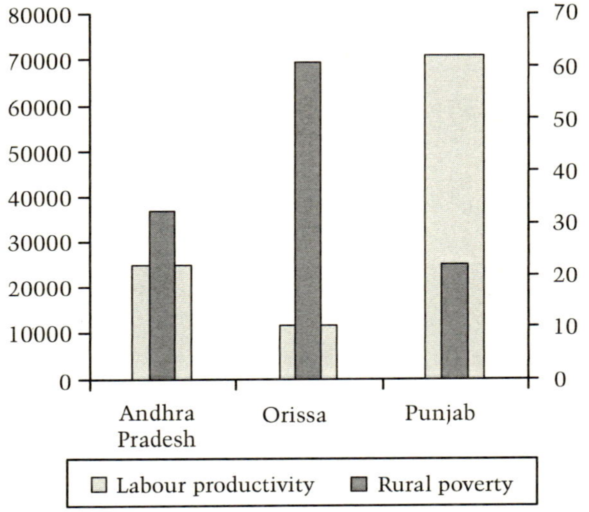

Figure 4.4

Land Productivity and Capital Intensity of Land

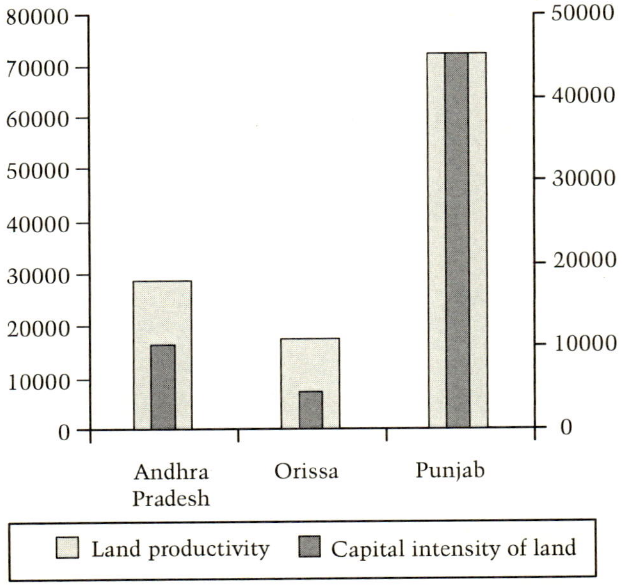

Figure 4.5

Labour Productivity and Capital Intensity of Labour

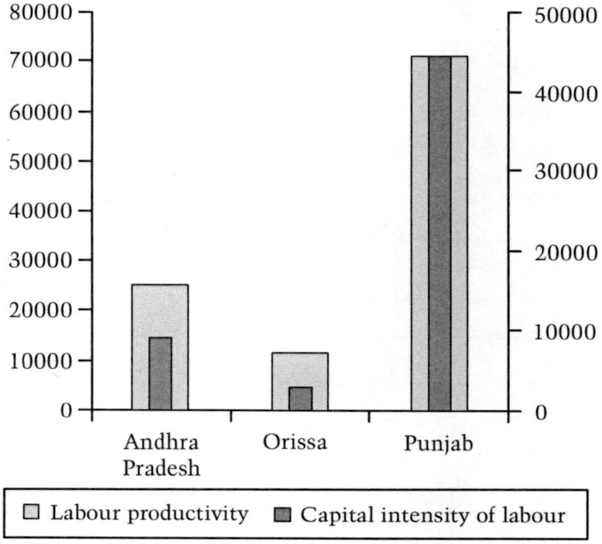

Aggregative Analysis

In this section, results from aggregative analysis of capital growth rates, composition, intensity, productivity, and determinants of GVO, productivity of labour and capital formation are examined.

Capital Growth Rate Analysis

An analysis of aggregative growth rates and of growth rates of sample states (Table 4.3) would lead to four major inferences. First, among non-land capital, the growth rates of animal capital (-0.74%) and farm machinery (-2.13%) are found to be negative, while the growth rate of irrigation capital is found to be positive (1.56%). Second, the growth rate of farm machinery is negative in both Andhra Pradesh and Punjab, but there is a positive growth trend in Orissa (1.33%). Third, Punjab recorded a very strong positive growth rate of irrigation capital (7.21%), whereas high negative growth trend is found in the other two states. Fourth, overall negative growth rate of operated landholding (in hectare) is recorded in Punjab with the highest rate of negative growth, followed by Orissa. However in Andhra Pradesh there is a positive growth rate of land capital.

Fifth, a little below 1 per cent negative growth rate is recorded in overall of non-land capital assets, with high negative growth in Andhra Pradesh, and small positive growth rate in other two states. Sixth, the negative growth rate in farm machinery and irrigation capital together is found to have occurred in sample states, because some positive growth rates in Punjab and Orissa are more than offset by negative growth rate (-4.07%) in Andhra Pradesh.

Table 4.3

Compound Growth Rates of Capital Stock: Aggregative and Individual State Analysis

Capital Asset	*Growth Rates (%)*			
	Overall	*Punjab*	*Andhra Pradesh*	*Orissa*
Land	-0.06	-0.62	0.25	-0.02
Animal capital	-0.74	0.21	-2.02	-0.49
Farm machinery	-2.13	-1.99	-3.79	1.33
Irrigation capital	1.56	7.21	-4.26	-10.30
All non-land capital assets	-0.74	0.52	-3.35	0.13
Farm machinery and irrigation capital	-0.74	0.61	-4.07	1.13

Shifts in Composition of Capital Stock

Temporal and spatial analysis of trends in composition of four components of total capital stock and three components of non-land capital stock is the basic focus of this section. It could be observed from (Table 4.4) and the corresponding figures that:

- The overall results on composition of total stock suggest that the percentage share (94%) of land capital assets was dominant during the first period (P.I) and the share dominance continued during the second period (P.II) also (95%). There was no change in percentage share (2%) of animal capital as well as irrigation capital (1%) during the period of 13 years, with farm machinery experiencing fall in its share by 1 per cent during the same period of 13 years. In this regard it is reported (Personal communication from S. Mahendra Dev, Director, Indira Gandhi Institute of Development Research, Mumbai) that land formed about 68 per cent of total assets in case of cultivator households during 2002; but this analysis includes assets such as land, building (which alone accounts for about 20 per cent), livestock and poultry, machinery and equipment, household durables, financial assets, and dues receivable. But the present study has considered only land, farm machinery, irrigation capital and animal capital. This is the reason for differences in the percentage share of land in total assets.

- The capital composition analysis of non-land capital assets reveals that there was a fall in the share of farm machinery from 48 per cent to 40 per cent during the period, and of irrigation capital from 22 per cent to 15 per cent, whereas the share of animal capital had remained almost the same.
- The state-wise results indicate that:
  - o The share of land capital in total capital stock is found to be 95 per cent and above in all the three sample states during 2007-08, and the remaining 5 per cent accounted by AC, FM and IC.
  - o In case of non-land capital stock, the share of animal capital is more dominant in Orissa, irrigation capital in Andhra Pradesh, and farm machinery in Punjab.

Table 4.4

Shifts in Composition of Capital Stock: Aggregative and Individual State Analysis

Capital Stock	*Composition (%): Percentage Share*							
	Overall		*Punjab*		*Andhra Pradesh*		*Orissa*	
	P.I	*P.II*	*P.I*	*P.II*	*P.I*	*P.II*	*P.I*	*P.II*
1. *Total Capital Stock:*								
Land	94	95	95	96	91	97	95	96
Animal capital	2	2	1	1	3	1	3	2
Farm machinery	3	2	3	2	2	1	2	2
Irrigation capital	1	1	1	1	4	1	-	-
Total	100	100	100	100	100	100	100	100
2. *Non–Land Capital Stock:*								
Animal capital	30	29	23	22	32	39	64	59
Farm machinery	48	40	63	45	28	26	35	40
Irrigation capital	22	31	14	33	40	35	1	1
Total	100	100	100	100	100	100	100	100

Notes: P.I = 1994-95; P.II = 2007-08.

Figure 4.6

Shifts in Composition of Total Capital Stock

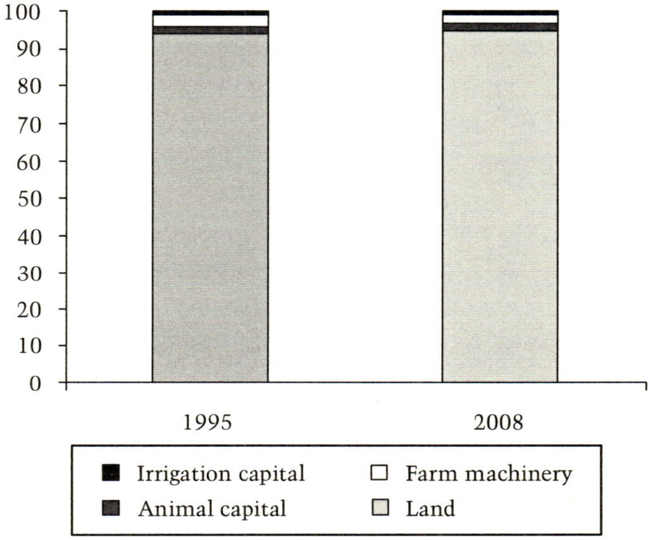

Figure 4.7

Shifts in Composition of Total Capital Stock

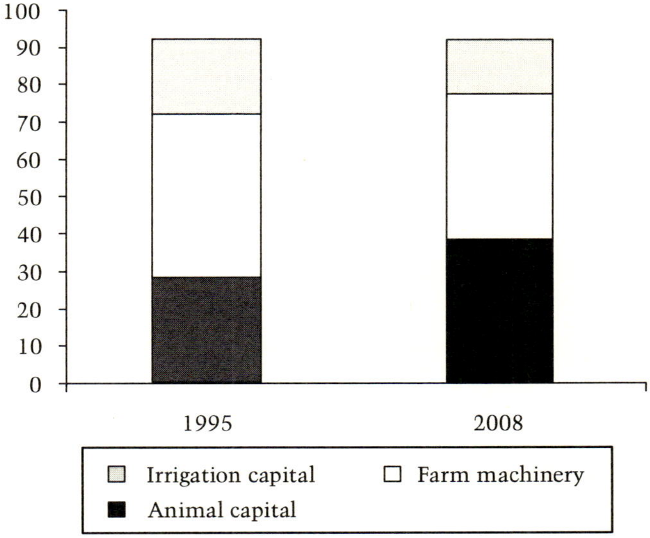

Factor Intensity and Factor Productivity

It could be seen from Table 4.5 that:

- In overall, both capital stock per hectare and farm machinery plus irrigation capital (FM+IC) per hectare had declined during second period (P.II) *vis-à-vis* P.I. Further, there was a marginal decline in capital per unit of labour also.
- The 'behaviour' of these ratios varies across states. Punjab represents a typology of increasing capital per unit of land and labour. On the other hand, there is a considerable amount of decline in these ratios during P.II in Andhra Pradesh. As against these two contrasting typologies, Orissa presents a typology of marginal changes (either increase or decrease) in these ratios.
- With reference to factor productivity ratios, ignoring differences across states, there is an increase in output per unit of labour, per unit of capital, and per unit of land during P.II. Obviously, change in

Table 4.5

Factor Intensity and Factor Productivity in Sample Farms: Overall and State-wise Analysis

Factor-Intensity and Productivity	*Ratios*							
	Overall		*Punjab*		*Andhra Pradesh*		*Orissa*	
	P.I	*P.II*	*P.I*	*P.II*	*P.I*	*P.II*	*P.I*	*P.II*
Factor-Intensity Ratios:								
Land-capital (C/A)	19055	17443	38903	45097	16525	10283	4437	4525
Land-(FM+IC)/A	13443	12303	29861	35020	11179	6311	1597	1854
Labour-capital (C/L*)	14410	14393	3s7341	44246	11423	9025	3163	3053
Labour-(FM+IC)/L*	10166	10152	28662	34359	7728	5538	1138	1251
Land-Labour (L/A)	132	121	104	102	145	114	140	148
Factor-Productivity Ratios:								
Labour-output (GVO/L*)	23628	30126	43955	70855	21412	25333	13025	11783
Non-land capital–output (GVO/C)	1.64	2.09	1.18	1.6	1.87	2.81	4.12	3.86
Land-output (GVO/A)	31244	36510	45793	72217	30973	28866	18272	17468

Notes: P.I = 1994-95; P.II = 2007-08.

A = Land in hectare; L = Labour in man-days; L* = Labour in 100 man-days.

factor productivity ratios across states differ. Punjab has registered the pattern of increased output per unit of labour, capital and land during P.II. In Andhra Pradesh, the pattern is one of increasing output per unit of labour, per unit of capital and decline in output per hectare. In Orissa, there is a decline in all the three factor-productivity ratios.

Empirical Results on Determinants of Gross Value of Output (GVO), Productivity of Labour and Capital Formation in Sample States

This section is concerned with addressing three issues using empirical results. First, what are the determinants of GVO at farm level? Related to that is the issue what is the relative importance of capital stock *vis-à-vis* other determinants? Second, what are the determinants of productivity of labour engaged in agriculture? Added to this issue is the relative importance of capital *vis-à-vis* other determinants? Third, what are the determinants of capital formation (non-land capital assets) at farm level? To answer these issues, three functions *viz.*, GVO, labour productivity and capital formation have been specified in earlier discussion. These functions have been estimated with aggregative as well as disaggregative data set. The data of both Punjab and Andhra Pradesh have been pooled for estimating aggregative GVO function. In view of data constraint, the data of Orissa have not been pooled. However, GVO functions have been estimated for each state. The same procedure has been followed in estimating labour productivity function as well as capital formation function. In addition to state-wise functions, further disaggregative farm group-wise estimates will be discussed later on.

GVO Function Estimates

- The results derived with pooled data analysis of Andhra Pradesh and Punjab (Table 4.6) suggest that:
  - o Animal capital, farm machinery, land, labour, literacy and credit availment—all have positive and significant impact on GVO.
  - o The explanatory power of the estimated model is validated by high Adj. R^2 of 71 per cent.

Table 4.6

Elasticities of GVO: Analysis of Results from Pooled Data of Andhra Pradesh and Punjab

Variables	*Regression Coefficients/Elasticities*	*t–Value*
Constant (A)	5.41	22.79
AC	0.016	2.13
FM	0.024	1.66
A	0.216	5.45
L	1.008	23.69
DVL	0.161	2.83
DVIR	-0.352	-6.25
DVCR	0.165	3.03
DVY	0.325	6.87
DVS_1	-0.811	-2.14
Adj. R^2 = 0.71	Number of samples: 900	

- State-wise elasticities of GVO are presented in Table 4.7.
  - o With respect to Punjab:
    - (a) Animal capital, farm machinery, land, labour and credit availment are found to have positive and significant impact on GVO. The literacy variable, even though insignificant, has positive influence on GVO.
    - (b) High Adj. R^2 of 90 per cent validates the explanatory power of the estimated model.
  - o With respect to Andhra Pradesh:
    - (a) Elasticities of output with respect to animal capital, land, labour, literacy and credit availment are all positive and significant. Elasticity of output with respect to farm machinery, although insignificant, is positive.
    - (b) Adj. R^2 of 63 per cent supports the explanatory power of the independent variables included in the model.
  - o With respect to Orissa:
    - (a) Output elasticities of farm machinery and labour are positive and significant. But regression coefficients of

animal capital and literacy, even though negative, are not significant.

(b) Due to 'inadequacy' of data, the value of Adj. R^2 is low at 43 per cent.

Table 4.7

Elasticities of GVO: Analysis of Results from Individual States

Variables	*Regression Coefficients*		
	Punjab	*Andhra Pradesh*	*Orissa*
Constant (A)	8.712 (29.78)	4.234 (14.78)	0.666 (1.13)
AC	0.015 (1.2)	0.020 (2.13)	-0.039 (-0.78)
FM	0.041 (2.78)	0.007 (0.34)	0.172 (2.08)
A	0.759 (16.24)	0.142 (2.76)	-0.72 (-4.61)
L	0.287 (5.26)	1.107 (21.06)	1.651 (10.27)
DVL	0.039 (0.87)	0.177 (2.2)	-0.205 (-0.77)
DVIR	-0.096 (-1.34)	-0.386 (-5.52)	NA
DVCR	0.055 (1.38)	0.143 (1.71)	NA
DVY	0.474 (11.66)	0.274 (4.19)	-0.036 (-0.23)
Adj. R^2	0.90	0.63	0.43

Note: t-Values in parenthesis.

Number of samples: Punjab: 300; Andhra Pradesh: 600; Orissa: 443.

Labour Productivity Function Estimates

- The values of estimated coefficients derived with the pooled data of Andhra Pradesh and Punjab for labour productivity function are presented in Table 4.8.
  - o Animal capital, farm machinery, literacy and credit availment are all found to have positive and significant impact on labour productivity.
  - o The Adj. R^2 of 38 per cent, even though low, appears to support the validity of the model.
- State-wise results on labour productivity function are not reported, in view of inadequacy of fitness of the model. Further, it needs to be stated that the coefficient of irrigation dummy variable is negative and significant. It is not clear whether this 'surprising' result is due

to 'improper' specification, or due to irrigation management practices, and other associated factors.

Table 4.8

Results on Labour Productivity Function: Pooled Data Analysis of Punjab and Andhra Pradesh

Variable	*Regression Coefficients/Elasticities*	*t–Value*
Constant (B)	5.73	45.2
AC/A	0.007	1.01
FM/A	0.021	1.63
DVIR	-0.202	-4.26
DVL	0.118	2.41
DVCR	0.192	4.08
DVY	0.311	7.72
DVS (Andhra Pradesh)	-0.801	-14.17
Adj. R^2	0.38	

Note: Number of samples: 900.

Capital Formation Function Estimates

From the results on capital formation function (Table 4.9) with pooled data analysis of Punjab and Andhra Pradesh sample farmers, following observations could be made:

- The coefficient of land, credit availment and literacy are positive as well as statistically significant.
- The Adj. R^2 of 0.34 suggests that the independent variables could explain only 34 per cent of variation in capital formation at the farm level.
- The state-wise results on capital formation function are not reported in view of inadequate 'fit' of the specified model.

Disaggregative Analysis: Farm Size-wise

The focus of this section is farm size-wise analysis of results on growth rates of capital stock, shifts in composition of capital stock, factor intensity as well as factor productivity and determinants of GVO, productivity of labour and capital formation. Marginal and small farms are defined as those with upto 2 hectare of land, semi-medium and medium farms from 2 to 10 hectare, and large farms with more than 10 hectare.

Table 4.9

Results on Capital Formation Function: Pooled Data Analysis of Punjab and Andhra Pradesh

Variable	*Regression Coefficients/Elasticities*	*t–Value*
Constant (C)	10.35	54.48
A	0.967	14.19
DVCR	0.325	2.38
DVL	0.163	1.12
DVY	-0.263	-2.24
DVS (Andhra Pradesh)	-1.689	-12.62
Adj. R^2	0.34	

Note: Number of samples: 900.

Capital Growth Performance of Farm Groups

It could be observed from Table 4.10 that:

- Cutting across differences in capital growth performance of marginal and small farms in sample states, the overall growth rate is the highest (2.00%) in case of irrigation capital, followed by less than 1 per cent positive growth rate in farm machinery, leading to 1.51 per cent positive growth rate of farm machinery and irrigation capital put together. The negative growth rate (-1.17%) of animal capital is a cause of concern, because animal capital would be quite crucial for this farm group with small size of landholding. Further, positive growth rates of irrigative capital in all the three states put together are because of high growth rate (9.58%) of irrigation capital in marginal and small farms of Punjab.
- In overall, the semi-medium and medium farms of sample states are found to have experienced negative growth rates of all types of capital assets, excepting irrigation capital. The positive growth rate of irrigation capital (1.55%) is again due to high positive growth rate (6.74%) of irrigation capital in Punjab.
- In case of large farms also, the growth rates of land, animal capital and farm machinery are negative in general, and positive growth of rate is observed in case of irrigation capital alone, due to high growth rate (6.72%) of irrigation capital in Punjab only. In Andhra Pradesh, positive growth rate (2.49%) of land capital is observed.

Table 4.10

Compound Growth Rates of Capital Stock: Farm Size-wise Analysis

	Growth Rates (%)			
Farm Size/ Capital Asset	*Overall*	*Punjab*	*Andhra Pradesh*	*Orissa*
Marginal/Small:				
Land	-0.08	-0.34	0.08	-0.12
Animal capital	-1.17	-0.45	-2.50	0.19
Farm machinery	0.98	0.90	1.07	1.27
Irrigation capital	2.00	9.58	-4.80	NA
All non-land capital assets	0.32	2.61	-2.62	0.41
Farm machinery and irrigation capital	1.51	4.5	-2.72	1.08
Semi-Medium/Medium:				
Land	-0.04	-0.6	-0.08	0.47
Animal capital	-0.35	0.67	-1.60	-0.51
Farm machinery	-1.94	-1.76	-4.01	3.10
Irrigation capital	1.55	6.74	-3.64	-7.94
All non-land capital assets	-0.62	0.5	-3.07	0.75
Farm machinery and irrigation capital	-0.72	0.45	-3.80	2.87
Large:				
Land	-0.20	-0.83	2.49	-7.11
Animal capital	-2.71	-1.45	-4.12	-7.97
Farm machinery	-5.19	-4.49	-14.06	-4.95
Irrigation capital	1.08	6.72	-6.80	NA
All non-land capital assets	-2.79	-1.3	-7.27	-5.62
Farm machinery and irrigation capital	-2.81	-1.28	-8.44	-5.10

Farm Group Analysis of Composition of Capital Structure

The results on compositional shifts between two periods of time and of differences in composition of capital stock across three farm groups are in Table 4.11 and 4.12. It is observed from the tables that:

- In marginal and small farms, the share of land capital in total capital stock would come to 95 per cent during 2007-08, and other three capital assets would account for the remaining 5 per cent. With respect to non-land capital composition of this farm group (Table 4.12), animal capital alone would account for 40 per cent in overall during second period, with as high as 75 per cent in Orissa and as low as 30 per cent in Punjab. In brief, the share of animal capital varies inversely with growth stage of agriculture in these states, the growth stage defined in terms of productivity of land.

- In semi-medium and medium farms, the share of land capital in total capital stock is found to be as high as 97 per cent in overall during second period (Table 4.11), and it is almost not any thing different in three states, and as a result the share of non-land capital assets in total capital stock is found to be less than 4 per cent. Further, the share of animal capital in non-land capital stock (Table 4.12) varies inversely with growth stage of agriculture, defined in terms of productivity of land.

Table 4.11

Shifts in Composition of Total Capital Stock: Farm Size-wise Analysis

Farm size and Capital Asset	*Composition (%): Percentage Share*							
	Overall		*Punjab*		*Andhra Pradesh*		*Orissa*	
	P.I	*P.II*	*P.I*	*P.II*	*P.I*	*P.II*	*P.I*	*P.II*
Marginal/Small:								
Land	93	95	95	94	89	96	95	94
Animal capital	3	2	2	2	5	2	4	4
Farm machinery	2	1	2	2	2	1	1	2
Irrigation capital	2	2	1	2	4	1	-	NA
Total	100	100	100	100	100	100	100	100
Semi-Medium/Medium:								
Land	95	97	95	96	92	97	96	96
Animal capital	1	1	1	1	2	1	3	2
Farm machinery	3	1	3	2	3	1	1	2
Irrigation capital	1	1	1	1	3	1	-	-
Total	100	100	100	100	100	100	100	100
Large:								
Land	95	97	94	97	89	98	91	91
Animal capital	1	1	1	1	2	1	2	1
Farm machinery	3	1	4	1	3	-	7	8
Irrigation capital	1	1	1	1	5	1	-	NA
Total	100	100	100	100	100	100	100	100

Notes: P.I = 1994–95; P.II = 2007–08.

- The value share of land in total capital stock of large farms has come to 97 per cent during second period (Table 4.11). Among non-land capital stock, (Table 4.12) the overall share of animal capital is found to be 16 per cent, of farm machinery 43 per cent and of irrigation capital 41 per cent. Hence, the share of animal capital varies inversely with farm size (Table 4.12).

Table 4.12

Shifts in Composition of Non-Land Capital Stock: Farm Size-wise Analysis

Farm size/Non-Land Capital Asset	Composition (%): Percentage Share							
	Overall		Punjab		Andhra Pradesh		Orissa	
	P.I	P.II	P.I	P.II	P.I	P.II	P.I	P.II
Marginal/Small:								
Animal capital	48	40	45	30	46	46	77	75
Farm machinery	26	28	38	31	15	24	22	25
Irrigation capital	26	32	17	39	39	30	1	NA
Total	100	100	100	100	100	100	100	100
Semi-Medium/Medium:								
Animal capital	28	29	22	22	30	37	67	57
Farm machinery	50	42	65	48	32	28	32	43
Irrigation capital	22	29	13	30	38	35	1	-
Total	100	100	100	100	100	100	100	100
Large:								
Animal capital	16	16	14	13	22	34	21	15
Farm machinery	58	43	72	47	25	9	78	85
Irrigation capital	26	41	14	40	53	57	1	NA
Total	100	100	100	100	100	100	100	100

Notes : P.I = 1994–95; P.II = 2007–08.

Factor Intensity and Factor Productivity: Farm Group-wise Analysis

The factor intensity analysis (Table 4.13) suggests that:

- During 2007-08, the marginal and small farms, in overall, are found to have more capital stock per hectare than other two groups of farms, whereas large farms have far more capital stock per unit of labour.

- Number of labour employed per unit area cultivated is the highest in marginal and small farms (163), followed by semi-medium and medium farms (120) and then large farms (81). In other words, labour employed per unit of land varies inversely with farm size.
- Marginal and small farms of Punjab have about four times more capital per hectare than those of Andhra Pradesh and about 10 times more capital than those of Orissa.

Table 4.13

Factor Intensity: Farm Size-wise Analysis

Farm size and Factor Intensity	*Overall*		*Punjab*		*Andhra Pradesh*		*Orissa*	
	P.I	*P.II*	*P.I*	*P.II*	*P.I*	*P.II*	*P.I*	*P.II*
Factor intensity:								
Marginal and Small:								
C/A	21200	22327	42972	62812	23613	16561	5713	6119
FM + IC/A	10930	13418	23598	43706	12865	8901	1311	1532
C/L*	11782	13711	28009	42722	11309	9765	3520	3735
FM + IC/L*	6075	8240	15381	29727	6162	5248	807	935
L/A	180	163	153	147	209	170	162	164
Semi-Medium and Medium:								
C/A	17982	16672	39991	46178	14990	10096	3882	4027
FM + IC/A	12980	11871	31291	35905	10476	6395	1272	1729
C/L*	13718	13846	37535	46933	10514	8873	2875	2771
FM + IC/L*	9903	9858	29370	36492	7347	5621	942	1190
L/A	131	120	107	98	143	114	135	145
Large:								
C/A	22872	20705	33101	31094	17875	4867	6898	8493
FM + IC/A	19149	17326	28604	26953	13972	3225	5471	7227
C/L*	27617	25694	47667	35537	25278	8385	4930	6353
FM + IC/L*	23122	21500	41191	30804	19758	5556	3911	5406
L/A	83	81	69	88	71	58	140	134

Note: P.I = 1994–95; P.II = 2007–08; A = Land in hectare; L = Labour in man-days; L* = Labour in 100 man-days.

Similarly, these farms of Punjab have about four times more capital per unit of labour than in Andhra Pradesh, and about 11 times more capital than in Orissa. This is also the case with respect to semi-medium and large farms of Punjab *vis-à-vis* those of Andhra Pradesh and Orissa. These differences in capital stock per unit of land and labour are bound to have differences in productivity of land of these three states, discussed previously in this chapter.

The results on factor productivity analysis (Table 4.14) are suggestive of the inference that:

- Productivity of labour in marginal and small farms of Punjab is more than two times than in Andhra Pradesh and more than four times than in Orissa. Similarly, these farms of Punjab are found to have harvested about two times more GVO per hectare than those of Andhra Pradesh and about four times more than those of Orissa. But productivity of capital in marginal and small farms is the highest in Orissa followed by Andhra Pradesh and Punjab.
- Almost the same pattern in productivity of labour, land and capital is found in semi-medium and medium farms and large farms of Punjab *vis-à-vis* those of Andhra Pradesh and Orissa.

Table 4.14

Factor Productivity: Farm Size-wise Analysis

Farm size and Factor Productivity	*Overall*		*Punjab*		*Andhra Pradesh*		*Orissa*	
	P.I	*P.II*	*P.I*	*P.II*	*P.I*	*P.II*	*P.I*	*P.II*
Factor Productivity:								
Marginal and Small:								
GVO/L*	17622	22756	29854	48650	16611	21215	12359	11439
GVO/C	1.50	1.66	1.07	1.14	1.47	2.17	3.51	3.06
GVO/A	31708	37055	45803	71528	34684	35980	20062	18744
Semi-Medium and Medium:								
GVO/L*	23267	29693	41771	72666	21993	26498	12994	11886
GVO/C	1.70	2.14	1.11	1.55	2.09	2.99	4.52	4.29
GVO/A	30498	35755	44503	71497	31357	30150	17549	17272
Large:								
GVO/L*	42396	45729	72032	85775	32549	25626	15137	11285
GVO/C	1.54	1.78	1.51	2.41	1.29	3.06	3.07	1.78
GVO/A	35111	36850	50021	75052	23018	14873	21178	15086

Notes: P.I = 1994–95; P.II = 2007–08; A = Land in hectare; L* = Labour in 100 man-days.

Determinants of GVO, Productivity of Labour and Capital Formation: Farm Size-wise Analysis

On determinants of GVO of three farm groups, the analysis is performed with the pooled data of these farms. The state-wise results on GVO of these farm groups are not reported in view of low explanatory power of the estimated GVO functions. It is observed from Table 4.15 that:

- In case of marginal and small farms, farm machinery, labour and literacy are found to have positive and significant impact on GVO. The regression coefficients of animal capital and land, even though negative, are not significant, and of credit availment, even though insignificant, is positive. The relative high Adj. R^2 of 59 per cent validates the explanatory power of the model estimated.
- In case of semi-medium and medium farms, the output elasticities of farm machinery, labour and credit availment are significant and positive. The regression coefficients of animal capital and literacy, even though insignificant, are positive.

Table 4.15

Elasticities of GVO: Farm Group-wise Results

Variables	*Marginal and Small Farms*	*Semi-Medium and Medium Farms*	*Large Farms*
Constant	3.20 (8.86)	5.39 (10.24)	7.24 (4.48)
AC	-0.007 (-0.44)	0.007 (0.38)	-0.126 (-0.98)
FM	0.067 (2.06)	0.065 (2.06)	0.160 (3.2)
A	-0.112 (-0.9)	-0.138 (-1.13)	0.558 (1.43)
L	1.409 (18.44)	1.068 (12.82)	0.594 (4.88)
DVL	0.223 (1.58)	0.082 (0.74)	0.245 (1.6)
DVIR	-0.340 (-2.63)	-0.421 (-3.27)	0.004 (0.02)
DVCR	0.038 (0.29)	0.234 (1.86)	0.058 (0.39)
DVY	0.342 (3.76)	0.169 (1.93)	0.064 (0.47)
DVS (AP)	-0.829 (-5.39)	-0.733 (-4.66)	-0.778 (-3.67)
DVS (Orissa)	-1.607 (-8.63)	-1.773 (-8.66)	-1.460 (-4.81)
Adj. R^2	0.59	0.35	0.83

Note: t-values in parenthesis.

Number of samples: Marginal and small: 552; Semi-medium and medium: 746; Large: 45.

- In case of large farms, the output elasticities of farm machinery, land, labour and literacy are both positive and statistically significant. Regression coefficient of animal capital, even though negative is insignificant, and of credit availment, even though positive, is not significant. Adj. R^2 of 83 per cent validates the explanatory power of the model estimated.
- On determinants of labour productivity, the results on only farm group-wise are reported, and those on state-wise are not reported in view of inadequate explanatory power of the model. As shown in Table 4.16.

Table 4.16

Results on Labour Productivity: Farm Group-wise Results

Variables	*Marginal and Small Farms*	*Semi-Medium and Medium Farms*	*Large Farms*
Constant (B)	4.57 (22.91)	5.81 (29.96)	6.85 (6.39)
AC/A	0.017 (1.7)	0.003 (0.27)	-0.181 (-1.31)
FM/A	0.117 (5.5)	0.489 (2.73)	0.123 (2.26)
DVIR	-0.320 (-3.5)	-0.375 (-5.19)	0.0249 (0.11)
DVL	0.251 (2.64)	0.129 (2.08)	0.185 (1.1)
DVCR	0.089 (0.96)	0.234 (3.32)	0.036 (0.22)
DVY	0.334 (5.15)	0.165 (3.38)	-0.016 (-0.12)
DVS (Andhra Pradesh)	-0.590 (-5.63)	-0.752 (-8.58)	-0.829 (-3.61)
DVS (Orissa)	-1.337 (-10.28)	-1.619 (-14.39)	-1.774 (-5.62)
Adj. R^2	0.37	0.48	0.71

Note: t–values in parenthesis.

Number of samples: Marginal and small: 552; Semi-medium and medium: 746; Large: 45.

- In case of marginal and small farms, the coefficients of animal capital, farm machinery and literacy are not only significant, but are also found to have positive impact on labour productivity. Credit availment, even though insignificant, is found to have positive impact on labour productivity in marginal and small farms.
- With regard to semi-medium and medium farms, the coefficients of farm machinery, literacy and credit availment are both positive and significant. The coefficient of animal capital, even though insignificant, is positive.

- In case of large farms, the elasticities of labour productivity with respect to farm machinery and literacy are found to be positive and almost significant. But the negative coefficient of animal capital is disturbing, and it is almost significant. The coefficient of credit availment variable, even though insignificant, is found to have positive impact on labour productivity.

The results on determinants of capital formation are in Table 4.17.

- In case of marginal and small farms, the coefficients of land, credit availment and literacy are positive as well as statistically significant.
- With regard to semi-medium and medium farms, the coefficient of land alone is both positive and significant. The coefficient of credit availment is positive, but insignificant, and that of literacy negative but insignificant.
- In case of large farms, credit availment alone is found to be both positive and significant. The coefficients of literacy and land are both positive, but statistically insignificant.

Summary of Results and Inferences

The overwhelmingly dominant share of farm household investment in agriculture has made it imperative for examining the farm level capital growth, composition of capital stock, factor intensity as well as factor

Table 4.17

Results on Capital Formation: Farm Group-wise Analysis

Variables	*Marginal and Small Farms*	*Semi-Medium and Medium Farms*	*Large Farms*
Constant (C)	9.34 (30.07)	10.65 (45.39)	12.03 (6.22)
A	1.027 (5.14)	0.985 (8.38)	0.273 (0.36)
DVCR	0.549 (2.29)	0.124 (0.91)	0.420 (1.45)
DVL	1.09 (4.26)	-0.119 (-0.99)	0.187 (0.63)
DVY	0.009 (0.05)	-0.215 (-2.29)	-0.567 (-2.39)
DVS (Andhra Pradesh)	-1.647 (-7.05)	-1.798 (-13.4)	-1.241 (-4.26)
DVS (Orissa)	-2.135 (-8.08)	-2.452 (-15.96)	-1.885 (-4.51)
Adj. R^2	0.20	0.41	0.56

Notes: t–values in parenthesis.

Number of samples: Marginal & small: 552; Semi-medium and medium: 746; Large: 45.

productivity, and determinants of GVO, labour productivity and capital formation. These farm level issues have been examined with 1,350 farm samples, spreading across high, moderate and low agriculture productivity states. Some of the major findings of the study both at aggregative (pooling the data) and disaggregative (farm group wise) levels are summarised as below:

At aggregative level, cutting across all sample states and farm levels, some of the major findings with policy implications are detailed as below:

- Capital intensity and productivity of land as well of labour vary directly, and prevalence of poverty varies inversely with productivity of land and labour, implying the importance of capital formation in agriculture.
- Between 1994-95 and 2007-08, growth rates of non-land capital stock as a group is found to be negative, but the growth rate of irrigation capital as such is found to be positive.
- In total capital stock, the share of land capital alone would account for 94 per cent, and among non-land capital stock the share of farm machinery is found to be the highest (40 per cent).
- With respect to factor intensity, there has been a decline in capital stock per hectare and per unit of labour, but there has been an increase in GVO per unit of land, labour and capital perhaps due to increased efficiency in resource use.
- Animal capital, land, labour, literacy and credit availment are found to have positive influence on GVO, and animal capital, farm machinery, literacy and credit availment have positive impact on productivity of labour. With respect to farm level capital formation, with incomplete specification of the model due to data constraint, land, literacy and credit availment are found to have positive impact.

From disaggregative of analysis with data on three farm groups, following are the major concluding inferences:

- Marginal and small farms have experienced positive growth rate of irrigation capital as well as farm machinery, but negative growth rate of animal capital. In total capital stock, land forms 95 per cent, and among non-land capital stock animal capital would account for 40 per cent.

- These farms are endowed with highest capital stock per hectare, and lowest capital stock per unit of labour. Labour use per hectare is the highest. GVO per unit of land is the highest, but GVO per unit of labour is the lowest as well as per unit of capital. Farm machinery, land, literacy and credit availment are found to have positive impact on GVO, and animal capital, farm machinery, literacy and credit availment have positive impact on labour productivity. Land, credit availment and literacy have positive impact on capital formation.
- In case of semi-medium and medium farms, all types of capital stock excepting of that of irrigation have recorded negative growth rates. Land would account for 97 per cent of total capital stock, and farm machinery with highest percentage share among non-land capital stock.
- With respect to capital intensity in these farms, there is lowest capital stock per hectare, but lower capital stock per unit of labour than in large farms. GVO per unit of land is the lowest, of capital highest, and GVO per unit of labour is higher than what it is in marginal and small farms, but far lower than what it is in large farms.
- Animal capital, farm machinery, labour, literacy and credit availment are the positive determinants of GVO. Animal capital, farm machinery, literacy and credit availment have turned out to be positive determinants of labour productivity. Only land and credit availment are found to have positive impact on capital formation.
- With regard to large farms, growth rates of all types of capital assets, excepting that of irrigation capital, are negative. Land accounts for 97 per cent of total capital stock, and among non-land capital stock farm machinery would account for the highest percentage share.
- Capital stock per hectare is more than in semi-medium and medium farms (but lower than in small and marginal farms), and capital per unit of labour is the highest. But labour employment per hectare is the lowest. These farms have realised highest level of GVO per unit of labour but GVO per unit of land is marginally lower than marginal and small farms (but higher than in the other farm group). GVO per unit of capital is lower than what it is in semi-

medium and medium farms, and marginally higher than what it is in the other farm group.

- Farm machinery, land, labour, literacy and credit availment have positive impact on GVO. The variables which have positive impact on labour productivity are animal capital, farm machinery, literacy and credit availment. Land, credit availment and farmer literacy are found to have positive impact on capital formation.

Following these results/inferences derived from the analysis of farm level data, pathways and needed policy directions and interventions will be discussed in Chapter 6.

5 Capital Formation in Irrigated and Rainfed Farms

Micro Level Evidences

The present chapter is a continuum of Chapter 4 which has focussed on farm level capital growth, composition, intensity as well as productivity of capital, importance of capital *vis-à-vis* other factors in influencing gross value of output (GVO) and productivity of labour, and on determinants of farm level capital formation. Six major results are extracted from Chapter 4 to provide a backdrop to the present chapter:

First, the overall growth rates of non-land capital assets (animal capital, irrigation capital and farm machinery) has decelerated between 1994-95 and 2007-08. Second, with respect to composition of total capital stock (including land), land is the dominant capital asset forming 95 per cent of total capital stock. Third, non-land capital stock per unit of land and labour has registered a decline between two periods of time. Excepting some variations, the same patterns of capital growth rates, composition and factor intensity (i.e., capital per unit of land and labour) are observed across states and farm size groups. Fourth, cutting across states and farm size groups, animal capital, farm machinery, land, labour and credit availment are the major determinants of farm level GVO, measured in terms of output elasticities. Fifth, animal capital, farm machinery, literacy and credit availment are found to have positive impact on labour productivity. Sixth, in general land, credit availment and literacy level of farmers are found to be major determinants of farm level capital formation. It is realised that technology and terms of trade are other major determinants of capital formation. But lack of data at farm level prevented the inclusion of these variables in capital formation function.

The present chapter is based on subset of data set used in the earlier study (Bisaliah and Dev, 2010a). The data subset consists of data on irrigated farms of Punjab and Andhra Pradesh, and rainfed farms of Andhra Pradesh.

As in the case of Chapter 4, the specific issues addressed in this chapter are five. First, how have been the growth rates of different capital components? Second, how is the composition of total capital assets and non-land capital assets? Third, what patterns could be observed in factor intensity and factor productivity? Fourth, how is the importance of capital *vis-à-vis* other factors in influencing GVO and productivity of labour, and what are the determinants of farm level capital formation? Fifth, with respect to all the four issues stated above how comparable is the performance of irrigated and rainfed farms? The issues have been addressed both in aggregative (pooled data analysis) and disaggregative frame (farm size-wise analysis).

Data Base and Analytical Tools

Farm level data are required to address the issues of this chapter. Under Comprehensive Cost of Cultivation Scheme (CCCS), instituted by the Directorate of Economics and Statistics (DES), Government of India, farm level data are collected by agriculture universities and other research institutions, spread across agro-climatic regions of the country, following cost accounting data collection method. Out of 1,350 samples drawn from a pooled data set of 8,000 farm households (details in Chapter 4), data on a total of 831 irrigated farms of Punjab (high agricultural productivity state) and Andhra Pradesh (medium agricultural productivity state) are drawn to develop the data set. Data on 831 irrigated farms would form pooled data for the years 1994-95 and 2007-08. The sample structure for the present study is as detailed below:

State/Farm-Size Groups	*Number of Irrigated Farms*
Punjab	300
Andhra Pradesh	531
Total	831
Marginal and small farms: upto 2 hectare	319
Semi-medium and medium farms: 2 to 10 hectare	476
Large farms: more than 10 hectare	36
Total	831
Andhra Pradesh	
Irrigated farms	531
Rainfed farms	69

Added to data on 831 irrigated farms of both the states, data on 69 rainfed farms of Andhra Pradesh are also considered for the performance analysis of irrigated and rainfed farms of the state with respect to capital growth, composition of capital stock, factor intensity and factor productivity, determinants of gross value of farm level crop output, labour productivity and capital formation. However, the present study is basically a study of irrigated farms of Punjab and Andhra Pradesh. In view of data problem on irrigation, data from Orissa (a low agricultural productivity state) is not considered in the present study on irrigated farms. The analytical tools used in this chapter are the same as the ones employed in Chapter 4.

Trends in Growth Rates, Compositional Shifts and Ratio Analysis of Capital Stock in Irrigated Farms

The focus of the present section is to analyse results on trends in growth rates, compositional shifts, factor intensity and factor productivity ratios of irrigated farms of Punjab and Andhra Pradesh. The analysis in this section is performed both at aggregative (overall results for both the sample states) and at disaggregative levels (state level).

Growth Rate Analysis

It could be seen from Table 5.1 that:

- In general, excepting some positive compound growth rate (CGR) of irrigation capital, in case of all other capital assets, negative CGRs have been recorded between 1994-95 and 2007-08.
- The irrigated farms of Punjab has experienced a high level of positive CGR (7.21%) in irrigation capital, but about 2 per cent of negative growth in farm machinery. With respect to non-land capital assets, the growth rates are positive, but very small.
- In Andhra Pradesh, the irrigated farms have experienced negative growth rates in all types and combinations of capital assets, excepting very small positive growth in land capital asset.

Table 5.1

Compound Growth Rates of Capital Stock: Aggregative and Individual State Analysis of Irrigated Farms

Capital Asset	Growth Rates (%)		
	Overall	Punjab	Andhra Pradesh
Land	-0.16	-0.62	0.15
Animal capital	-0.72	0.21	-1.95
Farm machinery	-2.40	-1.99	-4.02
Irrigation capital	1.76	7.21	-4.04
All non-land capital assets	-0.77	0.52	-3.31
Farm machinery and irrigation capital	-0.78	0.61	-4.03

Compositional Shifts in Capital Structure between 1994-95 and 2007-08

As could be seen from Table 5.2 that,

- The dominant share (over 90%) of land in total capital stock both in aggregate (overall) and disaggregate form (state-wise) is quite obvious. Further, there has been a decline in the share of animal capital as well as farm machinery between 1994-95 and 2007-08.

Table 5.2

Shifts in Composition of Capital Stock: Aggregative and Individual State Analysis of Irrigated Farms

Capital Stock	Composition (%): Percentage Share					
	Overall		Punjab		Andhra Pradesh	
	P.I	P.II	P.I	P.II	P.I	P.II
1. *Total Capital Stock:*						
Land	94	96	95	96	91	97
Animal capital	2	1	1	1	3	1
Farm machinery	3	2	3	2	2	1
Irrigation capital	1	1	1	1	4	1
Total	100	100	100	100	100	100
2. *Non-Land Capital Stock:*						
Animal capital	27	27	23	22	32	38
Farm machinery	49	40	63	45	28	25
Irrigation capital	24	33	14	33	40	37
Total	100	100	100	100	100	100

Note: P.I = 1994-95; P.II = 2007-08.

Figure 5.1

Shifts in Composition of Total Capital Stock

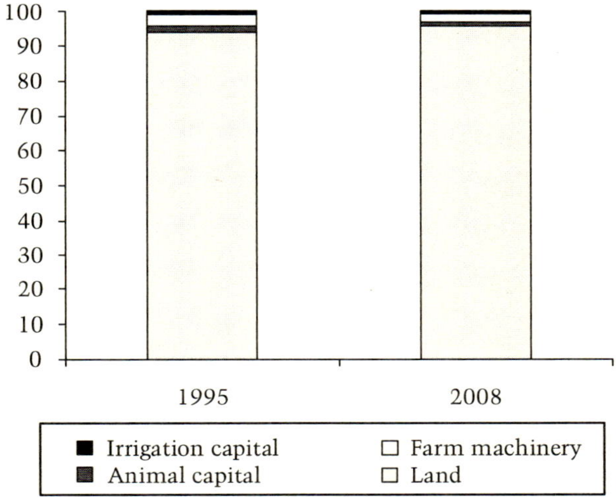

Figure 5.2

Composition of Non-Land Capital Stock: Temporal Shift

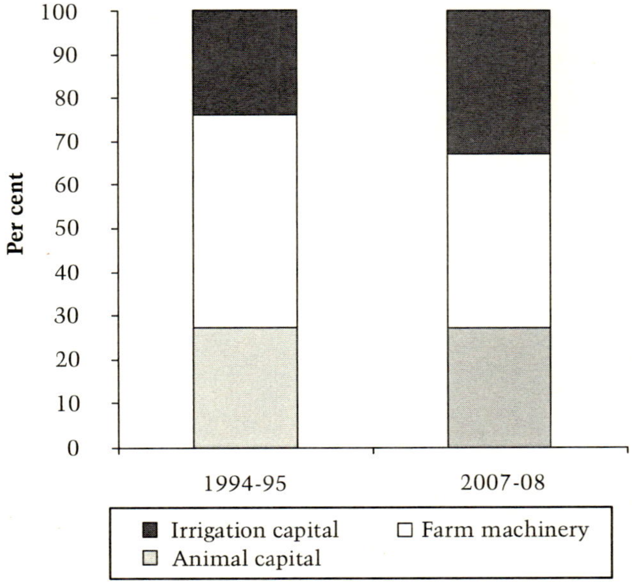

- Among non-land capital stock, there is a decline in the share of farm machinery in general between two periods of time. The decline is much more in Punjab than in Andhra Pradesh. On the other hand, the share of irrigation capital has increased from 14 per cent to 33 per cent in Punjab, with a marginal fall in Andhra Pradesh. In case of animal capital, there is not much of a change in the percentage share in non-land capital assets.

Factor Intensity and Factor Productivity: Aggregative and Disaggregative Analysis

It is observed from Table 5.3 that:

- Land-capital ratios (measured in two ways) have declined in general, and much more so in Andhra Pradesh, whereas in Punjab these ratios has increased between two periods of time. In other words, there is less capital per hectare during second period in Andhra Pradesh, whereas in Punjab there is more of capital stock per unit area cultivated. Less of labour per hectare of land is employed both in aggregative and disaggregative terms (i.e., fall in land-labour ratio).

Table 5.3

Factor Intensity and Factor Productivity in Sample Farms: Overall and State-wise Analysis of Irrigated Farms

Factor Intensity and Productivity	*Ratios*					
	Overall		*Punjab*		*Andhra Pradesh*	
	P.I	*P.II*	*P.I*	*P.II*	*P.I*	*P.II*
Factor Intensity Ratios:						
Land-capital (C/A)	26445	24440	38903	45097	17570	11126
Land-(FM + IC)/A	19431	17917	29861	35020	12000	6893
Labour-capital (C/L*)	20104	21645	37341	44246	11633	9272
Labour-(FM + IC)/L*	14771	15868	28662	34359	7945	5745
Land-labour (L/A)	132	113	104	102	151	120
Factor Productivity Ratios:						
Labour-output (GVO/L*)	28917	41384	43955	70855	21527	25250
Non-land capital–output (GVO/C)	1.44	1.91	1.18	1.60	1.85	2.72
Land-output (GVO/A)	38038	46728	45793	72217	32514	30299

Note: P.I = 1994–95; P.II = 2007 – 08; A = Land in hectare, L = Labour in mandays; L* = Labour in 100 man-days.

- Labour-capital ratio analysis suggests that there has been an increase in capital per unit of labour in Punjab during second period, and a fall in Andhra Pradesh.

With respect to results on factor productivity (Table 5.3):

- GVO per unit of labour, capital and land has increased substantially in Punjab, whereas in Andhra Pradesh, there is a marginal increase in the output per unit of labour and considerable increase in GVO per unit of capital, but a marginal fall in the output per unit area of land. In brief, higher the stock of capital per hectare, larger the volume of output (GVO) per hectare and per unit of labour. These results establish the inference that there is a positive association between capital stock intensity and productivity of land and labour.

Determinants of Gross Value of Output, Productivity of Labour and Capital Formation: Aggregative and State-wise Results

The present section discusses empirical results to answer three questions. First, what do the estimated regression coefficients tell about determinants of GVO? Second, what do the estimated regression coefficients reveal about the determinants of labour productivity in irrigated agriculture? Third, what do the estimated capital formation functions reveal about determinants of capital formation? These questions are addressed by examining both aggregative and disaggregative results.

Determinants of GVO

The estimated elasticities (regression coefficients) of GVO with respect to animal capital, farm machinery, irrigation capital, land, labour, literacy and credit availment are in Tables 5.4 and 5.5. It can be observed from Table 5.4 that:

- The estimated GVO function, using pooled data of 831 samples of irrigated farms of Punjab and Andhra Pradesh (Table 5.4), validates the inference that 71 per cent of variation (Adj. R^2=0.71) in GVO is explained by the explanatory variables specified in the model. The three broad results are:

- o The elasticities of GVO with respect to labour, land, credit availment, farmer literacy, and farm machinery are significant, with a t-value of more than one.
- o The surprising result is negative and significant elasticity of GVO with respect to irrigation capital.
- o Even though the elasticity of GVO with respect to animal capital is positive, it is not statistically significant.

Table 5.4

Elasticities of GVO: Analysis of Results from Pooled Data of Andhra Pradesh and Punjab

Variables	*Regression Coefficients/Elasticities*	*t–Value*
Constant (A)	6.011	25.32
AC	0.007	0.94
FM	0.016	1.09
IC	-0.032	-5.76
A	0.271	6.95
L	0.940	22.39
DVL	0.173	3.13
DVCR	0.235	4.63
DVS_1	-0.789	-12.48
Adj. R^2 = 0.71	Number of samples: 831	

The state-wise estimates of GVO function are given in Table 5.5.

- In case of Punjab, the high Adj. R^2 of 0.86 validates the model in the sense that 86 per cent of variations in GVO are explained by the explanatory variables included *viz.*, farm machinery, irrigation capital, land, labour, literacy and credit availment. The coefficients/output elasticities are not only positive, but also statistically significant. The elasticity of GVO with respect to animal capital is positive, but not statistically significant.
- The explanatory power of the estimated GVO model for Andhra Pradesh is quite satisfactory with Adj. R^2 of 0.64. Animal capital, land, labour, literacy and credit availment are found to have positive and significant influence on GVO, with a t-value of more than one. But the surprising result is negative and statistically significant

elasticity of GVO with respect to irrigation capital. With respect to farm machinery, elasticity coefficient is negative, but statistically insignificant.

Table 5.5

Elasticities of GVO: Analysis of Results from Individual States

Variables	*Regression Coefficients*	
	Punjab	*Andhra Pradesh*
Constant (A)	8.826 (25.18)	4.794 (16.098)
AC	0.005 (0.38)	0.015 (1.64)
FM	0.044 (2.49)	-0.012 (-0.62)
IC	0.015 (1.87)	-0.040 (-5.92)
A	0.742 (13.21)	0.176 (3.56)
L	0.250 (3.82)	1.067 (20.89)
DVL	0.126 (2.39)	0.159 (2.03)
DVCR	0.246 (5.6)	0.113 (1.44)
Adj. R^2	0.86	0.64

Note: t-Values in parenthesis.
Number of samples: Punjab: 300; Andhra Pradesh: 531.

Labour Productivity Function Estimates

The aggregative and disaggregative (state-wise) labour productivity functions are estimated with animal capital per hectare, farm machinery per hectare, irrigation capital per hectare, literacy and credit availment as explanatory variables. The empirical results are in Tables 5.6 and 5.7.

- In case of pooled data analysis of Punjab and Andhra Pradesh (Table 5.6), only coefficients of literacy and credit availment are both positive and statistically significant; the coefficient of farm machinery is positive, but not statistically significant and the coefficient of animal capital is negative, but not statically significant. The coefficient of irrigation capital is negative, but highly significant. Adj. R^2 of 36 per cent is not high enough to validate the explanatory power of the model.
- With respect to state-wise estimates (Table 5.7) of labour productivity functions, Adj. R^2 values are very low; but in case of Punjab, farm machinery, irrigation capital, literacy and credit

availment are found to have statically positive impact on labour productivity. In case of irrigated farms of Andhra Pradesh, animal capital, literacy and credit availment are found to have positive and significant impact on labour productivity, whereas farm machinery and irrigation capital have negative and significant impact.

Table 5.6

Labour Productivity Function Estimates: Pooled Data Analysis of Punjab and Andhra Pradesh

Variables	*Regression Coefficients/Elasticities*	*t–Value*
Constant (B)	6.061	45.95
AC/A	-0.006	-0.8
FM/A	0.011	0.84
IC/A	-0.023	-4.24
DVL	0.122	2.46
DVCR	0.240	5.25
DVS (Andhra Pradesh)	-0.817	-14.58
Adj. R^2	0.36	

Note: Number of samples: 831.

Table 5.7

Results on Labour Productivity Functions: State-wise Results

Variables	*Regression Coefficients*	
	Punjab	*Andhra Pradesh*
Constant (B)	5.413 (20.14)	5.448 (46.98)
AC/A	-0.053 (-2.95)	0.009 (1.13)
FM/A	0.090 (4.01)	-0.027 (-1.73)
IC/A	0.014 (1.21)	-0.032 (-5.25)
DVL	0.132 (1.91)	0.137 (2.08)
DVCR	0.0.309 (5.29)	0.113 (1.72)
Adj. R^2	0.18	0.07

Note: t – Values in parenthesis.
Number of samples: Punjab: 300; Andhra Pradesh: 531.

Estimated Capital Formation Functions

Tables 5.8 and 5.9 present results on determinants of capital formation in irrigated sample farms.

- It is seen from Table 5.8 that only land and credit availment are statistically significant to have positive impact on capital formation.
- As could be seen from the state-wise disaggregative analysis presented in Table 5.9, land, credit availment and literacy are found to have statistically significant positive impact on capital formation in Punjab, whereas in Andhra Pradesh only the coefficient of land is both positive and statistically significant, and coefficient of credit availment even though positive, is not statistically significant.

Table 5.8

Results on Capital Formation Function: Pooled Data Analysis of Punjab and Andhra Pradesh

Variables	*Regression Coefficients/Elasticities*	*t–Value*
Constant (C)	10.529	60.12
A	0.869	13.49
DVCR	0.132	1.06
DVL	0.037	0.27
DVS (Andhra Pradesh)	-1.542	-12.53
Adj. R^2	0.33	

Note: Number of samples: 831.

Table 5.9

Results on Capital Formation Function: State-wise Results

Variable	*Regression Coefficients*	
	Punjab	*Andhra Pradesh*
Constant (C)	10.289 (67.72)	9.113 (42.96)
A	0.928 (14.68)	0.830 (8.70)
DVCR	0.230 (2.09)	0.037 (0.19)
DVL	0.193 (1.46)	-0.052 (-0.26)
Adj. R^2	0.43	0.12

Note: t–Values in parenthesis.

Number of samples: Punjab: 300; Andhra Pradesh: 531

Farm Group-wise Analysis of Results on Irrigated Farms

This section is concerned with the examination of empirical results on capital growth, composition of capital stock, factor intensity as well as factor productivity, and determinants of GVO, productivity of labour and capital formation of three farm groups of irrigated farms.

Capital Growth Analysis

Table 5.10 provides results on CGRs of three farm groups—overall as well as state-wise. The results on overall and state-wise growth rates suggest that:

- In overall, excepting negative growth rates of land and animal capital, the growth rates are found to be positive in marginal and small farms with a little above 2 per cent growth rates of irrigation capital. In marginal and small farms of Punjab, the same growth pattern is observed, excepting high positive growth rate (9.58%) of irrigation capital. But in Andhra Pradesh, excepting farm machinery all other capital assets has experienced negative growth rates with the highest negative growth rate (-4.80%) being observed in irrigation capital.
- With regard to semi-medium and medium farms, the overall growth rates of capital assets are negative, excepting positive growth rate (1.74%) of irrigation capital. But in Punjab, excepting the growth rates of land and farm machinery, the other growth rates are positive, with highest growth rate (6.74%) in case of irrigation capital. In case of Andhra Pradesh, the semi-medium and medium farms are found to have experienced negative growth rates of all capital assets, the highest being farm machinery (-4.24%) followed by irrigation capital (-3.41%).
- Large farms in general have experienced negative growth rates of capital assets excepting in case of irrigation capital and land capital. In case of farm machinery the negative growth rate is very high (-5.25%). The large farms of Punjab are found to have registered a high positive growth rate (6.72%) of irrigation capital with negative growth rates in case of all other items of capital stock. In Andhra

Pradesh, excepting land, there is a high negative (as high as -15.6 per cent in case of farm machinery) growth rates of capital assets.

Table 5.10

Compound Growth Rates of Capital Stock: Farm Size-wise Analysis of Irrigated Farms

Farm Size/Capital Asset	*Growth Rates (%)*		
	Overall	*Punjab*	*Andhra Pradesh*
Marginal/Small:			
Land	-0.35	-0.34	-0.36
Animal capital	-1.57	-0.45	-2.81
Farm machinery	0.95	0.90	1.08
Irrigation capital	2.05	9.58	-4.80
All non-land capital assets	0.29	2.61	-2.78
Farm machinery and irrigation capital	1.54	4.50	-2.76
Semi-Medium/Medium:			
Land	-0.26	-0.60	-0.05
Animal capital	-0.16	0.67	-1.29
Farm machinery	-2.28	-1.76	-4.24
Irrigation capital	1.74	6.74	-3.41
All non-land capital assets	-0.66	0.50	-2.97
Farm machinery and irrigation capital	-0.83	0.45	-3.78
Large:			
Land	0.48	-0.83	2.08
Animal capital	-2.67	-1.45	-5.14
Farm machinery	-5.25	-4.49	-15.61
Irrigation capital	1.46	6.72	-6.26
All non-land capital assets	-2.62	-1.30	-7.49
Farm machinery and irrigation capital	-2.61	-1.28	-8.26

Composition of Capital Stock

Tables 5.11 and 5.12 provide results on compositional shifts in capital stock of different farm-size groups:

- With respect to all the farm groups, the dominant share (over 90%) of land in total capital assets is quite obvious. The share of all other capital assets would form less than 10 per cent. This is perhaps a measure of 'under capitalisation' of irrigated farms. The declining/ constant share of animal capital, farm machinery and irrigation capital in total capital stock supports the inference of 'under capitalisation'. (Table 5.11)

Table 5.11

Shifts in Composition of Total Capital Stock: Farm Size-wise Analysis of Irrigated Farms

Farm Size and Capital Asset	*Composition: Percentage Share*					
	Overall		*Punjab*		*Andhra Pradesh*	
	P.I	*P.II*	*P.I*	*P.II*	*P.I*	*P.II*
Marginal/Small:						
Land	93	95	95	94	89	96
Animal capital	3	2	2	2	5	2
Farm machinery	2	1	2	2	2	1
Irrigation capital	2	2	1	2	4	1
Total	100	100	100	100	100	100
Semi-Medium/Medium:						
Land	94	96	95	96	92	97
Animal capital	2	1	1	1	2	1
Farm machinery	3	2	3	2	3	1
Irrigation capital	1	1	1	1	3	1
Total	100	100	100	100	100	100
Large:						
Land	95	97	95	97	90	98
Animal capital	1	1	1	1	2	1
Farm machinery	3	1	3	1	3	-
Irrigation capital	1	1	1	1	5	1
Total	100	100	100	100	100	100

Note: P.I = 1994–95; P.II = 2007–08.

- The analysis of compositional shifts of non-land capital assets (Table 5.12) suggests that:
  - o In case of marginal farms of both the states put together (overall), there has been a decline in the share of animal capital from 45 per cent to 35 per cent between two periods of time, and increase in the share of irrigation capital from 29 per cent to 36 per cent. The irrigated farms of Punjab has followed the same pattern of composition, excepting quite an increase in the share of irrigation capital from 17 per cent to 39 per cent. On the other

hand, the marginal and small farms of Andhra Pradesh are found to have experienced a fall in the share of irrigation capital and rise in the share of farm machinery.

Table 5.12

Shifts in Composition of Non-Land Capital Stock: Farm Size-wise Analysis of Irrigated Farms

Farm Size/Non-Land Capital Asset	*Composition: Percentage Share*					
	Overall		*Punjab*		*Andhra Pradesh*	
	P.I	*P.II*	*P.I*	*P.II*	*P.I*	*P.II*
Marginal/Small:						
Animal capital	45	35	45	30	45	45
Farm machinery	26	29	38	31	15	24
Irrigation capital	29	36	17	39	40	31
Total	100	100	100	100	100	100
Semi-Medium/Medium:						
Animal capital	25	26	22	22	29	37
Farm machinery	52	42	65	48	32	27
Irrigation capital	23	32	13	30	39	36
Total	100	100	100	100	100	100
Large:						
Animal capital	16	16	14	13	21	29
Farm machinery	59	41	72	47	26	8
Irrigation capital	25	43	14	40	53	63
Total	100	100	100	100	100	100

Note: P.I = 1994–95; P.II = 2007–08.

- In general, there has been a fall in the share of farm machinery and a rise in the share of irrigation capital, with almost a constant share of animal capital in semi-medium and medium farms. In Punjab, the same pattern of shifts in composition of non-land capital had taken place. On the other hand, in Andhra Pradesh, there has been a fall in the share of both farm machinery and irrigation capital, and a rise in the share of animal capital.
- Large irrigated farms in overall, are found to have recorded a fall in the share of farm machinery from 59 per cent to 41 per cent,

and a rise in the share of irrigation capital from 25 per cent to 43 per cent. Punjab has experienced the similar pattern of composition, with quite a fall in the share of farm machinery (from 72 per cent to 47 per cent), and a quite a rise in the share of irrigation capital (from 14 per cent to 40 per cent). The large farms of Andhra Pradesh has followed the same pattern.

Factor Intensity and Factor Productivity

The results on factor intensity in different farm groups are in Table 5.13:

- In case of marginal and small farms of Punjab, capital per hectare and per unit of labour are found to be not merely higher than in

Table 5.13

Factor Intensity: Farm Size-wise Analysis of Irrigated Farms

Farm Size and Factor Intensity	*Overall*		*Punjab*		*Andhra Pradesh*	
	P.I	*P.II*	*P.I*	*P.II*	*P.I*	*P.II*
Marginal and Small:						
C/A	32710	35536	42972	62812	26629	19334
FM + IC/A	17997	22989	23598	43706	14677	10684
C/L*	16456	20644	28009	42722	11801	10336
FM + IC/L*	9054	13355	15381	29727	6504	5712
L/A	199	172	153	147	226	187
Semi-Medium and Medium:						
C/A	25164	23887	39991	46178	15757	10727
FM + IC/A	18954	17598	31291	35905	11127	6790
C/L*	19036	21403	37535	46933	10614	8984
FM + IC/L*	14338	15768	29370	36492	7495	5687
L/A	132	112	107	98	148	119
Large:						
C/A	27394	18238	33101	31094	19025	5291
FM + IC/A	23082	15385	28604	26953	14984	3735
C/L*	39483	25227	47667	35537	27456	9285
FM + IC/L*	33268	21280	41191	30804	21625	6554
L/A	69	72	69	87	69	57

Note: P.I = 1994–95; P.II = 2007–08; A = Land in hectare; L = Labour in man-days; L* = Labour in 100 man-days.

Andhra Pradesh during both the periods, the ratios have also increased substantially during second period *vis-à-vis* first period. But in Andhra Pradesh these ratios are not merely lower, but also have declined further during second period. Labour use per hectare of land has declined in both the states during second period.

- The semi-medium and medium farms have also experienced the same pattern of land-capital, labour-capital and land-labour ratios over a period of time both in Punjab and Andhra Pradesh, similar to the ones observed in the case of marginal and small farms.
- But in the large farms of Punjab, there has been a marginal decline in the capital stock per hectare and per unit of labour, but an increase in labour per unit of land. In Andhra Pradesh, there has been a considerable amount of decline in capital stock per unit of land and per unit of labour, and marginal decline in labour use per hectare.

With regard to factor productivity across farm groups (Table 5.14):

- In Punjab, there was an increase in GVO per unit of labour, capital and land in marginal and small farms. In Andhra Pradesh, GVO per unit of labour and land, even though lower than in Punjab, there was a trend towards rise during second period. But output (GVO) per unit of capital was not merely higher in Andhra Pradesh, it had also registered an increase during second period.
- In case of semi-medium and medium farms of Punjab, there was an increase in GVO per unit of labour, capital and land. In Andhra Pradesh of these farms, there was a marginal increase in GVO per unit of labour, but marginal decline per unit of land. Partial productivity of capital had increased during second period *vis-à-vis* first period.
- There was an increase in output per unit of labour, capital and land in large farms of Punjab. In large farms of Andhra Pradesh there was a decline in GVO per unit of labour and land, but a considerable increase in GVO per unit of capital.

Table 5.14

Factor Productivity: Farm Size-wise Analysis of Irrigated Farms

Farm Size and Factor Productivity	*Overall*		*Punjab*		*Andhra Pradesh*	
	P.I	*P.II*	*P.I*	*P.II*	*P.I*	*P.II*
Marginal and Small:						
GVO/L*	20478	29968	29854	48650	16701	21247
GVO/C	1.24	1.45	1.07	1.14	1.42	2.06
GVO/A	40706	51587	45803	71528	37685	39742
Semi-Medium and Medium:						
GVO/L*	28301	41441	41771	72666	22169	26250
GVO/C	1.49	1.94	1.11	1.55	2.09	2.92
GVO/A	37411	46249	44503	71497	32913	31344
Large:						
GVO/L*	55998	62372	72032	85775	32434	26186
GVO/C	1.42	2.47	1.51	2.41	1.18	2.82
GVO/A	38852	45092	50021	75052	22473	14922

Note: P.I = 1994–95; P.II = 2007–08; A = Land in hectare; L* = Labour in 100 man-days.

Estimates of Gross Value of Output

The results on farm group analysis are in Table 5.15:

- In case of marginal and small farms, GVO elasticities with respect to land, labour, literacy and credit availment are positive as well as statistically significant. But elasticity of irrigation capital is significant, but the sign is negative and thereby not in accordance with the postulated sign. The elasticities of other two capital assets *viz.*, animal capital and farm machinery are not statistically significant. Adj. R^2 of 0.64 is high enough to validate the estimated function, in terms of its explanatory power.
- With regard to semi-medium and medium farms, animal capital, farm machinery, labour, literacy and credit availment have positive elasticities, somewhat statistically significant with t-values of more than one. But the elasticity with respect to irrigation capital is negative, and statistically significant. Adj. R^2 of 0.58 is adequate enough to vindicate the validity of estimated GVO function.

- In respect to large farms, the elasticities of GVO with respect to farm machinery, land, labour and literacy are found to be positive, and statistically significant with t-values of more than one. But elasticities with respect to irrigation capital and animal capital are negative, and statistically significant with t-values of more than one. The elasticity with respect to credit availment is positive, but not statistically significant. With a high Adj. R^2 of 85 per cent, the explanatory power of the model is validated.

Table 5.15

Elasticities of GVO: Farm Group-wise Results

Variables	*Marginal and Small Farms*	*Semi-Medium and Medium Farms*	*Large Farms*
Constant	7.723 (25.25)	5.291 (14.62)	9.572 (6.11)
AC	-0.002 (-0.25)	0.021 (1.73)	-0.327 (-2.44)
FM	-0.009 (-0.56)	0.027 (1.22)	0.183 (3.21)
IC	-0.019 (-3.03)	-0.038 (-4.47)	-0.033 (-1.15)
A	0.577 (7.97)	0.070 (0.76)	0.495 (1.25)
L	0.623 (10.64)	1.070 (18.42)	0.601 (4.4)
DVL	0.227 (2.99)	0.169 (2.14)	0.283 (1.94)
DVCR	0.179 (3.07)	0.277 (3.55)	0.116 (0.73)
DVS (AP)	-0.664 (-9.43)	-0.778 (-7.68)	-0.841 (-3.88)
Adj. R^2	0.64	0.58	0.85

Note: t-Values in parenthesis.
Number of samples: Marginal and small: 319; Semi-medium and medium: 476; Large: 36.

Labour Productivity Function Estimates

- The estimates on labour productivity functions for three farm groups are in Table 5.16. In case of marginal and small farmers only two elasticities *viz.*, literacy and credit availment are found to have positive and significant impact on labour productivity and in case of three capital components unexpected negative impact is observed.
- With regard to labour productivity function of semi-medium and medium farms, the coefficient of farm machinery, literacy and credit availment are both positive and statistically significant. The coefficient of irrigation capital is both negative and significant.

- In case of large farms, the coefficients of farm machinery and literacy are positive as well as significant. But coefficients of animal capital and irrigation capital are negative as well as significant.
- Adj. R^2 for labour productivity functions of marginal and small, and semi-medium and medium farms is just moderate, and in case of large farms, it is found to be 69 per cent.

Table 5.16

Results on Labour Productivity: Farm Group-wise Results

Variables	*Marginal and Small Farms*	*Semi-Medium and Medium Farms*	*Large Farms*
Constant (B)	6.174 (35.29)	5.928 (32.12)	8.430 (7.73)
AC/A	-0.007 (-0.82)	0.008 (0.71)	-0.364 (-2.48)
FM/A	-0.031 (-1.71)	0.029 (1.62)	0.157 (2.51)
IC/A	-0.018 (-2.63)	-0.037 (-4.83)	-0.054 (-1.46)
DVL	0.118 (1.51)	0.185 (2.94)	0.218 (1.38)
DVCR	0.184 (2.91)	0.278 (4.46)	0.124 (0.70)
DVS (Andhra Pradesh)	-0.822 (-11.33)	-0.770 (-9.62)	-0.826 (-3.48)
Adj. R^2	0.35	0.40	0.69

Note: t–Values in parenthesis.
Number of samples: Marginal and small: 319; Semi-medium and medium: 476; Large: 36.

Estimates of Capital Formation Function

- The farm group-wise capital formation estimated functions are presented in Table 5.17. Land has turned to be both a positive and significant variable in influencing capital formation in all the three farm groups. Credit availment has both positive and statistically significant impact on capital formation in large farms, and in case of other two farm groups credit availment has positive impact but not statistically significant. Literacy variable is found to have positive impact on capital formation in case of marginal and small farms and large farms, where as its impact is negative with respect to semi-medium and medium farms.

Table 5.17

Results on Capital Formation: Farm Group-wise Analysis

Variables	*Marginal and Small Farms*	*Semi-Medium and Medium Farms*	*Large Farms*
Constant (C)	10.135 (30.83)	10.310 (34.41)	9.969 (5.40)
A	0.915 (3.95)	1.192 (7.42)	0.983 (1.35)
DVCR	0.204 (0.89)	0.066 (0.43)	0.331 (1.21)
DVL	0.351 (1.17)	-0.172 (-1.10)	0.242 (0.91)
DVS (Andhra Pradesh)	-1.289 (-5.76)	-1.715 (-11.28)	-1.198 (-4.40)
Adj. R^2	0.15	0.34	0.53

Note: t – Values in parenthesis.

Number of samples: Marginal and small: 319; Semi-medium and medium: 476; Large: 36.

Comparison of Results on Capital Formation in Irrigated and Rainfed Farms of Andhra Pradesh

It is recalled from earlier discussion that one of the objectives is to address the issue of performance of irrigated and rainfed farms of Andhra Pradesh with respect to capital growth, composition of capital stock, factor intensity and factor productivity, and estimates of GVO function, labour productivity function, and capital formation function. It is also recalled from earlier section that the results for comparative study is derived from a sample of 531 irrigated farms and 69 rainfed farms. It needs to be stated that results on irrigated farms of Andhra Pradesh have already been discussed earlier, but a brief reference to these results for the purpose of comparison is made.

Capital Stock Growth Analysis

As seen from Table 5.18 that excepting land, the growth rates of all other capital assets and their groups are negative in case of irrigated farms, whereas in rainfed farms the growth rates of both farm machinery and land capital assets are found to be positive.

Table 5.18

Compound Growth Rates of Capital Stock in Irrigated and Rainfed Farms of Andhra Pradesh

Capital Asset	*Growth Rates (%)*		
	Overall	*Irrigated*	*Rainfed*
Land	0.25	0.15	1.11
Animal capital	-2.02	-1.95	-3.30
Farm machinery	-3.79	-4.02	3.86
Irrigation capital	-4.26	-4.04	-15.49
All non-land capital assets	-3.35	-3.31	-4.30
Farm machinery and irrigation capital	-4.07	-4.03	-5.36

It is observed (Table 5.19) from farm group-wise analysis of capital growth that excepting the positive CGR of farm machinery, the growth rates of all other items/groups of capital stock are found to be negative in marginal and small irrigated farms, whereas in case of rainfed farms the growth rates of land, animal capital and farm machinery are positive. With regard to semi-medium and medium irrigated and rainfed farms, the growth rates of all items of capital are negative, excepting the positive growth rate of farm machinery in rainfed farms of this group. The large irrigated farms of Andhra Pradesh have experienced negative growth rates of different items of capital stock, excepting the positive growth rate of land. On the other hand, rainfed farms have recorded positive growth rates of land, animal capital and farm machinery assets.

Composition of Capital Stock

Compositional difference in capital stock between irrigated and rainfed farms, and shifts in composition between two periods of time (between 1994-95 and 2007-08) are shown in Tables 5.20–5.22.

- The share of land in total capital stock had increased to 97 per cent in case of both irrigated and rainfed farms. With regard to the percentage shares of other three types of capital stock, there was a decline between two periods of time. Further, among non-land capital stock, the share of animal capital was 38 per cent in irrigated farms, whereas it was 55 per cent in rainfed farms during 2007-08. During the same period, the percentage share of farm machinery

Table 5.19

Compound Growth Rates of Capital Stock: Farm Size-wise Analysis of Irrigated and Rainfed Farms of Andhra Pradesh

Farm Size/Capital Asset	*Growth Rates (%)*		
	Overall	*Irrigated*	*Rainfed*
Marginal/Small:			
Land	0.08	-0.36	2.36
Animal capital	-2.50	-2.81	2.41
Farm machinery	1.07	1.08	0.92
Irrigation capital	-4.80	-4.80	-4.58
All non-land capital assets	-2.62	-2.78	1.50
Farm machinery and irrigation capital	-2.72	-2.76	-0.64
Semi-Medium/Medium:			
Land	-0.08	-0.05	-0.40
Animal capital	-1.60	-1.29	-9.01
Farm machinery	-4.01	-4.24	4.68
Irrigation capital	-3.64	-3.41	-14.56
All non-land capital assets	-3.07	-2.97	-6.52
Farm Machinery and irrigation capital	-3.80	-3.78	-4.71
Large:			
Land	2.49	2.08	5.02
Animal capital	-4.12	-5.14	2.41
Farm machinery	-14.06	-15.61	5.11
Irrigation capital	-6.80	-6.26	NA
All non-land capital assets	-7.27	-7.49	-
Farm machinery and irrigation capital	-8.44	-8.26	-

was higher (37%) in rainfed farms than in irrigated farms (25%). Obviously, the share of irrigation capital was higher in irrigated farms (Table 5.20).

- The results on difference in composition of four components of capital stock in total capital across farm groups are presented in Table 5.21. The share of land across three farm groups is found to be over 96 per cent during 2007-08. The percentage share of animal capital is higher in marginal and small rainfed farms than it is in other two farm groups during the same period.

Table 5.20

Shifts in Composition of Capital Stock in Irrigated and Rainfed Farms of Andhra Pradesh

Capital Stock	Composition: Percentage Share					
	Overall		Irrigated		Rainfed	
	P.I	P.II	P.I	P.II	P.I	P.II
1. *Total Capital Stock:*						
Land	91	97	91	97	92	97
Animal capital	3	1	3	1	4	2
Farm machinery	2	1	2	1	1	1
Irrigation capital	4	1	4	1	3	-
Total	100	100	100	100	100	100
2. *Non–Land Capital Stock:*						
Animal capital	32	39	32	38	48	55
Farm machinery	28	26	28	25	13	37
Irrigation capital	40	35	40	37	39	8
Total	100	100	100	100	100	100

Note: P.I = 1994-95; P.II = 2007-08.

Table 5.21

Shifts in Composition of Total Capital Stock: Farm Size-wise Analysis of Irrigated and Rainfed Farms in Andhra Pradesh

Farm Size and Capital Asset	Composition: Percentage Share					
	Overall		Irrigated		Rainfed	
	P.I	P.II	P.I	P.II	P.I	P.II
Marginal/Small:						
Land	89	96	89	96	94	96
Animal capital	5	2	5	2	4	3
Farm machinery	2	1	2	1	1	1
Irrigation capital	4	1	4	1	1	-
Total	100	100	100	100	100	100
Semi-Medium/Medium:						
Land	92	97	92	97	92	97
Animal capital	2	1	2	1	4	1
Farm machinery	3	1	3	1	1	2
Irrigation capital	3	1	3	1	3	-
Total	100	100	100	100	100	100
Large:						
Land	89	98	90	98	81	97
Animal capital	2	1	2	1	6	2
Farm machinery	3	-	3	-	1	1
Irrigation capital	5	1	5	1	12	-
Total	100	100	100	100	100	100

Note: P.I = 1994–95; P.II = 2007–08.

- The difference in composition of non-land capital stock across farm groups is presented in Table 5.22. The percentage share of animal capital is found to be 74 per cent in rainfed marginal and small farms, and it is 45 per cent in case of irrigated farms. In case of large rainfed farms also, the same pattern of the dominant share (77%) of animal capital stock is observed. For obvious reasons, the share of irrigation capital in irrigated farms is more dominant. In brief, the percentage share of animal capital is quite substantial in case of rainfed farms.

Table 5.22

Shifts in Composition of Non–Land Capital Stock: Farm Size-wise Analysis of Irrigated and Rainfed Farms in Andhra Pradesh

Farm Size/Non-Land Capital Asset	*Composition: Percentage Share*					
	Overall		*Irrigated*		*Rainfed*	
	P.I	*P.II*	*P.I*	*P.II*	*P.I*	*P.II*
Marginal/Small:						
Animal capital	46	46	45	45	66	74
Farm machinery	15	24	15	24	22	20
Irrigation capital	39	30	40	31	12	6
Total	100	100	100	100	100	100
Semi-Medium/Medium:						
Animal capital	30	37	29	37	49	34
Farm machinery	32	28	32	27	12	53
Irrigation capital	38	35	39	36	39	12
Total	100	100	100	100	100	100
Large:						
Animal capital	22	34	21	29	31	77
Farm machinery	25	9	26	8	6	23
Irrigation capital	53	57	53	63	63	-
Total	100	100	100	100	100	100

Note: P.I = 1994–95; P.II = 2007–08.

Factor Intensity and Factor Productivity Analysis

Table 5.23 presents evidences on differences in factor intensity and factor productivity, as between irrigated and rainfed farms of Andhra Pradesh. Irrigated farms are found to have 3.40 times more capital stock per hectare than rainfed farms, and a unit of labour working in irrigated farms has 1.8 times more capital than in rainfed farms, during 2007-08. It is also observed that an average irrigated farm employs 120 units of labour per hectare, whereas an average rainfed farm employs 64 units of labour. In brief, both capital intensity and labour intensity are higher in irrigated farms. But in both categories of farms, both labour intensity and capital intensity are found to have declined substantially within a span of 13 years, i.e., between 1994-95 and 2007-08. This declining intensity is a situation of disturbing trend.

Table 5.23

Factor Intensity and Factor Productivity in Irrigated and Rainfed Farms of Andhra Pradesh

Factor Intensity and Productivity	*Ratios*					
	Overall		*Irrigated*		*Rainfed*	
	P.I	*P.II*	*P.I*	*P.II*	*P.I*	*P.II*
Factor Intensity Ratios:						
Land-capital (C/A)	16525	10283	17570	11126	6670	3265
Land-(FM + IC)/A	11179	6311	12000	6893	3443	1458
Labour-capital (C/L*)	11423	9025	11633	9272	7891	5139
Labour-(FM + IC)/L*	7728	5538	7945	5745	4073	2294
Land-labour (L/A)	145	114	151	120	85	64
Factor Productivity Ratios:						
Labour-output (GVO/L*)	21412	25333	21527	25250	19461	26640
Non-land capital-Output (GVO/C)	1.87	2.81	1.85	2.72	2.47	5.18
Land-output (GVO/A)	30973	28866	32514	30299	16450	16926

Note: P.I = 1994–95; P.II = 2007–08; A = Land in hectare; L = Labour in man-days; L* = Labour in 100 man-days.

With regard to factor productivity, output per unit of labour and capital is higher in an average irrigated and rainfed farm of 2007-08 than of 1994-95.

Further during 2007-08, productivity of both labour and capital is higher in rainfed farms than in irrigated farms. However, productivity of land per hectare is double in an average irrigated farm *vis-à-vis* rainfed farms, due to higher capital and labour intensity, among others, in irrigated farms.

Factor intensity analysis of three farm groups is presented in Table 5.24:

- In case of marginal and small farms, an average irrigated farm is endowed with over 4 times more capital stock per hectare compared to an average rainfed farm, and about 2 times more capital per unit of labour. There is about 2 times more labour employment found in an average irrigated farm than in an average rainfed farm.

Table 5.24

Factor Intensity Analysis of Irrigated and Rainfed Farms of Andhra Pradesh: Farm Size-wise Analysis

Farm Size and Factor Intensity	*Overall*		*Irrigated*		*Rainfed*	
	P.I	*P.II*	*P.I*	*P.II*	*P.I*	*P.II*
Marginal and Small:						
C/A	23613	16561	26629	19334	5041	4517
FM + IC/A	12865	8901	14677	10684	1706	1160
C/L*	11309	9765	11801	10336	4799	4816
FM + IC/L*	6162	5248	6504	5712	1624	1236
L/A	209	170	226	187	105	94
Semi-Medium and Medium:						
C/A	14990	10096	15757	10727	6665	2923
FM + IC/A	10476	6395	11127	6790	3405	1916
C/L*	10514	8873	10614	8984	8470	5851
FM + IC/L*	7347	5621	7495	5687	4327	3835
L/A	143	114	148	119	79	50
Large:						
C/A	17875	4867	19025	5291	9358	2691
FM + IC/A	13972	3225	14984	3735	6475	613
C/L*	25278	8385	27456	9285	11514	4242
FM + IC/L*	19758	5556	21625	6554	7967	967
L/A	71	58	69	57	81	63

Note: P.I = 1994–95; P.II = 2007–08; A = Land in hectare; L = Labour in mandays; L* = Labour in 100 mandays.

- With regard to semi-medium and medium farms, there is 3.6 times more capital per hectare of an irrigated farm, one and a half times more capital per unit of labour, and more than double the labour employed per hectare.
- An average large irrigated farms has about two times more capital per hectare and per unit of labour, employing less labour per hectare.

- Both in irrigated and rainfed farms, capital stock per hectare has declined during 2007-08 compared to that of 1994-95. Labour employment per hectare has also declined.

Factor productivity analysis of three farm groups is presented in Table 5.25:

- GVO per unit of labour and land is more in marginal and small irrigated farms, but GVO per unit of capital is more in rainfed farms. But GVO per unit of land is double in irrigated marginal and small farms.
- Both labour and capital productivity is more in rainfed farms than irrigated semi-medium and medium farms. But GVO per hectare is more in irrigated farms.

Table 5.25

Factor Productivity Analysis of Irrigated and Rainfed Farms of Andhra Pradesh: Farm Size-wise Analysis

Farm Size and Factor Productivity	*Overall*		*Irrigated*		*Rainfed*	
	P.I	*P.II*	*P.I*	*P.II*	*P.I*	*P.II*
Marginal and Small:						
GVO/L*	16611	21215	16701	21247	15428	20942
GVO/C	1.47	2.17	1.42	2.06	3.21	4.35
GVO/A	34684	35980	37685	39742	16204	19642
Semi-Medium and Medium:						
GVO/L*	21993	26498	22169	26250	18402	33204
GVO/C	2.09	2.99	2.09	2.92	2.17	5.68
GVO/A	31357	30150	32913	31344	14481	16591
Large:						
GVO/L*	32549	25626	32434	26186	33280	23049
GVO/C	1.29	3.06	1.18	2.82	2.89	5.43
GVO/A	23018	14873	22473	14922	27051	14624

Note: P.I = 1994–95; P.II = 2007–08; A = Land in hectare; L* = Labour in 100 man-days.

- In case of large farms, GVO per unit of labour and per hectare of land is found to be more in irrigated farms, but capital is found to be more productive in rainfed farms.

- The interesting observation is that capital is found to be more productive (in terms of output per unit of capital) in rainfed farms of all three farm groups during 1994-95 as well as 2007-2008. This implies that additional stock of capital could be more productive in rainfed farms.

Determinants of GVO, Labour Productivity and Capital Formation Comparison between Irrigated and Rainfed Farms

Estimates of GVO elasticities of irrigated and rainfed farms are presented in Table 5.26. With regard to irrigated farms, animal capital, land, labour, literacy and credit availment are found to have positive and statistically significant influence on GVO. The explanatory power of the estimated GVO function is sound enough with an Adj. R^2 of 64 per cent. But the elasticity of GVO with respect to irrigation capital is negative as well as highly significant. In case of rainfed farms, the estimated GVO function (following bootstrapping Davison and Hinkley, 1997) suggests that farm machinery, land, labour, literacy and credit availment are significant variables to have positive influence on GVO. Adj R^2 is also moderately high (40%), validating the explanatory power of the estimated model.

Table 5.26

Elasticities of GVO in Andhra Pradesh: Analysis of Results from Irrigated and Rainfed Farms

Variables	*Regression Coefficients*	
	Irrigated	*Rainfed*
Medium farms	4.794 (16.98)	5.043 (3.68)
AC	0.015 (1.64)	-0.005 (-0.18)
FM	-0.012 (-0.62)	0.109 (1.58)
IC	-0.040 (-5.92)	NA
A	0.176 (3.56)	0.385 (2.73)
L	1.067 (20.89)	0.764 (3.08)
DVL	0.159 (2.03)	0.349 (1.35)
DVCR	0.1013 (1.44)	0.423 (1.96)
Adj. R^2	0.64	0.40

Note: t-Values in parenthesis.
Number of samples: Irrigated: 531; Rainfed: 69.

Table 5.27 provides estimated GVO functions for three farm groups of irrigated farms. It is observed that land, labour, literacy and credit availment have positive significant influence on GVO of marginal and small farms. In case of semi-medium and medium irrigated farms, animal capital, labour and literacy are found to have positive and significant influence. Credit availment and animal capital have positive influence on GVO, but statistically insignificant. But the elasticity of GVO with respect to irrigation capital is both negative and highly significant. Coefficients of farm machinery, labour, and literacy are positive as well as significant in case of large irrigated farms. Land is found to have positive influence on GVO of large irrigated farms, but the coefficient is statistically insignificant.

Table 5.27

Elasticities of GVO of Irrigated Farms in Andhra Pradesh: Farm Group-wise Results

Variables	*Marginal and Small Farms*	*Semi-Medium and Medium Farms*	*Large Farms*
Constant	6.862 (19.03)	4.118 (9.80)	6.972 (2.54)
AC	0.005 (0.55)	0.024 (1.69)	-0.265 (-1.48)
FM	-0.036 (-1.80)	0.010 (0.36)	0.206 (2.61)
IC	-0.029 (-4.04)	-0.045 (-4.44)	-0.023 (-0.35)
A	0.557 (6.32)	-0.095 (-0.75)	0.483 (0.58)
L	0.688 (10.15)	1.206 (17.15)	0.714 (3.72)
DVL	0.279 (2.77)	0.133 (1.18)	0.511 (1.83)
DVCR	0.122 (1.52)	0.104 (0.84)	-0.411 (-1.04)
Adj. R^2	0.60	0.55	0.72

Note: t-Values in parenthesis.

Number of samples: Marginal and small: 207; Semi-medium and medium: 307; Large: 17.

Even though number of samples of rainfed farms is small for marginal and small farms and semi-medium and medium farms, the estimated GVO function (following boot strapping method) results are considered for comparison with those of irrigated farms. It could be observed from Table 5.28 that farm machinery, land and labour are major determinants of GVO of marginal and small farms under rainfed farming, and the coefficients of animal capital, literacy and credit availment, even though positive, are not statistically significant. In case of semi-medium and medium rainfed farms, labour, literacy and credit availment are found to have significant positive influence on GVO, and the coefficients of farm machinery and land, even though positive, are not statistically significant. However low Adj. R^2 of the estimated equations does not validate adequately the explanatory power of the model.

Table 5.28

Elasticities of GVO of Rainfed Farms in Andhra Pradesh: Farm Group-wise Results

Variables	*Marginal and Small Farms*	*Semi-Medium and Medium Farms*	*Large Farms*
Constant	4.007 (1.64)	7.578 (4.36)	-
AC	0.015 (0.37)	-0.033 (-0.58)	-
FM	0.127 (1.34)	0.031 (0.23)	-
A	0.566 (1.21)	0.335 (0.80)	-
L	0.964 (1.87)	0.425 (1.19)	-
DVL	0.318 (0.62)	0.551 (1.77)	-
DVCR	0.410 (0.76)	0.659 (2.24)	-
Adj. R^2	0.12	0.23	-

Note: t-Values in parenthesis.
Number of samples: Marginal and small: 40; Semi-medium and medium: 26; Large: 3.

Empirical results on labour productivity functions and on capital formation functions for comparison are not reported, in view of extremely low Adj. R^2.

Concluding Observations

The present chapter has focussed on the performance of irrigated farms with respect to various dimensions of capital at farm level, *viz.*, growth of capital stock, composition of capital stock, capital intensity, as well as productivity (in addition to other intensity and productivity ratios), and determinants of GVO, productivity and capital formation. A comparison of performance of irrigated and rainfed farms has also been attempted, using the same performance indicators of agricultural capital stock at farm level. The needed policy interventions to impact these aspects of agricultural capital stock will be discussed in the next chapter.

6 Substantive Inferences and Policy Directions

The objectives set out for the study are to document and analyse cross-country experiences on capital, growth and poverty, to analyse macro evidences on trends in various aspects of investment in agriculture in India, agriculture growth and poverty, to analyse the micro (farm level) evidences on growth of capital stock and its composition, intensity and productivity, and role of capital in determining farm level gross value of output and productivity of labour engaged in agriculture, as well as to identify the determinants of investment in agriculture by farm households. The present chapter is to recapitulate the substantive inferences of the analysis of macro and micro evidences on investment in agriculture and to derive the pathways and policy directions. While recapitulating the inferences from micro evidences, the focus is mainly on overall inferences (ignoring differences across states), and to some extent on three farm groups *viz.*, marginal and small, semi-medium and medium and large farms.

Substantive Inferences

The major conclusions and substantive inferences drawn in previous chapters are recapitulated in this section.

Capital, Growth and Poverty

The major conclusions and inferences derived from the analysis of relationships between capital, growth and poverty and cross-country empirical evidences on these relationships (Chapter 2) are:

- The concept of capital has been broadened to envelope physical capital, human capital, social capital, natural capital, knowledge capital (R&D), institutional capital (governance) and infrastructure capital.

- Various growth models have recognised different variants of capital as one of the major deep drivers of growth.
- Growth accounting studies with growth regression methodology have provided three results, which are quite valuable for developing countries in their policy and programme designs. First, capital accumulation is by far the most important contributor to measured growth in output in developing countries in addition to labour, human capital and TFP. Second, variations in TFP have been explained in terms of human capital, physical capital, natural capital, macroeconomic management, governance, knowledge development and dissemination through R&D, institutional factors like land distribution and tenure and economic integration with outside world. Third, the positive interaction between technological advance, capital accumulation and TFP catch-up, contributes for 'bridging idea' gap between countries to facilitate movement towards growth convergence. Hence convergence of labour productivity, narrowing differences in capital: labour ratios and convergence of TFP are crucial for growth convergence.
- Cross-country experiences of developing countries regarding the nexus between growth and poverty suggest that the impact of growth on poverty depends on sectoral pattern of growth, initial distribution inequalities and employment generation pattern of chosen growth pattern.
- There are many imperatives for reinstating agriculture/rural sector at the centre of development agenda of developing countries. First, poverty is dominantly a rural phenomenon, and agro-rural sector is still a dominant provider of employment for rural people. Second, high growth performance of agriculture would lead to more non-farm activities and generation of more employment opportunities for the rural poor, and to higher real wages due to fall in prices of food articles. Third, it is concluded that agriculture R&D, rural infrastructure, irrigation, rural growth centres to provide non-farm employment and income opportunities, increase in rural labour productivity and high TFP are crucial for improving the performance

of rural growth and for reducing rural poverty. All these would need increase in investment in agriculture for capital formation as a major driver of rural growth and poverty reduction.

- In support of the need for investment in agriculture, it is necessary to keep in view the major inference on the positive relationship between agriculture capital stock and productivity of labour engaged in agriculture, and inverse relationship between productivity of labour and prevalence of poverty and hunger.
- While emphasising the importance of capital accumulation in enhancing growth performance and poverty reduction, it is absolutely important to recognise the difference between capital accumulation and capital assimilation (Nelson and Pack, 1999). The growth/development experiences of South Korea, China and Singapore have experienced not merely rapid growth of physical stock, but also high rate of investment in human capital which has facilitated capital assimilation through entrepreneurship, learning by doing and innovation.

Macro Evidences on Capital Formation, Agriculture Growth and Poverty in India

This part of the study (Chapter 3) has focussed on examination of analytical constructs and empirical evidences related to data set, investment behaviour of public and private sector, trends in the pace and composition of capital formation in/for agriculture, complementarity, between public and private investment, and impact of capital formation on agriculture growth and poverty. Following are the substantive inferences and conclusions on this theme:

- Loss of momentum in capital formation, particularly led by public sector investment, has become one of the binding constraints on the performance of agriculture and on the realisation of other development policy goals. It is recalled from the recent compilation by HLC (2009) that the share of agriculture in total investment in the economy has been declining more rapidly in 1990s (7.9%) and further declined to 7.4 per cent between 2000-2006. This decline is significant compared to share of 11.4 per cent share in 1980s and 15.3 per cent in 1970s.

- In addition to loss of momentum in capital formation in agriculture, compositional shift in the share of public sector and private sector in total investment in agriculture has also taken place. The share of public sector in total investment in agriculture has declined, and the decline has been more pronounced in 1990s (28%) and further to 23 per cent in 2005-06, as compared to 45 per cent in 1980s. It is quite obvious that public and private sector investment cannot be treated as substitutes.
- The investment behaviour of public sector and private sector is not the same. Public sector investment is deemed to be exogenously determined by the political economy compulsions, whereas private investment is found to be positively impacted by public investment, terms of trade, technology and institutional credit, and negatively impacted by incidence of rural poverty and percentage of area under marginal holdings.
- There are contradictory inferences drawn on the impact of public investment on private investment, i.e., the complementarity issue. With all the differences in inferences drawn, depending on choice of data set and choice of methodological construct for estimation, the broad inference suggests that there is positive inducement effect of public investment on private investment.
- The analysis of impact of capital formation on the growth performance of agriculture has become one of the methodological issues such as time lag between investment and growth response, choice of measurement of capital investment in agriculture and choice of equation. With all these methodological controversies, the major inference drawn is that investment in agriculture, rural literacy, terms of trade, institutional credit, cropping intensity and other infrastructural variables are found to have positive impact on agricultural productivity and production. This establishes the nexus between investment in agriculture and growth performance of the sector.
- Private investment is found to have direct and positive impact on poverty reduction via improved growth performance of agriculture; whereas public investment has positive impact on agriculture

productivity which in turn contributes for poverty reduction through employment, wages and fall in the price of food articles. It is also true that there are other determinants of poverty *viz.*, rural literacy, village electrification, terms of trade, rural roads and credit flow. In addition to investment in agriculture, these are also found to have positive impact on poverty reduction.

All these evidences and inferences lead to the conclusion that high rate of growth in capital stock in agriculture would lead to high rate of growth in agricultural productivity and poverty reduction. It is recalled that trend growth rates in capital stock, technology, gross irrigated area, electricity use and cropping intensity in agriculture have decelerated between 1980-81 and 1990-91 and between 1996-97 and 2005-06, and these trends have impacted adversely growth performance of agriculture and tempo of poverty reduction in India.

Micro (Farm Level) Evidences on Capital Structure: Impact and Determinants

Micro level evidences on various aspects of capital formation through investment in agriculture have been derived from the analysis of farm level two data sets, obtained from the Directorate of Economics and Statistics (DES), Ministry of Agriculture, Government of India (Chapter 4). The first data set consists of data of 15 states of India on land, animal capital, irrigation capital and farm machinery for the years 1994-95 and 2007-08. The second data set consists of data of three sample states *viz.*, Punjab (high productivity state), Andhra Pradesh (medium productivity state) and Orissa (low productivity state), with a total sample of 1,350 for two years *viz.*, 1994-95 and 2007-08. This data set is amenable for estimating growth rates of capital stock at farm level, composition of capital stock, factor intensity, factor productivity and determinants of farm level GVO, productivity of labour engaged in agriculture and farm level capital formation. Deflators developed by CSO have been used for converting the values of capital stock at current prices to values at constant prices, and deflator reported in NAS has been used for converting GVO at current prices to GVO at constant prices.

Broad Trends from the Analysis of Data of 15 States

- Growth rate analysis of non-land capital stock suggests that there has been hardly 0.72 per cent growth rate per annum.
- In the total capital stock, the share of land is found to be about 95 per cent. Among non-land capital assets, there has been a decline in the share of animal capital and an increase in the share of both farm machinery and irrigation capital.
- There been a decline in animal capital stock for every unit of farm machinery and irrigation capital. Farm machinery has established its increasing importance over irrigation capital.

Broad Results on Capital Formation in 3 Sample States

- As stated in earlier Section, the overall results on three states are recapitulated (ignoring the differences across states), and the overall results on three farm groups (ignoring differences across states).
- Four development experiences from the analysis of agro-economic features are extracted. First, per hectare productivity of land is found to vary directly with non-land capital stock per hectare. Second, productivity of labour and non-land capital stock per unit of labour are also found to vary directly. Third, productivity of land and percentage area irrigated are also positively related. Fourth, poverty is negatively related to intensity of capital stock, productivity of land, productivity of labour and intensity of irrigation.
- Among non-land capital assets, the growth rates of animal capital and farm machinery are found to be negative, while the growth rate of irrigation capital is found to be positive.
- The share of land in total capital stock is 95 per cent; irrigation capital, among non-land capital stocks, has increased its share, and farm machinery continues to enjoy the dominant share of 40 per cent.
- There has been a decline in non-land capital stock per hectare and per unit of labour.
- With respect to overall results from the disaggregative analysis of farm groups:

- o Marginal and small farms have experienced negative growth rates of land animal capital, and positive growth rates of irrigation capital and farm machinery. The share of land in total capital stock is found to be around 94 per cent. In case of composition of non-land capital assets, there has been a fall in the share of animal capital and increase in the share of irrigation capital and farm machinery. With respect to capital intensity, there has been marginal increase in capital stock per hectare and per unit of labour. Further with respect to productivity ratios, there has been an increase in GVO per unit of labour, land and capital during 2007-08 *vis-à-vis* 1994-95.
- o In case of semi–medium and medium farms, the growth rates of all capital components, excepting that of irrigation capital (due to high rate of irrigation capital growth in Punjab), are found to be negative. In total capital stock, land continues to dominate with a share of 96 per cent. In respect of composition of non-land capital stock, there has been a fall in the share of farm machinery and rise in the share of irrigation capital. Regarding factor intensity ratio, there has been a marginal decline in capital stock per unit of land and increase per unit of labour. There has been an increase in GVO per unit of land, labour and capital during 2007-08.
- o The large farms have experienced negative growth rates of all capital components, excepting that of irrigation capital. In total capital stock, 96 per cent share of land establishes the dominance of the asset. In case of non-land capital assets, there has been a decline in the share of farm machinery and increase in the share of irrigation capital. In the sample states, there has been a decline in the capital stock per unit of land and labour. However, GVO per unit of land, labour and capital has experienced an increase.

- In aggregative terms (cutting across the results from individual states and farm groups); animal capital, farm machinery, land, labour and credit availment have turned out to be important positive determinants of farm level GVO; animal capital, farm machinery, literacy and credit availment are found to have positive impact on labour productivity; land, credit availment and literacy level of farmers are identified as major positive determinants of capital formation at farm level. Even though macro results place importance on terms of trade and technological status as yet other important determinants of capital formation, these variables could not be included in farm level capital formation function due to same values for all the sample farms as well as lack of data availability.

Capital Formation in Irrigated and Rainfed Farms

The present section recapitulates results (Chapter 5) on capital formation in irrigated farms of Punjab and Andhra Pradesh (with a pooled sample of 831), and irrigated (531) and rainfed (69) farms of Andhra Pradesh.

- On irrigated farms (sample of 831).
- In overall there has been a negative growth rates of capital assets, excepting that of irrigation capital.
- Land is the most important asset in total capital stock, forming about 96 per cent.
- Among non-land capital stock, the share of farm machinery is the highest (40%), followed by irrigation capital (33%) and animal capital (27%).
- There has been a decline in capital stock per hectare of land, and marginal increase per unit of labour.
- There has been an increase in output (GVO) per unit of labour and per unit of land, and marginal increase in GVO per unit of non-land capital stock.
- Labour, land, credit availment, farmer literacy, farm machinery and animal capital have positive impact on GVO.
- Literacy, credit availment and farm machinery have positive impact on productivity of labour.
- The major determinants with positive impact on capital formation are land, credit availment and literacy.
- With regard to results on farm groups:

- o In case of marginal and small farms, there have been positive growth rates of irrigation and farm machinery and negative growth rates of land and animal capital; The share of land in total capital stock of these farms comes to 95 per cent. Among non-land capital assets, the share of animal capital and irrigation capital is over 30 per cent, and that of farm machinery 29 per cent, with regard to capital intensity, there has been an increase in capital stock per hectare and per unit of labour. These farms have also experienced an increase in GVO per unit of land, labour and capital. Land, labour, literacy and credit availment are found to have positive impact on GVO, literacy and credit availment have positive impact on productivity of labour, and land, credit availment and literacy are to found to have positive impact on capital formation at marginal and small farms.
- o In case of semi-medium and medium farms, there have been negative growth rates of all capital assets, excepting that of irrigation capital. The share of land in total capital stock is 96 per cent, and the share farm machinery in non-land capital assets 52 per cent and of animal capital and irrigation capital 25 per cent and 23 per cent respectively. There has been an increase in capital stock per unit of labour, but a decrease per unit of land, with regard to factor productivity, these farms have experienced an increase in GVO per unit of labour, land and capital. Animal capital, farm machinery, land, labour, literacy and credit availment are found to have positive impact on GVO, animal capital, farm machinery, literacy and credit availment have positive impact on productivity of labour and land, credit availment and literacy are the major determinants of capital formation with positive impact.
- o In case of large farms, there have been negative growth rates of farm machinery and animal capital, and positive growth rates of irrigation capital and land (marginal). Land forms 97 per cent of total capital stock, and farm machinery, among non-land capital assets with 59 per cent share. These farms have experienced a decline in capital stock per hectare and per unit of labour; with regard to factor productivity, there have been an increase in GVO

per unit of land, labour and capital. Farm machinery, land, labour, literacy and credit availment have positive impact on GVO, literacy, farm machinery and credit availment have positive impact on productivity of labour, and land, credit availment and literacy are found to be positive determinants of capital formation.

- On irrigated and rainfed farms of the sample state:
  - o The growth rates of all types and groups of capital have been found to be negative in case of irrigated farms of Andhra Pradesh, excepting that of a low positive growth of land; but in case of rainfed farms, excepting that of land and farm machinery, the growth rates of other capital assets are negative.
  - o Land forms 97 per cent of total capital stock in both irrigated and rainfed farms. Among non-land capital stock, animal capital shares 55 per cent in rainfed farms and 38 per cent in irrigated farms.
  - o With regard to capital intensity, there has been a decline in capital stock per hectare of land and marginal increase per unit of labour in irrigated farms. In case of rainfed farms, there has been a decline in capital stock per hectare as well as per unit of labour.
  - o With regard to factor productivity, both irrigated and rainfed farmers are found to have experienced an increase in GVO per unit of labour and capital, but a marginal fall in GVO per unit of land of irrigated farms and a marginal increase in GVO per unit of rainfed farms.
  - o The marginal and small irrigated as well as rainfed farms have experienced a fall in capital stock per hectare. The same trends are observed in case of irrigated and rainfed farms of other two groups. There has also been a fall in capital stock per unit of labour in irrigated as well as rainfed farms of all three farm groups, excepting marginal increase in case of rainfed marginal farms.
  - Regarding factor productivity of different farm groups, all the three farm groups have experienced an increase in GVO per unit of labour, capital and land.

- Animal capital, land, labour, literacy and credit availment are the major positive determinants of GVO of irrigated farms, and in case of rainfed farms, farm machinery, land, labour, literacy and credit availment have positive impact on GVO. Farm group-wise analysis of irrigated farms suggests that animal capital, land, labour, literacy and credit availment have positive impact on GVO of marginal and small farms, animal capital, labour, literacy and credit availment in case of semi-medium and medium irrigated farms, and farm machinery, land, labour and literacy in case of large farms. With respect to rainfed marginal and small farms and semi-medium and medium farms, farm machinery, land, labour, literacy and credit availment are found to have positive impact on GVO.

Pathways and Policy Directions

It has been rightly argued (HLC, 2009) that declining investment in agriculture over time at macro level has emerged as one of the binding constraints on the performance of Indian agriculture. At micro (farm) level also, capital growth in general is found to be negative, even though in case of capital assets like irrigation it has been positive. The disquieting trends in capital formation through investment in agriculture both at macro and micro level have slowed down the pace and pattern of agriculture growth and poverty reduction. Hence, the realisation that there is a need for identifying pathways and policy directions for accelerating investment in agriculture as a prime trigger for achieving the 'desired' rate of growth of rural sector. There are some important pathways and policy directions derived from the examination of macro and micro evidences on various aspects of capital formation.

It is recalled from earlier discussion that decline in investment in agriculture has been mainly public sector investment-led. In other words, there has been a decline in the share of public sector in capital formation from 45 per cent in 1980s to 23 per cent in 2005-06. Further, share of TFP in output growth has not merely been low, but also it has declined over a period of time. TFP growth depends on public policies such as investment in research, extension, education, natural resource management, and infrastructure such as irrigation, roads, electricity and so on. The studies by Fan *et al.* (2000; 2002) has brought out significant returns on public investment through its impact on poverty reduction. The public investment provides a kind of 'public goods', which impact positively investment in agriculture by private sector. Added to all these is the argument that public and private sector investments are not perfect substitutes. The next issue is what are the priority areas of investment by public sector in agriculture.

Public Investment Policies and Priorities

In formulating policies towards public investment in agriculture, many areas of priority have been suggested (Panagariya, 2008; Bisaliah, 2010a; Chand, 2011): irrigation, rural electrification, technology development and transfer, rural economic diversification, marketing system, roads, sunrise sectors, dryland agriculture, and reduction of regional and farm group-wise agriculture development disparities and rural human capital. All these lines of public investment are needed for faster growth of rural sector as well as more inclusive growth. Few elaborations on some of these priority areas of public investment are in order:

- The enhancement of public investment in irrigations needs to be coupled with some reforms, because the public sector investment portfolio in agriculture irrigation constitutes the single largest component and there is much to be desired in the management and operational efficiency of irrigation projects. Policy initiatives are required for coordinating the choice between new projects and better utilisation of existing ones. There has been a persistent gap between irrigation potential created and actual utilisation of irrigation water. Adequate investment has to be made for increasing operational efficiency of irrigation systems so as to reduce conveyance losses, distribution and utilisation of water. Further, efficiency of irrigation would also depend on promotion of institutional structures like water user association, water syndicates like the ones in France, and village level committees for management of tank irrigation system. Public investment for renovation of water bodies initiated by Government of India recently could prove to be a right step for rehabilitating tanks and other traditional method of water harvesting and storages, if the gap between public investment outlay and outcome is reduced through proper governance including public private participatory mode.

- It has been very well established that rural electrification impacts agricultural productivity through farm household investment in electric pumps. But there are regions where groundwater potential is underexploited, and others where it is overexploited, causing environmental concerns. Yet another problem with respect to rural electrification is transmission and distribution losses (estimated to be as high as 40%). Any effective implementation of rural electrification projects needs the support/involvement of local bodies like village *panchayats* and other people's organisations. Further, public investment will have to be made for promotion of solar and wind energy for tiding over the problems like hike in prices of conventional sources, uncertainties in supply and growing scarcity. The efficiency of public investment in providing subsidies to users of non-conventional energy sources especially for irrigation could be increased by providing subsidies to village as a unit.
- Another important area of public investment is for rural economic diversification as a part of rural transformation. There is much for India to learn how public investment could be an important instrument for rural socioeconomic transformation through the 'support' to rural non-farm sector (RNFS). The term 'rural' is no longer synonymous with agriculture or food production system (Planning Commission, 2010: 55). China has demonstrated the evolution of a new concept of 'rurality' within agriculture sector, and operationalised it for rural transformation with the support of public policies and investment for RNFS. Some of the major development premises, strategies and impacts of Chinese model of rural transformation through public policies and investment are as follows:
    - o Rural development does not have to live in the shadows of urban development; instead, there can be deliberate public investment in rural social and economic structure for rural growth.
    - o Rural economic diversification is a major driver of job creation and poverty alleviation.

- o Evolve rural economic diversification through the growth of rural towns.
- o Promote innovation and R&D through focussing on the needs of rural people, rural producers and firms.
- o Couple hard investment with better governance, institutions, social participation and policy process.
- o Rural transformation is about human development, as opposed to simply development of assets. It is recalled from previous Section of this chapter that in addition to capital accumulation in the form of physical assets, capital assimilation through investment in human capital is crucial for growth/development in any sector. This requires not only social support system through investment in social sectors, but also a special focus is needed for skill development of rural people though the provision of technical literacy, so that there can be occupational mobility of rural people at least first in the rural sector.
- o In addition to heavy investments for inclusive, sustainable and diversified rural growth, and right governance system and policy process, the institutional structures for improving the efficiency and effectiveness of public policies and programmes could be yet another important pillar of rural transformation (Planning Commission, 2010). The RNFS in China (covering informal manufacturing sector, trade and construction and so on) is closely connected to the development of small towns. It is premised in the Chinese model that public investment for developing towns can contribute for job creation, occupation mobility, food security and for improving public service delivery in rural areas. In fact, rural economic diversification in China (Ibid.) has been achieved through support to township and village enterprises (TVEs). TVEs have grown from 1.5 million in 1978 to 23 million in 2006, providing 119 million jobs and contributing 40 per cent of China's export products. Further, it is reported (Ibid.) that during 1983-1993, the share of farm job was 60 per cent and of non-farm 40 per cent. But in 1999-2004, the share of farm job was about 40 per cent, and of non-farm almost 60 per cent.

In a move for shared learning (Ibid.) from the emerging areas such as China, India, Brazil and South Africa, many useful development lessons have emerged for the promotion of rural economic diversification and rural socioeconomic transformation through the development of RNFS (Dev, 2008; Bisaliah, 2010a). In addition to China, Brazil has also realised that new opportunities for agri-based enterprises is one key element to employment and economic diversification (details in Planning Commission, 2010). South Africa has launched a policy of subsidy for light manufacturing sector so that they can survive in rural areas (Ibid.). In Vietnam, experience of crop diversification by farmers to shift from low value to high value crops with the support of public investment for technology and market development would offer yet another development perspective on rural growth and poverty alleviation. The Chinese model of implementation has provided a useful lesson for other countries.

That is, diversification of the rural economy beyond its agrarian tradition is one of the major drivers of rural transformation. The provision of infrastructure including information and communication technologies (ICTs), and development of new economic alternatives such as small scale manufacturing, and agro-processing feature as major enablers of economic diversifications in China. In India, agri-rural industry relationships are yet to be triggered on a scale needed for this country. It is reported that only about 2 per cent of India's raw materials from agriculture are processed compared to 80-90 per cent in North America. Further, value addition by processing is only 7 per cent in India compared to 23 per cent in China (Chadha and Gulati, 2007). With low processing of perishable commodities like fruits and vegetables it is not surprising that post-harvest losses in India range from 30-40 per cent. Hence, Chinese model focussing on institutions, innovations, market reform and infrastructure could be critical for the development of both agriculture and RNFS in India. All these would need the support of 'big push' in public investment to address the development policy goals of faster and more inclusive growth.

- It is realised that TFP has to be a major source of productivity and output growth in crop and livestock sectors in India. As TFP increases, the cost of production decreases benefitting both the producers and consumers, and the lower cost of production would enhance the competitive edge of Indian agriculture. But TFP growth rate has been falling over time (Ranjita *et al.*, 2005; Chand *et al.*, 2011). In yet another study (Tripathi, n.d.), covering data for a period of 37 years (1969 to 2005), it has concluded that agriculture growth in India has relied almost on increase in conventional factors—land, labour and capital, while TFP growth was negative with some positive value for the period 1990-91 to 1995-96. TFP growth for the entire period of 37 years in agriculture was negative (-11), and for the period between 1996-97 to 2005-06, it was -1.87. Further it has been estimated (Mittal *et al.*, 2005) that TFP growth has been declining in wheat farming, a major staple food grain. There are many other studies (Dholakia *et al.*, 1993; Desai and Namboodiri, 1998; Chand *et al.*, 2005; Kumar *et al.*, 2005) which have highlighted the importance of TFP growth. In a recent study (Chand *et al.*, 2011), it is reported that TFP in Indian agriculture is not merely low, but also it is on the decline. This implies small and declining share of TFP in output growth in crop and livestock sector in India, and output growth has been mainly input growth-led. But in order to sustain food security and other development goals of agriculture, the achievement of the projected rise in production of food and non-food commodities will have to be effected through the enhancement of productivity per unit of land for which a steady positive growth in TFP is essential. There are many sources of TFP growth such as agriculture R&D, education, extension, infrastructure, irrigation, natural resource management and so on. Of these sources, investment in agriculture research is considered as quite crucial for developing land, capital and labour augmenting technologies by increasing their productivity and thereby shifting production function upward and unit cost function downward. The returns to investment in agriculture research have been estimated as 42 per cent which is quite a significant contribution to national economy, and research investment is to be considered a priority area of public investment in agriculture. It is also reported (Alston *et al.*, 1998) that return to investment in agriculture research is about 50 per cent to Asian region implying under investment in agriculture research. It is also reported (Golait *et al.*, 2008) that out of the total investment made in the world on agriculture science and technology during 2000, developed countries shared about 62 per cent, and developing countries about 38 per cent. The present level of public investment in agriculture in India is a little over 0.5 per cent of AGDP, whereas in western countries it is about 2 per cent.

It is argued (Chand *et al.*, 2011) that public funding for research in agriculture should be raised to at least one per cent of AGDP, implying a big push in the allocation of public resources to agriculture research system. Coupled with jump in public investment in agriculture, research is the needed reform in agriculture research management system.

In addition to TFP growth at national level, regional variations in TFP growth to the extent of negative/low TFP growth in some crops and regions (states or cluster of states like Eastern India) have to be kept in view while allocating public investment. This is in tune with the argument that public policies including investment policies are to be designed and implemented for addressing the growth problems of regions such as Gangetic of different growth centres plains, Eastern India and rainfed regions. For example compared to northern states, ICORs are lower in eastern states (Bisaliah, 2004) where more public investment is required, not merely because of low ICORs, but also because majority of the rural poor are concentrated. (details on this issue in Chand *et al.*, 2011). Unless the situations of negative/low/stagnant/moderate/high growth rates in TFP growth rates across regions and crops are considered while allocating public investible resources, it will be difficult to maintain the tempo of agriculture growth at the national level. Hence, public investment in lagging regions, farm groups and crops should receive high priority. It is suggested that public investment in less favoured regions not only offers the largest poverty reduction per unit of spending, but also leads to the highest economic returns (HLC 2009: 267-68).

- Small holders of India and rainfed farming are two major areas of priority for public investment. Among others, small holders of India need innovative institutions such as 'clustering approach', and support to linking these farmers with processors and retailers. If the concept of agri-business is to be applied to small holders, public policies and investment will have to focus on 'farmers group' as a development unit for support from the government.

Yet another important concern is the low productivity of rainfed farming (occupying over 60 per cent of cropped area in India) due to hostile agro-climatic regime, and where the majority of the rural poor live. These 'non-elite' farmers need to be oriented to assimilate technology, management and marketing dimensions of agriculture growth. Farmers in these regions are confronted with degraded and depleted natural resource base, biological disequilibrium, and adverse effects of climate change. If the farmers of these rainfed farming regions are oriented in development culture through development education with public policy support and participation of voluntary organisations, production potential of dry farming itself could be a new source of agriculture growth in India (Dwarakinath, 2009). Reaching these 'unreached' through the strategy of 'building on the rest' (not merely 'building on the best') through public investment could help Indian agriculture to overcome the stagnant/ decelerated growth in agriculture. Hence in the absence of 'big push' in agriculture investment with enhanced public investment and with favourable policy environment for private sector to invest in agriculture, the problems of food insecured regions and people (not merely in terms of food availability but also in terms of accessibility with adequate purchasing power), widely prevalent malnourishment and undernourishment (accelerated further by food price inflation) especially of children and women, and high intensity of hunger among lower strata of Indian society would continue to persist.

Related to this issue of public investment to support less favoured regions and farm groups is to make public investment for meeting the challenges of climate change and its profound adverse impact on the poor. The public investment can be made to set up Climate Risk Management, Research and Training Centres so as to address the problems of technology generation and transfer systems in 128 agro-climate zones of the country. Further, public investment is needed for rebuilding of natural resource base to minimise the potential risks from climate change.

- It has already been discussed in the preceding sections that public investment in irrigation (both development and management reforms), rural electrification, rural economic diversification, agricultural research (for steady growth of TFP), small holder development, rainfed regions and other growth centres is crucial for faster and more inclusive growth in rural sector. There are many other areas of rural infrastructure such as roads, market yards, storage, public credit system, processing of farm products so as to add value and to promote value chain, and supply chain in input market which need public policy support and investment.

All these would validate the proposition that public and private investments cannot be substitutes in many critical areas, mainly because of differences in their objective function and their investment project portfolio. Public investment is imperative for 'honouring' many policy development goals like development support for lagged/bypassed regions, farm groups, non-farm sector in rural areas, and provision of adequate and quality supportive services for agriculture as a part of 'public good' component. There is no basis for complacency about the role of public sector investment in agriculture which is vital for inducing both farm household and corporate investment. The Structural Adjustment Programme of Economic Reform Regime prescribing reduction in the development role of the state, assumes that private investment will rise when public investment declines (i.e., crowding-in/out effects). This assumption may be valid if immediate profitability of investment is considered. The larger development agenda is not expected to be addressed by private sector, and that continues to be the domain of public sector investment. It is difficult to expect private investment in areas like watershed development, rebuilding natural resource base, large irrigation projects, investment in social sectors, certain areas of technology development and transfer, development of backward regions and lagging farm households, market support system, sound biological environment for farming, rural roads and other rural infrastructural facilities. Hence, in the absence of adequate public investment in many critical areas and regions, the strategy of fast-track privatisation will not occur. Private corporate sector may be willing to branch into favoured regions, and into other regions only when adequate public investment in rural infrastructure is made. Even though it is mainly the responsibility of the public sector to address the problems of infrastructure deficit, participation of corporate sector may be encouraged with a regulatory framework to safeguard the interests of users. But the amount of public investment needed for making Indian agriculture is quite high. For example infrastructural investment was 19 per cent of GDP in China as compared to 2 per cent in India in the 1990s (Dev, 2008). Given this magnitude of gap, a huge amount of investible resources are required for public investment. There are two areas which need the review of public policy *viz.*, policy of input subsidy and the use of Rural Infrastructural Development Fund (RIDF) by state government.

- With the activisation of RIDF and further augmentation of funds, there is an increase in resource availability of funds for public investment. But the challenge is the choice of investment project portfolio by the public sector. In addition to providing funds under RIDF to the state government for the lines of investment governed by the guidelines on RIDF utilisation, funds could also be provided for setting up food processing units, production and export of medicinal and aromatic plants, and for recapitalisation of cooperative banks which provide funds for investment by farm households.
- Diversion of public resources from capital to current expenditure in the form of subsidies has been one of the reasons for decline in public investment in agriculture. Added to this is the failure to realise the importance of non-price interventions for agriculture growth. Redirecting public expenditure away from subsidies towards expenditure on non-price determinants of agriculture growth like R&D, rural economic diversification, irrigation development and management, infrastructure, and development of less favoured regions and farmers would contribute for both faster and more inclusive growth. These public investments, augmented through reduction in subsidies, will have positive impact on farm household and corporate investment.

The debate on the role of subsidies *vis-à-vis* investment in agriculture has generated enough research efforts (Mundle *et al.*, 1991; Gulati *et al.*, 1995; 1997; Roy *et al.*, 2001; Chand and Kumar, 2004; Thamarajakshi, 1999 and others). It is argued that subsidies in Indian agriculture, even though not high compared to developed countries, have become unsustainable. Subsidies especially on fertiliser, power and irrigation water are crowding out productive investment. The direct fiscal effect, cropping pattern effect, environmental effect and equity effects of subsidies are far from desirable. The desired fiscal discipline as a part of economic reforms in India has led to cut back on public investment in agriculture, but not cut back on input subsidies. For example, a modest subsidy reduction, say 20 per cent, would enable Government to double its investment in agriculture (Kapila, 2009). The study by Chand and Kumar (2004) has estimated that instant return on one rupee subsidy is about three rupees (in terms of impact of subsidy on AGDP), and less than one rupee return on one rupee public investment in capital stock. But this is the impact of only one year.

If one year return to investment in public sector capital stock is multiplied by the expected life of capital stock, the total impact is estimated to be more than double the impact of subsidies. These results would point towards downsising subsidies in a selective phased manner and plough back the resources to increase public investment in agriculture. Hence, it is possible to compensate the farmers through more public investment in other areas to enhance the role of non-price factors in productivity growth and thereby output growth. Added to the increased public investment is the needed institutional reform for improving terms of trade in agriculture, instead of treating downsising of subsidies as an independent policy instrument. In fact, the Tenth Five Year Plan of India (2002-2007) has called for a review of policies which led to the diversion of scarce resources away from the creation of productive assets, and the reversal of the declining trend of public sector investment by better targetting subsidies. Political economy compulsions appear to be still strong enough to prevent quick actions on this call for a revision of policies on allocation of public resources.

- Finally, public policy support is needed for institution transformation though social capital accumulation such as preparing stakeholders for collective management of agricultural development programmes such as extension services, water resource management, and management of other rural infrastructure. Mobilising farmer groups as a development unit for watershed/ catchment management/integrated pest management/credit delivery, and for forging the development alliance with corporate sector is quite a development support strategy. These local groups, guided by external professionals, could contribute for augmentation of human capital in rural areas which could be a major deep driver of rural growth and which could contribute for increasing marginal efficiency of both public and farm household investment. Both capital accumulation and assimilation of efficiency contents of capital stock will be facilitated by rural human capital.

With proper management of public sector assets such as their ICOR could be decreased, and with lower rate of investment, targetted agriculture output growth rate could be achieved (Bisaliah, 2004). For example, 12.6 per cent growth rate in investment is required (as against the current rate of 4 per cent). If ICOR is brought down to 3.0 through the improved efficiency in the use of public sector assets in agriculture sector, the investment growth rate of 7.91 per cent (as against 12.6%) is enough to attain targetted output growth rate (Roy *et al.*, 2001).

Public Policy Regime for Inducing Private Investment

There are many reasons for which an appropriate public policy regime is needed for 'inducing' private investment in agriculture. First, 90 per cent of private investment (see Bisaliah, 2004 for earlier estimate of 95 per cent) is from millions of farm households (HLC, 2009: Chapter XIII). Hence, the focus is mainly on building rationale for enabling public policy regime to support farm level investment by farmers. Second, the share of private sector investment in agriculture has increased from 55 per cent in 1980s to 77 per cent in 2005-06. Third, the trend of increased share of private investment has been accompanied by decrease in ICOR, one of the measures for increased efficiency of investment in the sector. Fourth, given the commitment of public funds to address broader development agenda, the possibility of considerable hike in public investment to reverse decelerated growth of investment in agriculture sector is not high. Hence, Government has to create a favourable policy and supportive development environment for private investment (both domestic and foreign) to fill the investment gap in agriculture sector. Fifth, there has been a paradigm shift from public sector dominance in infrastructure investment to public-private sector partnership.

There are some compelling reasons, based on micro level evidences on capital formation in agriculture, and for public policy support to 'induce' private sector investment in agriculture. First, in general negative/low growth rates of capital stock (excepting that of irrigation capital) at farm level, dominance of land capital forming over 90 per cent of total capital (implying under capitalisation of Indian agriculture), and decline in capital stock per unit of land and labour are compulsive enough to warrant public policy support to farm level capitalisation of agriculture. Second, farm level evidences from sample states also support the theorem that capital intensity and productivity of land as well as labour are positively related. This also implies the need for more policy support for capital deficit regions, where marginal productivity of capital could be more, particularly in rainfed regions. Third, the evidences from the analysis of results from rainfed farms leads to infer that the growth rates of capital assets are negative, land forms the dominant capital asset, and decline in capital stock per unit of land and labour (in case of all three farm groups).

This also is compulsive enough for public policy support in case of less favoured farmers of rainfed regions. Fourth, in sample state of Punjab, higher capital intensity per unit of land and labour than in Andhra Pradesh is found to have led to higher output per unit of land and labour. This establishes the theorem that capital intensity and productivity of land and labour are positively related. Further, output per unit of capital is more in Andhra Pradesh than in Punjab implying 'adequate' amount of capital stock with farmers of Punjab and inadequate amount of capital stock in Andhra Pradesh. Hence, is the need for policy support to 'capital deficit' regions where marginal productivity of capital could be more. In this context, particular reference to imperatives of policy support to rainfed farms is made, based on empirical evidences derived from the analysis of capital formation in irrigated and rainfed farms of Andhra Pradesh. Negative growth rates of capital stock in rainfed farms (in irrigated farms also), land farming 97 per cent of total capital stock and decline in capital stock per unit of land and labour (in case of all three farm groups), higher GVO per unit of capital, and lower capital intensity per unit of land and labour are yet another set of reasons for policy support for rainfed farms.

Yet another compelling reason for public policy support to farmers for capital formation is the saving behaviour of farmers in India. The relationship between savings and investment, and investment and economic growth have been well established (HLC, 2009: Chapter II). Growth rate in the farm economy depends largely on the stock of capital built by farmers, which in turn depends on savings at the farm level (details on farm level savings in HLC, 2009: Chapter XIII). At macro level, India continues to remain one of the highest saving economies among the emerging economies, with 98 per cent of investment funded by domestic savings. (See Chandra and Sen, 2004 for details on saving performance in India, also Mohan, 2008). But in case of farm sector, it has been estimated by NSSO Survey (2002-03) that there are dissavings in the farm sector (HLC, 2009: 303). Agricultural savings as a percentage of AGDP is estimated to be -16.3, and total amount of cash loan as a percentage of AGDP is estimated to be 19.2. This has widened the gap between the amount of savings and investment in the farm sector. Hence, generation and mobilisation of savings in the farm sector is crucial for enhancing the level of investment at farm level so as to realise the growth potential of farm sector. This reinforces the need for public policy support to enhance investment by farm households.

With these rationale for 'enabling public policy support' for private investment, there is a need for identifying critical areas where public policy support could 'induce' private investment in farm sector. The critical areas are identified, based on both macro and micro empirical evidences.

- It is recalled from earlier discussion on macro evidences on capital formation that private investment is found to be positively impacted by public investment, terms of trade, technology and institutional credit and negatively impacted by incidence of rural poverty and percentage of area under marginal holdings. These determinants of investment behaviour of farm households are suggestive of the needed enabling policy regime for increasing farm-household investment.
    - o With the positive impact of public investment on private investment, the public investment that will have more impact on private investment will have to find a place in the public sector investment portfolio like irrigation and power, in addition to other priority areas of public investment discussed earlier.
    - o The positive impact of terms of trade on private investment would call for review of input-output price policy. Gradual withdrawal of subsidies should be coupled with ploughing back the resources for public investment which could maintain a

steady growth of TFP, the determinants of which have been discussed earlier. With high TFP, unit cost of production of farm output will decrease to make Indian agriculture competitive both in domestic and international markets. That would tilt terms of trade in favour of farm sector.

- The result of positive impact of technology on private investment could make 'technology' as an instrument for increasing private farm investment. It has been discussed that fatigue in technology generation and transfer systems has slowed down technology flow to farming sector compared to early Green Revolution period in India. This establishes the need for a critical review of institutional structures established for the purpose, and 'appropriateness' of present research and extension priorities of public sector which is expected to provide technological support as a public good to farm sector.
- Private investment is also found to be positively impacted by flow of institutional credit. This has been reinforced by the micro evidences that credit availment has positive impact on farm level GVO, productivity of labour engaged in agriculture, and on capital formation by farm households. However, a review of interest rate, credit limit for various purposes of credit availment by farmers, eligible amount of availment, repayment schedule, and credit delivery mechanism would provide the directions for streamlining the institutional credit system. Further, there is a need for policy initiative to introduce 'supervised credit' system, especially in case of investment credit where some technical guidance is required for farmers to make choice of farm level investment projects.
- Farmers 'literacy' is found to have positive impact on farm level GVO, productivity of labour engaged in agriculture and farm level capital formation. This component of human capital used in the analysis of micro level evidences on capital formation would reinforce the widely agreed premise that human capital does 'matter' in farm sector also, and public policy support for more investment in rural literacy, among investment in other

components of social sector, is justified in view of its positive impact at the farm level.

- o The negative impact of percentage area under marginal holdings on private investment is in suggestive of 'group approach' policy design to increase investment. This is in line with 'clustering approach' to support these farmers by treating farmers group as a development unit.
- o It is recalled that productivity of labour engaged in agriculture is a major requisite for addressing the problem of prevalence of poverty and hunger. The pooled data analysis of labour productivity function of this study suggests the positive influence of farmer literacy, credit availment, irrigation capital (in case of Punjab) and farm machinery on productivity of labour. This result is also indicative of directions for policy interventions for promoting literacy among farmers, for placing the institutional credit system for proper credit delivery, for supporting irrigation infrastructure, and for supporting acquisition of farm machinery through credit support.

So far the focus of the discussion of this section has been to identify the factors which are vital for inducing investment by farm households, for increasing farm level GVO and productivity of labour engaged in agriculture. Yet, one more area of public policy support is for forging the development alliance between farmers and corporate sector (even though a minor player in total private investment in farm sector). It is obvious that the investment portfolio of corporate sector is different from that of farmers. The investment portfolio of corporate sector consists of production, processing and value addition in areas such as seed, bio-fertilisers, biopesticides, agricultural implements/machinery, food, and host of horticulture products such as vegetables, flowers and medicinal and aromatic plants. These could also be investment candidates for cooperative sector. In many of these investment projects, the scope for development tie-up between corporate sector and farmers is quite high, and it has emerged on a considerable scale in the various versions of contract production. This kind tie-up has backward and forward linkages between corporate sector and farmers. It is incontrovertible that this development alliance itself could be a source of growth in productivity and production in farm sector.

But public policy support should go beyond tax holidays for corporate sector investment in rural areas, one of which is a regulatory system with built-in-checks to ensure win-win game for all the stakeholders, and yet another is investment in rural infrastructure by public sector without which corporate sector will not venture into investment in rural sector.

References

Adelman, I. and C.T. Morris (1973). *Economic Growth and Social Equity in Developing Countries*. Stanford: Stanford University Press.

Aghion, P., E. Caroli and C. Garcia Penalosa (1999). "Inequality and Economic Growth: The Perspective of the New Growth Theories", *Journal of Economic Literature* XXXVII: 1615-60. December.

Aghion, P., and P. Howitt (1992). "A Model of Growth Through Creative Destruction", *Econometrica* 60(2): 323-51. March.

Ahluwalia, M.S., N.G. Carter and H.B. Chenery (1979). "Growth and Poverty in Developing Countries", *Journal of Development Economics* 6(2).

Ahluwalia, M. S. (1985). "Rural Poverty, Agricultural Production and Prices", in J.W. Mellor and G.M. Desai (eds.), *Agricultural Change and Rural Poverty*. Baltimore: Johns Hopkins University Press.

Alagh, Y. K. (1994). "Macro Policies for Indian Agriculture", in G.S. Bhalla (ed.), *Economic Liberalization and Indian Agriculture*. New Delhi: Institute for Studies in Industrial Development.

———. (1997). "Agricultural Investment and Growth Indian", *Journal of Agricultural Economics* 52(2).

Alauddin, M. and M. Hossain (2001). *Environment and Agriculture in a Developing Economy: Problems and Prospects for Bangladesh.* Chelten-Ham and Northampton. Edward Elgar.

Alston, J.M., B.J. Craig and P.G. Pardey (1998). "Dynamics in the Creation and Depreciation of Knowledge and the Returns to Research", *Discussion Paper* (35). Washington D.C: IFRI.

Aron, J. (2000). "Growth and Institutions", *A Review of the Evidence* 15(1), The World Bank Research Observer.

Arrow, K.J. (1962). "The Economic Implications of Learning by Doing", *Review of Economic Studies* 29(3)

Barro, R.J. and G.S. Becker (1989). "Fertility Choice in Model of Economic Growth", *Econometrica* 57(2), March.

Barro, R.J. and X. Sala-i-Martin (1995). *Economic Growth.* New York: McGraw-Hill.

Bathla, S., and S. Thorat (2006). "Trends and Determinants of Public Investment in Indian Agriculture at the Regional Level", *Man and Development* 28(2) June.

Baulch, B. and N. McCulloch (1999). *Tracking Pro-Poor Growth*. Sussex: Institute of Development Studies.

Becker, G.S. (1964). *Human Capital: A Theoretical and Empirical Analysis with Reference to Education*. New York: National Bureau of Economic Research.

Bezemer, D. and D. Headey (2008). "Agriculture Development and Urban Bias", *World Development* 36(8): 1342-64, August.

Bhaduri, A. (2008). "Growth and Employment in the Era of Globalisation: Some Lessons from the Indian Experience", *ILO Asia-Pacific Working Paper,* New Delhi, January.

Bhatia, M.S. (1999). "Rural Infrastructure and Growth in Agriculture", *Economic and political Weekly*. March 27.

Bils, M. and P.J. Klenow (2000). "Does Schooling Cause Growth?", *American Economic Review* 90(5).

Bisaliah, S. (2004). "Capital Formation in Indian Agriculture: Growth, Composition, Determinants and Policy Directions", *Consultancy Report to ADB*, Manila.

———. (2006). "Economic policy Cycle and Major Impact Dimensions of Indian Economic Reforms", (*Mimeo*).

———. (2009a). "Capital Formation In/For Agriculture: A Proposal for Cross Country Study", *Consultancy Report to FAO,* Rome.

———. (2009b). "Growth of Agriculture-Horticulture Sectors and Livelihood Security", *International Conference on Horticulture For Livelihood Security and Economic Growth.* Bangalore: PNASF.

———. (2009c). *The Context, Complexity and Concerns of Indian Agriculture: Growth Drivers and Directions*. Bangalore: Institute of Agricultural Technologists.

———. (2010a). "Capital Formation, Agriculture Growth and Poverty: Conceptual and Empirical Constructs", *Consultancy Report to FAO,* Rome.

———. (2011). *Capital Structure in Irrigated Farms of India*: *Growth, Composition, Intensity and Productivity*.

Bisaliah, S. *et al.* (2010). "Private Capital Formation in Indian Agriculture: An Analysis of Farm Level Data", *Consultancy Report to FAO, Rome.*

Blarcom, B.V., O. Knudsen and J.D. Nash (1993). "The Reform of Public Expenditures for Agriculture", *World Bank Discussion Papers* (216).

Bose, A. (2007). "Employment", in K. Basu (ed.), *The Oxford Companion to Economics in India.* New Delhi: Oxford University Press.

Borguignon, F. (2003). "The Poverty–Growth-Inequality Triangle", *Conference on Poverty, Inequality and Growth.* Paris.

Broadberry, S. and B. Gupta (2009). "The Historical Roots of India's Service-Led Development: A Sectoral Analysis of Anglo-India productivity Differences: 1870-2000", Department of Economics University of Warwick, United Kingdom.

Cairncross, A.K. (1966). *The Short Term and Long Term in Planning*. Economic Development Institute, Washington D.C. January 6.

Chadha, G.K. (2003). "Indian Agriculture in the New Millennium: Human Resource to Technology Challenges", *Indian Journal of Agricultural Economics* 58(1), January-March.

Chadha, G.K. and Ashok Gulati (2007). "Performance of Agro–Industries in India. Emerging Issues and Prospects", in P.K. Joshi *et al.* (eds.), *Agriculture Diversification and Small Holders in South Asia.* New Delhi: *Academic Foundation*.

Chakrabarti, S. and A. Kundu (2009). "Rural Non-Farm Economy: A Note on the Impact of Crop-Diversification and Land-Conservation in India", *Economic and Political Weekly* XLIV(12), March 21.

Chand, R. (2000). "Emerging Trends and Regional Variations in Agricultural Investment and their Implications for Growth and Equity", *Policy Paper,* National Center for Agricultural Economics and Policy Research, New Delhi.

———. (2001). "Emerging Trends and Issues in Public and Private Investment in Indian Agriculture: A State-wise Analysis", *Indian Journal of Agricultural Economics* 56(2). April-June.

———. (2005). "Exploring Possibilities of Achieving Four Percent Growth Rate in Indian Agriculture", *NCAP-WP-*(01) 2005, New Delhi.

Chand, R. and P. Kumar (2004). "Determinants of Capital Formation and Agriculture Growth: Some New Explorations", *Economic and Political Weekly,* December 25.

Chand, R. and S.S. Raju (2008). "Instability in Indian Agriculture: Different Phases of Technology and Policy", *Discussion Paper,* NPP 01/2008. National Centre for Agriculture Economics and Policy Research. New Delhi.

Chand, R., P. Kumar and S. Kumar (2011). "Total Factor Productivity and Contribution of Research Investment to Agriculture Growth in India", *Policy Paper* 25, National Centre for Agricultural Economics and Policy Research, New Delhi.

Chandra, Prema and K. Sen (2004). "The Determinants of Private Saving in India", *World Development* 32(3).

Chenery, H., Montek S. Ahluwalia, C.L.G. Bell, John H. Duloy and Richard Jolly (1974). *Redistribution with Growth.* New York: Oxford University Press.

Chenery, H.B. (1986). *Industrialization and Growth: A Comparative Study.* World Bank, Washington.D.C

Chow, G.C. (1993). "Capital Formation and Economic Growth in China", *The Quarterly Journal of Economics* 108(3).

Christensen, L.R. (1975). "Concepts and Measurement of Agricultural Productivity", *American Journal of Agricultural Economics* 57(5): 910-15.

Christaensen, L.R., L. Demery and J. Kuhl (2006). "The Role of Agriculture in Poverty Reduction", *Policy Research Working Paper* (4013), World Bank: Washington.D.C.

Clark, E. (1940). *The Conditions of Economic Progress.* London: Macmillan.

Cline, W.R. (2004). *Trade Policy and Global Poverty.* Washington D.C.: Center for Global Development and Institute for International Economics.

Collins, S. and Barry P. Bosworth (1996). "Economic Growth in East Asia: *Accumulation versus Assimilation", Brookings Papers on Economic Activity* 2: 135-91.

Correa, R. (2008). "Locking in Private Investment in Indian Agriculture", *Institute of South Asian Studies* (40), Singapore. November 12.

Craig, B.J., P.G. Pardey and J. Roseboom (1997). "International Productivity Patterns: Accounting for Input Quality, Infrastructure and Research", *American Journal of Agricultural Economics* 79.

Dantwala, M.L. (1986). "Strategy of Agricultural Development Since Independence", in M.L. Dantwala (ed.), *Indian Agricultural Development Since Independence.* New Delhi: Oxford and IBH Publishing Co.

Dasgupta, S. and Ajit Singh (2005). "Will Services be the New Engine of Economic Growth in India", *Working Paper* 310, Centre for Business Research, University of Cambridge U.K.

Datt, G. and M. Ravallion (1992). "Growth and Redistribution Components of Changes in Poverty Measures: A Decomposition with Applications to Brazil and India in the 1980s", *Journal of Development Economics* 38(2): 275-95.

———. (1995). "Why Have Some Indian States Done Better than Others in Reducing Poverty", *World Bank Paper*, Washington D.C.

———. (1999). "When is Growth Pro-Poor: Evidence from the Diverse Experiences of India's States", *World Bank Working Papers*.

Datt, G., V. Kozel and M. Ravallion (2003). "A Model- Based Assessment of India's Progress in Reducing Poverty in the 1990s", *Economic and Political Weekly*, 25 January.

Datt, R. (2006). "Agricultural Development and Capital Formation in Agriculture", *Young Indian*, March.

David, A.A. (1993). *Public Infrastructure Investment: A Bridge to Productivity Growth?* New York: Jerome Levy Economic Institute.

Davison, A.C. and D.V. Hinkley (1997). *Bootstrap Methods and Their Applications*. Cambridge: Cambridge University Press.

Deininger, K. and Lyn Squire (1998). "New Ways of Looking at Old Issues: Inequality and Growth", *Journal of Development Economics* 57.

Desai, B.M. and N.V. Namboodiri (1998). "Determinants of Total Factor Productivity in Indian Agriculture", *Economic and Political Weekly* 32(52).

Desai, B.M. and E. D'Souza (1999). "Economic Reforms, Terms of Trade, Aggregate Supply and Private Investment", *Economic and Political Weekly*, 15 May.

Desai, B.M. (2002). "Policy Framework for Reorientation of Agricultural Development", *Indian Journal of Agricultural Economics* 57(1). January-March.

———. (2006). "Investment Credit to Agriculture", *Economic and Political Weekly*, 25. February.

Dev, S.M. (1997). "Subsidies and Investments in Indian Agriculture: Issues and Perspectives", *Paper* (39). Rajiv Gandhi Institute for Contemporary Studies, New Delhi.

———. (2002). "Bold Initiatives Needed on Agriculture and Rural Employment", *Economic and Political Weekly* 37(12).

———. (2006). "Half-Hearted Attention to Agriculture", *Economic and Political Weekly*, April 8

———. (2008). *Challenges for Revival of Indian Agriculture*. New Delhi: National Centre for Agricultural Economics and Policy Research.

Dev, S.M. and A. Ranade (1998a). "Rising Food Prices and Rural Poverty: Going Beyond Correlations", *Economic and Political Weekly* 33(39). September 26.

Dhawan, B.D. (1996). "Trends and Determinants of Capital Formation in Indian Agriculture", *Indian Journal of Agricultural Economics* 51(4). April.

———. (1998). *Studies in Agricultural Investments and Rural Savings*. New Delhi: Common Wealth Publishers.

Dhawan, B.D. and S.S. Yadav (1997). "Public Investments in Indian Agriculture: Trends and Determinants", *Economic and Political Weekly* 32(14) April 5.

Dholakia, R.H. *et al.* (1993). "Growth of Total Factor Productivity in Indian Agriculture", *Indian Economic Review* 28(1).

Dollar, D. and A. Kraay (2002). "Growth is Good for the Poor", *Journal of Economic Growth* 7(3): 195-225.

Domar, E. (1947). "Expansion and Employment", *American Economic Review.* March.

Dougherty, C. and D. Jorgenson (1996). "International Comparison of Sources of Growth", *American Economic Association Papers and Proceedings.*

Dwarakinath, R. (2009). *Dry Farming as the Second Front in Agriculture Development.* Bangalore: Science and Technology Academy.

Easterly, W and R. Levine (1997). "Africa's Growth Tragedy: Policies and Ethnic Divisions", *Quarterly Journal of Economics* 112(4).

Easterly, W. (2001). *The Elusive Quest for Growth, Economists Adventures and Misadventures in the Topics.* Cambridge: MIT Press.

Eastwood, R. and M. Lipton (2000). "Pro-Poor Growth and Pro-Growth Poverty Reduction: Meaning, Evidence and Policy Implications", *Asian Development Review* 18(2).

Engle, R.F. *et al.* (1997). "Co-integration and Error Correction", *Econometrica* 55(2).

ESCAP (2008). *Economic and Social Survey of Asia and Pacific.* United Nations.

Fan, S. *et al.* (2000). "Government Spending, Growth and Poverty in Rural India", *American Journal of Agricultural Economics.*

Fan, S. *et al.* (2002). "Growth, Inequality and Poverty in Rural China: The Role of Public Investment", *Research Report* 125. Washington D.C.: IFRI.

Fan, S. *et al.* (2003). *Impacts of Public Investments on Poverty Reduction in Thailand.* Washington.D.C.: IFRI.

FAO (1999). "Investment in Agriculture for Food Security", *Twenty Fifth Session of the World Food Summit,* 31 May-30 June, Rome.

———. (2001). "Mobilising Resources to Fight Hunger", Committee on World Food Security, Rome 28, May-June 1.

———. (2011). *Creating a Framework for Agricultural Investment Policy and Programme.* Development Support Division. Rome.

Fields, G.S. (2001). *Distribution and Development: A New Look at the Developing World.* New York: MIT Press.

Fisher, A.G.B. (1939). "Production: Primary, Secondary and Teritary", *Economic Record.* June.

Foster, J. and M. Szekely (2000). "How Good is Growth", *Asian Development Review* 18(2).

Gandhi, V.P. (1990). "Investment Behaviour in Developing Countries: The Case of Agriculture in India", IFRI Studies 22(1).

———. (1996). "Investment Behaviour in Indian Agriculture", *Indian Journal of Agriculture Economics* 51(4).

Ghose, A.K. (1989). "Rural Poverty and Relative Prices in India", *Cambridge Journal of Economics,* June 13.

Gill, R.S. (1976). "Economic Growth and Fixed Capital Formation in the Sixties", *EPW* 11(45), November 6.

Golait, R. *et al.* (2008). "Capital Adequacy in Indian Agriculture", *Reserve Bank of India Occasional Papers* 28(1).

Goudie, A. *et al.* (1999). "Economic Growth, Poverty and Inequality", *Journal of International Development.* II.

GoI (2003). *Report of the Committee on Capital Formation in Agriculture.* Directorate of Economics Statistics, Ministry of Agriculture. Government of India, New Delhi, March.

Granger, C.W.J. *et al.* (1974). "Spurious Regression in Econometrics", *Journal of Econometrics* 2(2).

Granger, C.W.J. *et al.* (1997). *Forecasting Economic Time Series.* New York: Academic Press.

Grossman, G.M. and E. Helpman (1991). *Innovation and Growth in Global Economy.* Cambridge: MIT Press.

Gulati, A. *et al.* (1995). "Subsidy Syndrome in Indian Agriculture", *Economic and Political weekly* 30(39) 30 September.

Gulati, A. *et al.* (1997). *Subsidies and Investments in Indian Agriculture.* Rajiv Gandhi Institute for Contemporary Studies July.

Gulati, A. *et al.* (2001a). "Capital Formation in Indian Agriculture Revisitng the Debate", *Economic and Political Weekly.* 19 May.

Gulati, A. *et al.* (2001b). "Capital Formation in Indian Agriculture", *Economic and Political Weekly* 36(20), May.

Gulati, A. *et al.* (2002). "Capital Formation in Indian Agriculture Trends: Composition and Implications for Growth", *Occasional Paper* 24. National Bank for Agriculture and Rural Development. Mumbai.

Hall, R.E. and C.I. Jones (1999). "Why do Some Countries Produce so much more Output Per Worker than Others", *Quarterly Journal of Economics* 114(1).

Harcourt, G.C. (1972). *Some Cambridge Controversies in the Theory of Capital.* Cambridge University Press.

Harcourt, G.C. and N. Laing (ed.) (1973). *Capital and Growth*. Harmonds-worth, Middlesex, England: Penguin Books.

Harrod, R.F. (1948). *Towards a Dynamic Economics.* London: MacMillan.

Hayami, Y. and V.W. Ruttan (1985). *Agricultural Development: An International Perspective.* Baltimore: Johns Hopkins University Press.

Hayami, Y. and R.W. Herdt (1977). "Market Price Effects of Technological Change on Income Distribution in Semi-Subsistence Agriculture", *American Journal of Agricultural Economics,* May.

Hayami, Y. (2002). "Induced Innovation and Agricultural Development in East Asia", in A. Mason (ed.), *Population Change and Economic Development in East Asia.* Stanford, University Press.

Hirashima, S. (2000). "Issues in Agriculture Reforms: Public Investment and Land Market Development", *Economic and Political Weekly* 35(20), May 19.

Hirschman, A.O. (1960). *The Strategy of Economic Development.* New Haven: Yale University Press.

Hooley, R.W. (1967). "The Measurement of Capital Formation in Underdeveloped Countries", *The Review of Economics and Statistics* 49(2), May.

HLC (2009). *Report of the High Level Committee on Estimation of Saving and Investment.* Ministry of Statistics and Programme Implementation, Government of India, New Delhi.

Hughes, B.B., M.T. Irfan, H. Khan, K.B. Kumar, D.S. Rothman and J.R. Solorzano (2008). *Patterns of Potential Human Progress.* New Delhi: Oxford University Press.

Hu, Zuliu and M. Khan (1997). "Why is China Growing So Fast", *IMF Staff Papers*. March.

Islam, Rizwanul (2004). "The Nexus of Economic Growth, Employment and Poverty Reduction: An Empirical Analysis", *Discussion Paper* 14. ILO, Geneva.

Jha, R. (2007). "Investment and Subsidies in Indian Agriculture", *SARC Working Paper* 2007/03.

Johnson, H.G. (1969). "Comparative Cost and Commercial Policy Theory in a Developing Economy", *The Pakistan Development Review, Supplement,* Spring.

Kakwani, N. (2000). "Growth and poverty Reduction: An Empirical Analysis", *Asian Development Review* 18(2).

Kakwani, N. and E.M. Pernia (2000a). "What is Pro-Poor Growth", *Asian Development Reviews* 18(1).

Kakwani, N., B. Prakash and H. Son (2000b). "Growth, Inequality and Poverty Reduction: An introduction", *Asian Development Review* 18(2).

Kakwani, N., S. Khardker and H.H. Son (2004). *Pro-Poor Growth: Concepts and Measurement with Country Case Studies.* International Poverty Centre, UNDP.

Kanbur, R. (2004). "The Development of Development Thinking", *Journal of Social and Economic Development* 6(2). July-December

Kapila, Uma (2009). "Output and Productivity Growth in Indian Agriculture", in K.L. Krishna *et al.* (Editors), *Readings In Indian Agriculture and Industry.* New Delhi: Academic Foundation.

Karmakar, K.G. (1998). "Capital Formation in Agriculture and Role of Institutional Credit", *Journal of Rural Development* 17(1).

Karry, A. (2004). "When is Growth Pro-Poor: Cross-Country Edividence", *IMF Working Paper* WP/04/47, New York.

Kawagoe, T. and Y. Hayami (1985). "An Inter-Country Comparison of Agricultural Production Efficiency", *American Journal of Agricultural Economics* 67.

Khan, Haider and John Weiss (eds.) (2006). *Poverty Strategies in Asia, Growth Plus Approach.* Cheltenham, UK: Edward Elgar.

Koichi, Emi (n.d.). *Long-Term Movement of Capital Formation–The Japanese Case, 1868-1940.*

Krugman, P. (1995). *The Development: Geography and Economic Theory.* Cambridge, Mass: MIT Press.

Kumar, A. *et al.* (2005). "Total Factor Productivity of the Livestock Sector in India", in P.K. Joshi *et al.* (ed.), *Impact of Agricultural Research.* National Centre for Agricultural Economics and Policy Research, New Delhi and International Crop Research Institute for Semi-Arid Tropics, Hyderabad.

Kumar, K.B. (2003). "Education and Technology in a Small Open Economy: Theory and Evidence", *Macroeconomic Dynamics* 7.

Kumar, K.B. and J.G. Medsusaka (2006). "Village *versus* Market Social Capital: An Approach to Development", *University of Sothern California Working Paper.*

Kuznets, S. (1955). "Economic Growth and Income Inequality", *American Economic Review XLV.*

———. (1963). *Quantitative Aspects of Economic Growth of Nations: Distribution of Income by Size Economic Development and Cultural Change.*

Landes, Maurice (2008). *The Environment for Agricultural and Agribusiness Investment in India*, EIB-37, USDA, Economic Research Service, July.

Lanjouw, J.O. and P. Lanjouw (1995). "Rural Non-Farm Employment-A Survey", *Background Paper for the World Development Report.*

Larson, D.F., R. Butzer, Y. Mundlak and A. Crejo (2000). "A Cross Country Database for Sector Investment and Capital", *The World Bank Economic Review* 14(2). May.

Lau, L. and P.A. Yotopoulos (1989). "The Meta-Production Function Approach to Technological Change in World Agriculture", *Journal of Development Economics* 31.

Lewis, A. (1954). *Economic Development with Unlimited Supplies of Labour.* Manchester School, May.

———. (1955). *The Theory of Economic Growth*. London: Allen and Unwin.

———. (1958). "Unlimited Supplies Labour", *Further Notes.* Manchester School. January.

Ligon, *et al.* (2007). "Estimating the Effects of Aggregate Agricultural Growth on the Distribution of Expenditures", *World Bank Report 2008.* Washington.D.C.: World Bank.

Lipsey, R.E. *et al.* (1996). "Wages and Foreign ownership: A Comparative Study of Mexico, Venezuela and the United States", *Journal of International Economics.* May.

Lipton, M. (1988). *Why Poor People Stay Poor*. London: Temple Smith.

Lipton, M. *et al.* (1995). "Poverty and Policy", *In Hand Book of Development Economics* III B. Amsterdam: North Holland.

Lucas, R.E. (1998). "On the Mechanics of Economic Development", *Journal of Monetary Economics* 22(1): 3-42.

———. (2002). *Lectures on Economic Growth.* Cambridge: Harvard University Press.

Maddala, G.S. (1992). *Introduction to Econometrics.* New York: MacMillan.

Majid, N. (2004). "Reaching Millennium Development Goals: *How well Does Agricultural Productivity Growth Reduce Poverty"?, Empolyment Strategy Papers* 2004/12 ILO, Geneva.

Mazumdar, T. (2005). "Capital Flows into India: Implications for its Economics Growth", *Economic and Political Weekly* May 21.

Majumdar, N.A. (2006). "Centrality of Agriculture to India's Economic Development", *Economic and Political Weekly.* January 7.

Mankiw, N.G., D. Romer and D.N. Weil (1992). "A Contribution to the Empirics of Growth", *The Quarterly Journal of Economics* 107(2): 407-37, May.

McCullockh, N., J. Leishrod and P. Timmer (2007). "Pathways out of Poverty during an Economic Crisis: An Empirical Assessment of Rural Indonesia", *Policy Research Working Paper* 4173. Washington D.C.: World Bank.

Mcekay, A. (1997). "Poverty Reduction through Economic Growth: Some Issues", *Journal of International Development* 9(4).

Meir, G.M. (1984). *Leading Issues in Economic Development.* Chapter 4. Mumbai: Oxford University Press.

Mellor, J. (1976). *The New Economics of Growth*: *A Strategy for India and the Developing World.* London: Crown University Press.

Mishra, S.N. *et al.* (1995). "Public and Private Capital Formation in Indian Agriculture: Comments on the Complementarity Hypothesis and Others", *Economic and Political Weekly* 30(25). June, 24.

Mishra, S.N. (1996a). "Capital Formation and Accumulation in Indian Agriculture Since Independence", *Indian Journal of Agricultural Economies* 51(1 and 2). January-June.

Mishra, S.N. *et al.* (1996b). "Terms of Trade, Rural Poverty, Technology and Investment", *Economic and Political Weekly* 31(13).

Misra, V.N. (1998). "Economic Reforms, Terms of Trade, Aggregate Supply and Private Investment in Agriculture: Indian Experience", *Economic and Political Weekly* 33(31).

Misra, U.N. *et al.* (1996). "Terms of Trade, Rural Poverty, Technology and Investment", *EPW*, 31, March 30.

Mitra, A. (1996). "Public and Private Investments in Agriculture", in B.M. Desai (ed.), *Agricultural Development Paradigm for the Ninth Plan under New Economic Environment*. New Delhi: Oxford and IBH.

Mittal, S. *et al.* (2005). "Total Factor Productivity and Sources of Growth of Wheat in India", in P.K. Joshi *et al.* (ed.), *Impact of Agricultural Research*. Centre for Agricultural Economics and Policy Research, New Delhi, and International Crop Research Institute for Semi-Arid Tropics, Hyderabad.

Mohan, Rakesh (2008). "The Growth Record of the Indian Economy, 1950-2008: A Story of Sustained Savings and Investment", *Reserve Bank of India Bulletin*, March.

Mundle, S. *et al.* (1991). "Volume and Composition of Government Subsidies in India 1987-88", *Economic and Political Weekly*. May 4.

Mukesh, E. *et al.* (2009). "Sectoral Labour Flows and Agricultural Wages in India: Has Growth Trickled Down", *Economic and Political Weekly*, January 10.

Murray, C.J. *et al.* (2000). "The Uncertain Trends in United States GDP", *Journal of Monetary Economics* 46(1).

Myrdal, G. (1957, 1963). *Economic Theory and Underdeveloped Regions*. London: Duckworth.

Naqvi, S.N.H. (1995). "The Nature of Economic Development", *World Development 23(4): 543-56*, April.

National Academy of Agricultural Sciences (2007). "Innovations in Rural Institutions: Drivers for Agricultural Prosperity", *Policy Paper* 39, NAAS, December. New Delhi.

Nayyar, D. (2006). "Transforming Growth Into Development: India's Unfinished Journey", *Modern Asian Studies* 40(3). University of Cambridge, U.K

Nelson, R.R. and H. Pack (1999). "The Asian Miracle and Modern Growth Theory", *The Economic Journal* 109 (457): 416-36 (July).

Osmani, S.R. (2000). "Growth Strategies and Poverty Reduction", *Asian Development Review* 18(2).

Pack, H. (1994). "Endogeneous Growth: Intellectual Appeal and Empirical Shortcomings", *Journal of Economic perspectives*. Winter.

Panagariya, A. (2008). *India: The Emerging Giant*. New Delhi: Oxford University Press.

Pasha, H. (2002). *Pro-Poor Policies*. United Nations.

Patterson, K. (2000). *An Introduction to Applied Econometrics*. Palgrave.

Perkins M. and L. Witt (1961). "Capital Formation: Past & Present", *Journal of Farm Economics* 43(2). May.

Planning Commission (2007). *Report of the Steering Committee on Agriculture for 11th Five Year Plan*. Yojana Bhavan, New Delhi.

Planning Commission (2010). "Dynamics of Rural Transformation in Emerging Economics", *International Conference Report* 14-16, April, Government of India, New Delhi.

Prasada, Rao D.S., T.J. Coelli and M. Alavddin (2004). *Agricultural Productivity Growth: Employment and Poverty in Developing Countries*. University of Queensland (Australia)/ILO, Geneva.

Raghavan, M. (1996). "Investment Lag in Agriculture", *Economic and Political Weekly,* October 26.

Presscott, E.C. (1998). "Needed: A Theory of Total Factor Productivity", *International Economic Review* 39.

Purohit, *et al.* (1999). *Capital Formation in Indian Agriculture: Issues and Concerns*. National Bank for Agriculture and Rural Development, Mumbai.

Ranson, B. (1987). "The Institutional Theory of Capital Formation", *Journal of Economic Issues* 21(3).

Ranjita, P. and Mruthyunjaya (2005). "Total Factor Productivity in Indian Agriculture: Impact of Research", in P.K. Joshi *et al.* (Editors), *Impact of Agricultural Research.* National Centre for Agricultural Economics and Policy Research, New Delhi and International Crops Research Institute for the Semi-Arid Tropics, Hyderabad.

Rao, C.H.H. (1997). "Agricultural Growth, Sustainability, and Poverty Alleviation in India", Lecture Presented at IFRI, Washington D.C. December 10.

Rao, C.H.H. and Ashok Gulati (1994). "Indian Agriculture: Emerging Perspectives and Policy Issues", *Economic and Political Weekly* XXIX (53), December 31.

Rao, D.S.P. *et al.* (2004). "Agricultural Productivity Growth: Employment and Poverty in Developing Countries: 1970-2000", *Employment Strategy Paper* No.2004/9.ILO Geneva.

Rao, N.C. *et al.* (2009). "Nature of Employment in Food Processing Sector", *Economic and Political Weekly.* April

Rao, N.C. (2005). "Trends and Determinants of Capital Formation in Andhra Pradesh Agriculture", *Indian Journal of Economics,* October.

———. (2002). "Capital Formation in Indian Agriculture: A Review", *Artha Vijnana* XLIV (3-40), September.

Rao, V.M. *et al.* (2000). *Modernizing Indian Agriculture*. Department of Economic Analysis and Policy. Mumbai: Reserve Bank of Indian.

Rath, N. (1989). "Agricultural Growth and Investment in India", *Journal of Indian School of Political Economy* 1(1). January-June.

Ravallion, M. *et al.* (1996). "How Important to India's Poor is the Sectoral Composition of Economic Growth", *World Bank Economic Review* 10.

Ravallion, M. and C. Shaohua (1997). "What Can New Survey Data Tell Us About Recent Changes in Distribution and Poverty", *World Bank Economic Review* 11.

Ravallion, M. *et al.* (2002). "Why Has Economic Growth been More Pro-Poor in some States of India than Others", *Journal of Development Economics* 68(2).

Ravallion, M. *et al.* (2003). "Measuring Pro-Poor Growth", *Economic Letters* 78.

Ravallion, M. (2000). "What is Needed for More Pro-Poor Growth Process in India", *Economic and Political Weekly,* March 25.

———. (2001). "Growth, Inequality, and Poverty: Looking Beyond Averages", *World Development* 29.

———. (2004). *Pro-poor Growth*: *A Primer.* Washington D.C.: World Bank.

———. (1997). "Good and Bad Growth: The Human Development Reports", *World Development* 25(5).

Rivera-Batiz,, L.A. and P.M. Romer (1990). "Economic Integration and Endogenous Growth", *National Bureau of Economic Research Working Paper* (3528).

———. (1953-54). "The Production Function and the Theory of Capital", *Review of Economic Studies* 21.

Robinson, J. (1956). *The Accumulation of Capital*. Macmillan.

Romer, P.M. (1986). "Increasing Returns and Long-Run Growth", *Journal of Political Economy* 94(5).

———. (1987). "Growth Based on Increasing Returns due to Specialization", *American Review Economic* 77(2).

———. (1989). "What Determines the Rate of Growth and Technological Change", *Working Paper, WPS 279*. Washington D.C.: World Bank.

———. (1990). "Endogenous Technological Change", *Journal of Political Economy* 98(5).

———. (1994). "The Origins of Endogenous Growth", *Journal of Economic Perspectives*. Winter.

Rostow, W.W. (1960). *The Stages of Economic Growth*. Cambridge: Cambridge University press.

Roy, B.C. *et al.* (2001). "Incremental Capital-output Ratio in Indian Agriculture", *Agricultural Economics Research Review* 14(1).

Roy, B.C. (2001). *Investment and Productivity in Indian Agriculture*. PhD Thesis Submitted to Post Graduate School, Indian Agriculture Research Institute, New Delhi.

Roy, T. (2002). "Economic History and Modern India", *The Journal of Economic Perspectives*. 16(3).

Ruttan, V. (1998). "New Growth Theory and Development Economics", *A Survey Journal of Development Studies*, December.

Sachs, J. *et al.* (1997). "Sources of Slow Growth in African Economies", *Journal of African Economics* (6).

Sadan, E. (1968). "Capital Formation and Growth in the Israeli Cooperative Farm", *American Journal of Agricultural Economics* 50(4).

Saibaba, P. (1996). "Investment Relations by Using Sectors NAS Data in MacroEconometric Modeling for India", II, Sectoral Studies, Institute of Economic Growth and Delhi School of Economics Research Team, New Delhi.

Saith, A. (1992). "The Rural Non-Farm Economy: Processes and Policies", *World Employment Programme ILO*, Geneva.

Sawanth, S.D. and V. Daptardar and S. Mhatre (2002). "Capital Formation and Growth in Agriculture: Neglected Aspects and Dimensions", *Economic and Political Weekly*, March 16.

Schmidhuber, J. *et al.* (2009). "Capital Requirements for Agriculture in Developing Countries to 2050", FAO Expert Meeting on *'How to Feed the World' in 2050*. 24-26 June, Rome.

Schultz, T.W. (1961). "Investment in Human Capital", *American Economic Review*, March.

———. (1963). *The Economic Value of Education*. New York: Columbia University Press.

Schumpeter, J. (1934). *The Theory of Economic Development*. Cambridge, Mass: Harvard University Press.

Sen, A. (1996). "Economic Reforms, Employment and Poverty: Trend and Options", *Economic and Political Weekly*, September 9.

Sen, Abhijit, *et al.* (2004). *State of the Indian Farmer: Millennium Study-Cost of Cultivation and Farm Income*. New Delhi: Academic Foundation.

Senhadji, A. (2000). "Sources of Economic Growth: An Extensive Growth Accountancy Exercise", *IMF Staff Papers* 47(1).

Shenngen, G. *et al.* (1999). *Impact of Public Investments in Agricultural Research and Infrastructure on Growth and Poverty Reduction in Rural India*. Washington. D.C.: IFRI.

Shetty, S.L. (1990). "Investment in Agriculture: Brief Review of Recent Trends", *Economic and Political Weekly*, February 17-24.

Shukla, Tara (1965). *Capital Formation in Indian Agriculture.* Bombay: Vora & Co.

Sing, J. *et al.* (2005). "Changing Patterns of Investments and its Impact on Growth in Punjab Agriculture", *Journal of Agriculture Development and Policy* 17(1).

Solow, R.M. (1956). "A Contribution to the Theory of Economic Growth", *Quarterly Journal of Economics* 70 (1).

———. (1957). "Technical Change and Aggregate Production Function", *Review of Economics and Statistics* 393.

———. (1994). "Perspectives on Growth Theory", *Journal of Economic Perspectives* 8.

Son, H. (2003). *A Note on Pro-Poor Growth*. Washington D.C.: World Bank.

Squire, L. (1993). "Fighting Poverty", *American Economic Review*, May.

Srinivasan, T.N. (1986). "Agricultural Production, Relative Prices, Entitlements and Poverty", in J.W. Mellor and G.M. Desai (eds.), *Agriculture Change and Rural Poverty: Variations on a Theme by Dharam Narain*. Bombay: Oxford University Press.

Stephan, VC-T *et al.* (2009). "Investment in Developing Countries", Food and Agriculture. Expert Meeting on *How to Feed the World in 2050*. Economic and Social Development, FAO, Rome.

Stern, N. (1989). "The Economics of Development: A Survey", *The Economic Journal* 99 (September).

Strokey, N. (1991). "Human Capital: Product Quality, and Growth", *Quarterly Journal of Economics*, May.

Storm, (1993). *Macroeconomic Considerations in the Choice of Agricultural Policy: A Study in Sectoral Independence with Reference to India.* Avenburgy, Aldershot, England.

Swan, T.W. (1956). "Economic Growth and Capital Accumulation", *Economic Record* 32(2).

Temple, J. (1999). "The New Growth Evidence", *Journal of Economic Literature* 37, March.

Thamarajakshi, (1999). "Agriculture and Economic Reforms", *Economic and Political Weekly*, August 14.

Tripathi, A. (n.d.). *Total Factor Productivity Growth in Indian Agriculture*. New Delhi: Institute of Economic Growth.

Thirlwall, A.P. (2003). *Growth and Development.* New York: Palgrave Macmillan.

Thirtle, C. and L. Lin and J. Piesse (2002). "The Impact of Research-Led Agricultural Productivity Growth on Poverty Reduction in Africa and Latin America", *Research Paper 016.* Kings College, University of London.

Thorat, S. *et al.* (2003). *Rural Public Investment in India: Lessons for Growth and Poverty Reduction.* India Habitat Centre, New Delhi.

Timmer, C.P. (2005). *Agriculture and Pro-Poor Growth: An Asian Perspective.* Centre for Global Development, Washington D C.

Tisdell, C.A. (1999). "Socio-Economic Policy and Change in South Asia: A Review Concentrating on Bangladesh", in M. Alauddin *et al.*: Development, *Governance and the Environment in South Asia: A Focus on Bangladesh*. UK: Macmillian.

Tostlebe, A.S. (1957). *Capital in Agriculture: Its Formation and Financing Since 1870*. New York: National Bureau of Economic Research.

UNWFP and MSSRF (2009). *Report of the State of Food Insecurity in Rural India*. Chennai (India).

UN Economic Commission for Latin America and the Caribbean (UNECLAC) (2005). *The Millennium Development Goals: A Latin American and Caribbean Perspective*.

Vaidyanathan, A. (2000). "India's Agricultural Development Policy", *Economic and political Weekly* 35(20), May 13.

Wagle, P. (1994). "Estimates of Aggregate Functions for Demand For Fertilizer", *Indian Journal of Agricultural Economics* 49(1). January-March.

Warr, P. (2000). "Poverty Reduction and Economic Growth: The Asian Experience", *Asian Development Review* 18(2).

———. (2001). "Poverty Reduction and Sectoral Growth: Evidence from South Asia", *WIDER Development Conference on Growth and Poverty*. Helsinki.

Weiss, J. and H.A. Khan (ed.) (2006). *Poverty Strategies in Asia: A Growth Plus Approach*. Edwad Elgar Publishing.

Wilcox, W.W. (1943). "Capital in Agriculture", *The Quarterly Journal of Economics* 58(1).

Wolff, E.N. (1991). "Capital Formation and Productivity Convergence over the Long Term", *The American Economics Review* 81(3). June.

World Bank (1990). *World Development Report 1990: Poverty*. New York: Oxford University Press.

———. (1991). *World Development Report 1991*. Washington D.C.: World Bank.

———. (1994). *World Development Report: Infrastructure for Development*. New York: Oxford University Press.

———. (2003). *Viet Nam Development Report*.

———. (2007). *World Development Report 2008*. Washington D.C.: World Bank.

World Development Report (2000-01). *Attacking Poverty*. New York: Oxford University Press.

Young, A. (1991). "Learning by Doing and the Dynamic Effects of International Trade", *Quarterly Journal of Economics*. May.

———. (1993). "Invention and Bounded Learning by Doing", *Journal of Political Economy*. June.

Young, R.R. *et al.* (1999). "The Tyranny of Numbers: Confronting Statistical Realities of the East Asian Growth Experience", *Quarterly Journal of Economics* 110 (3).

This publication was funded by the Food and Agriculture Organization of the United Nations (FAO) in the framework of a Japanese Trust Fund project *"Support to Study on Appropriate Policy Measures to Increase Investments in Agriculture to Stimulate Food Production"*. The project aims at identifying a policy framework for promoting, facilitating and supporting accelerated investment by the public and private sector for stimulating sustainable food production. It's activities include analytical work to understand the nature and the determinants of domestic capital formation, including capital formation at farm level. This book is the result of these analytical activities. The project has also developed data and information sets on agricultural investment. The data and information set, accessible at *http://www.fao.org/tc/policy-support/investment-policy/*, are designed to provide all relevant stakeholders with relevant data and information to assist them in grasping and analyzing the status and trend of agricultural investment as well as formulating investment strategy. More information can be found at website referred above.